PRAISE FOR ▮

"The Hanford site haunts the fu ▮▮▮▮▮ ▮▮ia River basin, its land, people, plants, and ▮▮▮als. It's a nuclear crime scene that once made atomic weaponry. Joshua Frank dissects that historical crime scene, tracing it back to the colonization of this land while also pointing to the future crimes that may have been unleashed by perpetual radioactive pollution—a silent killer that cannot be seen or smelled and takes thousands of lifetimes to fully neutralize. Frank issues an urgent call to action." **–NICK ESTES** (Lakota), author of *Our History Is the Future: Standing Rock Versus the Dakota Access Pipeline, and the Long Tradition of Indigenous Resistance*

"Joshua Frank's *Atomic Days* is a brilliantly written, explosive exposé of the most toxic site in the Western Hemisphere and most expensive environmental cleanup in world history. He has given us a terrifying look at the radioactive nuclear materials produced at Hanford for four decades, the environmental catastrophe left behind, and the disastrous cleanup efforts that generate huge profits for companies like Bechtel despite lies, fraud, and deadly accidents that only generate more corporate profits. But Frank also lifts up the courageous actions of whistleblowers, community watchdogs, and Indigenous leaders who can lead the way out of this morass. Read the book and take action to end the nuclear insanity." **–MEDEA BENJAMIN,** cofounder of CODEPINK

"With the environment at a tipping point, *Atomic Days* is a vital contribution to the urgent conversation about proposed solutions and the calamitous risks they carry." **–ABBY MARTIN,** creator of *The Empire Files*

"Nuclear power's significant carbon footprint is generated by carbon-intensive uranium mining. And what is overlooked by nuclear power boosters is the neocolonial impact of mining and refining nuclear fuel on Indigenous communities. . . . All of this makes reading Joshua Frank's *Atomic Days* more crucial than ever." **–JACQUELINE KEELER**, author of *Standoff: Standing Rock, the Bundy Movement, and the American Story of Sacred Lands*

"Joshua Frank takes us on a dangerous ride through Hanford, our most toxic site, where sewage waste from plutonium generation is actively chewing away at storage units full of the most poisonous stew on Earth. Frank peels back the layers of government secrecy that engulf the cleanup, the manipulations of the unions, the utter waste of cleanup contracts, and the Chernobyl-like disaster that awaits us all. *Atomic Days* is a crucial, timely book." **–DOUG PEACOCK**, author of *Was It Worth It?*

ATOMIC DAYS

THE UNTOLD STORY OF THE
MOST TOXIC PLACE IN AMERICA

JOSHUA FRANK

Haymarket Books
Chicago, Illinois

Published in 2022 by
Haymarket Books
P.O. Box 180165
Chicago, IL 60618
773-583-7884
www.haymarketbooks.org
info@haymarketbooks.org

ISBN: 978-1-64259-828-5

Distributed to the trade in the US through Consortium Book Sales
and Distribution (www.cbsd.com) and internationally through In-
gram Publisher Services International (www.ingramcontent.com).

This book was published with the generous support of Lannan
Foundation and Wallace Action Fund.

Special discounts are available for bulk purchases by organizations
and institutions. Please call 773-583-7884 or email
info@haymarketbooks.org for more information.

Cover design by Abby Weintraub.
Illustrations by Becky Grant.
Interior photos copyright Mark Ruwedel, 1992–1994.

Printed in Canada by union labor.

Library of Congress Cataloging-in-Publication data is available.

10 9 8 7 6 5 4 3 2 1

Hanford is located on Native grounds, the ancestral home of the Cayuse, Umatilla, Walla Walla, Yakama, Nez Perce, and Palouse peoples. We pay our respects to their elders, past and present, and acknowledge the ways that we have benefited from, and continue to benefit from, the ongoing theft of these lands and erasure of their cultures, voices, and lives.

This is their land, and this book is dedicated to their struggle.

CONTENTS

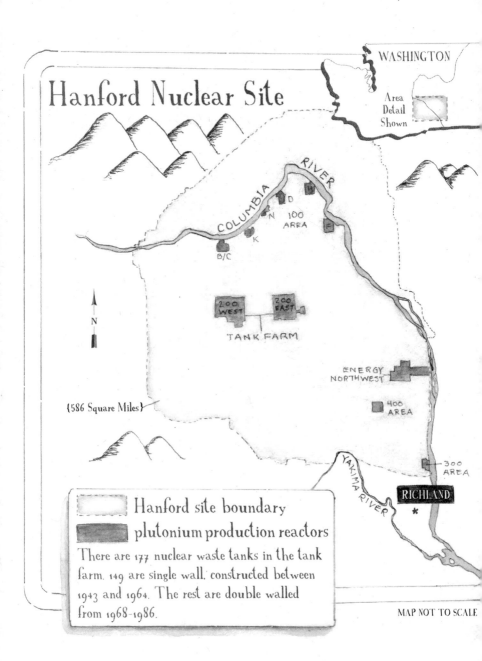

Hanford Nuclear Site

WASHINGTON

Area Detail Shown

COLUMBIA RIVER

N

D

100 AREA

K

F

B/C

N

200 WEST

200 EAST

TANK FARM

ENERGY NORTHWEST

400 AREA

(586 Square Miles)

300 AREA

YAKIMA RIVER

RICHLAND
*

Hanford site boundary

plutonium production reactors

There are 177 nuclear waste tanks in the tank farm. 149 are single wall, constructed between 1943 and 1964. The rest are double walled from 1968-1986.

MAP NOT TO SCALE

Illustrated map by Becky Grant.

WHY HANFORD?

A PROLOGUE

If you're like any number of people I've talked to over the last few years, you aren't really sure what Hanford is all about. Maybe you haven't even heard of the place; I certainly wouldn't blame you. It is, after all, off the beaten path. The Hanford Nuclear Site is located in eastern Washington State. It's far from Seattle, three hours to the Idaho border, on the banks of the Columbia River, and a couple of hundred miles upstream from Portland, Oregon.

I won't inundate you with all the details just yet; we'll get to all of that later. But here's a modest primer: Hanford was home to the US government's gargantuan plutonium operation. The site churned out nearly all of the radioactive fuel that was used in the country's nuclear arsenal. Like a ceaseless conveyer belt, Hanford generated plutonium for nearly four long decades, reaching maximum production during the height of the Cold War. Now, however, Hanford no longer produces plutonium. Instead, it's a sprawling wasteland of radioactive and chemical sewage, a landmass three times larger than Lake Tahoe. It's also the costliest environmental remediation project the world has ever seen and, arguably, the most contaminated place on the entire planet.

So, why, if this is all true, which it is, have you not heard much about this dismal atomic graveyard? It's hard not to think that the lack of awareness is intentional. How else to explain its obscurity? You've probably heard of Three Mile Island, Fukushima, and Chernobyl. Why not Hanford? Outside of the Pacific Northwest, you're not likely to read much about these wrecked lands, nor are you likely to catch any breaking news about what the hell is going on there. Not only is the site laced with huge amounts of radioactive gunk, but all that waste is also a ticking time bomb that could erupt at any given moment, creating a nuclear Chernobyl-like explosion, resulting in a singular tragedy that would be unlike anything the United States has ever experienced. It's a real and frightening possibility that I, for one, would rather not fathom.

I first heard of Hanford after I graduated from college in the early 2000s, while working for a nonprofit environmental group. One summer, I was tasked with the job of hiking up hidden, jagged canyons to survey the tributaries of Oregon's North Fork John Day River in search of salmon habitat. Hanford was just two hours north of where I bunked up for those few weeks in a small Forest Service cabin. Around the campfire, there was often talk that Hanford was a tough, toxic place. A couple of the crew members had even worked there in their younger years. "Don't bother with it," I remember one old-timer warning me, "I know people who died from working at Hanford. It's not worth the trouble." This guy also hid piles of money under his mattress, so I wasn't sure what to make of his alarmism. That was the extent of my knowledge back then. I knew Hanford was in bad shape, but didn't understand how it got that way or why it wasn't getting any better. Years later, while in graduate school, I read the definitive book on Hanford, *On The Home Front*, by historian Michele Gerber. I finally began to understand more fully what had transpired. Interestingly, despite her academic chops, Gerber was and remains a genuine Hanford booster. It was clear to me after reading the book that something was undeniably missing from her extensive research, which at times seemed like a revisionist take on Hanford's very deadly past. I needed to see, feel, and experience it for myself.

Having grown up in Billings, on the dry plains of eastern Montana, I felt on familiar ground when I first visited the town of Richland, Washington—just a stone's throw from Hanford's cordoned-off boundary. The town and its landscape reminded me of where I was raised. The topography was similar; the light blue sky was expansive, cloudless, and the air cold and crisp. The Columbia River cuts through Richland much like the great Yellowstone River does in Billings. It dragged me in. Unlike Billings, however, Richland had a different, darker, and more complex identity, and I could sense it. It wasn't a resource extraction town or an agricultural community like its neighbors Pasco or Kennewick. There were no ski slopes nearby, no fine dining or fancy vacation rentals packed full of well-heeled tourists. It was a town with an entirely different history—a past it is still openly proud of. Richland has heartily embraced the cruel bombs it helped to create, and with them, the destruction they caused. It was an odd thing, considering the thousands of lives these weapons shattered and the ecological ruin left in their wake, much of it in their own backyard. Even so, Richland's hubris is on display wherever one turns.

The local alehouse, boorishly named Atomic Ale Brewpub, showcases beers like Plutonium Porter, Half-Life Hefeweizen, and even the Atom Bustin' IPA. The kitschy logo over at the local Richland High School, home of "The Bombers," brandishes a mushroom cloud exploding out of a giant "R." And the local hardware store, which peddles T-shirts with the high school's emblem, sells out every time government officials fly in from Washington, DC. A fervent, mystifying patriotism still runs deep in Richland, and there is no mistaking that it's diehard Republican country. Benton County, where Richland is located, voted overwhelmingly for Donald Trump twice, most recently by a 20 percent margin over the Biden/Harris ticket.[1] Like other cities and regions across the United States, legislators in these parts have introduced anti-trans bills, and when protesters were bussed in from Portland for a recent anti-nuke rally, few, if any, locals joined in the festivities.[2]

However, what sets the place apart from other rural towns in the West that overwhelmingly vote Republican is that Richland is one of the most educated cities in the entire country, leading all others in PhDs per capita.[3] In other ways, too, Richland breaks the mold of what a rural, conservative stronghold looks like. That is, of course, until you peek under the hood to reveal that this place, with a population of nearly fifty thousand, was born out of the United States' nuclear ambitions during World War II and is still very much run like a covert military operation, fully dependent on government contracts to keep its economy steaming ahead.

My first visit to Richland was short, but I found myself enthralled. I spent two days roaming around town, drinking my fair share of the Half-Life Hefe, and hiking the White Bluffs Overlook above the Columbia River, which was once home to the Native Wanapum and Nez Perce. Having recently moved back to Oregon from New York, I knew I would return, and did a few years later, with my girlfriend Chelsea. I didn't share much about my intentions when I coaxed her to come along for a weekend getaway. I remember billing the trip as an exploration of sorts to the edge of Washington, where we would taste the wines of the Walla Walla region, one of the best grape-growing locales in the Pacific Northwest. Lucky for me, Chelsea likes wine. Also lucky for me, Walla Walla is just a short drive over to Hanford. I also conveniently forgot to tell Chelsea that this excursion was scheduled around the public opening of one of Hanford's oldest and most notorious buildings.

At noon on a chilly Saturday in September 2009, Chelsea and I joined a group of mostly elderly tourists. We packed ourselves onto a small bus in Richland to visit Hanford's B Reactor, which was designated a National Historic Landmark the year prior. Constructed by DuPont in just eleven months back in the early 1940s, B was the first full-scale plutonium production plant in the world. In the summer of 2009, the Department of Energy, along with the help of the Fluor Corporation, provided regular public tours of the reactor, hoping that one day the facility would turn into a twisted, national atomic museum of sorts—not a war memorial, mind you, but a full-fledged celebration of the Atomic Age. Today, nearly ten thousand tourists visit the B Reactor every year.[4]

"It was the perfect marriage of science and engineering," one of our guides expressed almost tearfully as we crawled on the bus. "The brave men that built this left us a history we should not ever forget."

Chelsea glared at me as the man's voice rang out over the crackling of the speakers. She was surely wondering what she'd signed up for when our little bus parked on a dirt path right next to a creepy, metallic structure that was flying an enormous US flag. At that point, she was also probably contemplating her future with a guy like me. The two-hour tour was fraught with pro-war symbolism, outlandish rhetoric, and crappy, salt-ridden snacks. I was ready for a glass of red wine or that Half-Life Hefe. Michele Gerber, author of *On The Home Front*, was in attendance that day, clipboard in hand, smiling behind us as some so-and-so explained the details of the reactor. "Thirty buildings and twenty service facilities were part of B operations," the guy explained, "for the last sixty years you wouldn't have been allowed in here. It was top secret!" He was jubilant. But there was no discussion of the disaster Hanford had become over that course of time. There was certainly no moment of silence for the casualties of our nuclear bombs. This was, instead, a time to rejoice in the ingenuity and superiority of the US war machine. Here, in the dark depths of the B Reactor, I did not feel at home or anywhere near it. I felt a sense of disgust and of urgency.

Not long after this trip, Chelsea and I decided to tie the knot. Luckily the B Reactor affair didn't scare her off. The bachelor weekend that followed our engagement wasn't so much a last hurrah as it was an exercise in listless meditation. My good friend and colleague Jeffrey St. Clair, with whom I co-edit *CounterPunch*, convinced me to stuff myself in the front seat of his inflatable kayak for the adventure of a lifetime, my last taste of freedom. We were to paddle Hanford's section of the Columbia River. Jeff and I didn't take part in any buffoonery, despite a cheap margarita or two at a local Mexican restaurant in Richland. Even though this was technically my bachelor party, we weren't there to party. We were on a mission to complete the fifty-mile stretch of the river in a mere two days. The float didn't require any real work. It allowed for ample downtime as we let the currents of the mighty river propel us downstream, hugging Hanford's border the entire way. For hours we gazed in a transcendental state at the tattered landscape and occasional coyote, with a fabulous panoramic view of Hanford's ominous buildings that sat scattered along the horizon. It was on this sublime river trip that I decided I needed to learn much more about what was happening out there.

While we baked ourselves in the blistering July sun, Jeffrey told me of one courageous and steadfast Hanford advocate, an attorney who lived up in Seattle. "Tom Carpenter runs the very best Hanford watchdog organization in the country, with the caveat that it's pretty much the only one," Jeff, who, for decades, has extensively covered regional environmental issues, told me. "He's sued the pants off of many of Hanford's villains and stood up to the DOE and its contractors more times than I can count."

I had to meet Tom Carpenter. First, I researched his group, Hanford Challenge, and the work they did, which included issuing in-depth reports on all things Hanford, from accidents to misallocation of resources to government fraud and abuse. The group protected whistleblowers and fought to ensure Hanford was a safe place to work. I remember ringing Tom one day while on the environmental beat for *Seattle Weekly*, asking if he had any scoops for a young, hungry journalist. He gave me a polite "no" but promised he'd get back to me if something came up. I didn't hear from Tom, but one day, months later, I received a phone call from a feisty union lawyer who told me he had some documents I might be interested in seeing. With funding support from The Nation Institute (now Type Media Center), I ended up writing two long investigative pieces for *Seattle Weekly* and a series of shorter reports on some of the biggest whistleblowers that Hanford had seen. One was a high-ranking DOE scientist named Donald Alexander. Another was a longtime contractor by the name of Walter Tamosaitis. It was during these two years of research that I learned about what kind of problems Hanford posed, not only to workers or the environment directly around it but to the entire country as well. I spoke to Indigenous activists like Russell Jim, whose lands were stolen to construct this atomic beast, and the lies the US government told along the way. I uncovered a history of hostility toward whistleblowers and the horrible dangers workers faced, and I've done my best to share their wild and gut-wrenching stories in this book.

This isn't to say I have Hanford all figured out. I certainly do not. If anyone tells you they do, they aren't straight shooters. It's an immensely complicated saga, and the Department of Energy intentionally makes it difficult to understand what is going on. In a world where there was actual, transparent accountability, the DOE would have a fancy website, database, and fat annual reports that detailed the intricacies of the money being spent on the cleanup. They would include flow charts, pie charts, and details about the endless contractors, the workers they employ, the jobs they carry out, and the science behind their decision-making. There would be frequent congressional testimonies, citizen councils, worker councils, and independent oversight committees. But none of this exists in any tangible form. Sure, we know the big numbers, the amount of cash that contractors like Bechtel score. The costs of the cleanup keep escalating, but the majority of radioactive sludge still sits right where it's always been. Currently, the DOE estimates the job could run anywhere between $316 and $662 billion.[5] To put it in perspective, their same estimate six years ago was around $110 billion.[6] Today, $2.6 billion is being spent annually.[7] That number, despite threats to cut it, continues to grow. Every few years, Bechtel signs another lucrative contract extension, with a ballooning bill attached, that we, the US taxpayer, write the checks for. Most recently, their work on one of the most important facilities at Hanford was projected to cost $41 billion.[8] Just five years ago, the same work was projected to run only $16 billion.[9] It's hard to keep up.

Even with these crazy, ever-changing cost projections, we aren't privy to the inner workings and technicalities of these huge contracts, which no doubt would invite the type of scrutiny they are hoping to avoid. Freedom of Information Act requests that would give journalists and activists insights into these affairs are often denied, with technicalities and issues of national security cited.[10] Or, like my own, are totally ignored.

* * *

The more I've looked into Hanford, the more I've come away frustrated, scratching my head, wondering how it's all come to this. How could a place be so profitable, so dangerous, and yet so under-reported outside of one or two regional papers? When my *Seattle Weekly* story of one whistleblower, Walter Tamosaitis, dropped, Rachel Maddow at MSNBC picked up the story. *The New York Times* followed, tailed by the *Los Angeles Times* and CNN. But like so much at Hanford, the mainstream spotlight faded as fast as it had appeared. There are reasons for this, no doubt, aside from DOE reluctance to let us in. The radio silence also has to do with the sheer volume of the work going on and its inherent complexities. Then there is the other big issue, that pulling back the curtain on the Hanford charade would expose the futility and senselessness not only of the United States' ugly past but of nuclear technology more generally. If the US public were made aware of the risks posed by Hanford's radioactive waste, we would surely question the validity of resurrecting the noxious nuclear power industry, which is now being heralded as a key weapon, so to speak, in the fight against climate change. As you will read here, atomic power and nuclear weapons—the mining that is needed, the waste they both produce, the Native lands they destroy, and the people they exploit—go hand in hand. They have a close, symbiotic relationship that is connected at a molecular level. One cannot have an honest discussion about the potential of nuclear power without fully acknowledging the ravages of the Hanford project. This would be tantamount to debating the future of our dying oceans without bringing up the topic of climate change.

My goal with *Atomic Days* is not to provide you with all the answers or to diminish every aspect of the remediation work currently being carried out at Hanford. Much of it is vitally important. There are incredibly gifted people I know personally who share the same goals many of us have about the site's remediation and future safety. My intentions are sincere. But I am deeply troubled as well. I am terrified by what a nuclear accident at Hanford would look like and by the lives and lands that such an incident would forever destroy. I am perplexed by the lack of accountability and angered by the enormous profit margins and corporate influence that plague nearly every aspect of the cleanup. I am upset that the DOE is understaffed and the contractors are so mismanaged. I am worried, too, about the workers who are putting their lives on the line every single day, and I am astonished that their unions don't do more to help out. Yet I am also hopeful: hopeful that, with a bit of knowledge about what is really going on at Hanford—which involves a true reckoning with its dreadful past—a youthful, grassroots movement, not unlike the struggle that rose up to fend off Big Oil at Standing Rock and elsewhere, can arise yet again to demand transparency, accountability, and radical change. The matter is vitally important to the future of the planet, to Hanford's Indigenous population, and to every US citizen who is paying for it. Because its radioactive threat is not only immediate, it's long-lasting and of atomic proportions.

40 Miles of Bad Roads

I've crossed the line
I've bent the rules
Home of the brave
Red, white, and blue
I've fought the fire
Running through my head
Stood by and watched
Believed in what they said

I'm 40 miles of bad road
A riverbed of potholes
I know, I know, I know
Where the money goes
Down a shaft of ratholes
Lowered by my ankles
Where dear dogs lie in the
Afterglow

—Dead Moon

Hanford nuclear reactor site, United States Department of Energy, 1960

CHAPTER ONE

ANATOMY OF AN ATOMIC WASTELAND

It is an atomic bomb. It is a harnessing of the basic power of the universe. The force from which the sun draws its power has been loosed against those who brought war to the Far East.

—President Harry S. Truman, August 6, 1945

The Columbia River basin in southeastern Washington is a desert land of sagebrush, sunshine, and coarse, silty soil. This beautiful landscape, however, has been radically altered by forces out of its control. Wild salmon, beacons of environmental health, have tenaciously hung on despite hydroelectric dams and overdevelopment. Human activity spans more than ten thousand years along this stretch of the mighty Columbia, known as *Wimahl* (the big river) to the Chinook tribe, who graciously welcomed the expedition of Meriwether Lewis & William Clark around 1805, the first time white colonialists visited the lands.[1] Archaeological evidence indicating that Indigenous people harvested the river's once plentiful salmon runs as far back as 7,000 BC. In 1962, archaeologists discovered the Marmes Rockshelter at the confluence of the Palouse and Snake rivers, the latter a tributary to the Columbia, where they unearthed some of the oldest signs of human activity in North America. Radiocarbon dating revealed that an industrious society of hunters thrived at this location for over eight thousand years, consuming elk and deer.[2] In 1996, on the muddy banks of the Columbia, downstream from the Marmes Rockshelter, the nearly intact skeletal remains of the nine-thousand-year-old Kennewick Man were found. Today, however, this landscape, scarred by decades of colonization and militarization, is a perverse version of its old self. It's home to the vast Hanford Nuclear Site, one of the most radioactive wastelands on earth and the costliest environmental remediation in world history, with a soaring price tag of $677 billion.[3]

When Lewis and Clark first laid eyes on the lower Columbia, they were astounded by the abundance of wildlife. Deer, elk, and wild horses flourished. Clark, who fancied himself the sportsman of the duo, seemed genuinely impressed by the wealth of salmon, some of which weighed over one hundred pounds. "The multitudes of this fish are almost inconceivable," he wrote, watching schools of salmon work their way upstream. Robert Stuart, the crew's intrepid scout, nicknamed this section of the river Priest Rapids after witnessing the Indigenous Wanapum (water people) hold a spiritual ceremony along the bank, giving thanks for the water's bounty, a river they called Ci Wana.[45] Upriver from Hanford, Priest Rapids today is hindered by a rickety dam. Where religious celebrants once assembled along the river's edge, you're now lucky to catch a glimpse of the occasional coyote or deer darting behind barbed wire fencing, as faded and rusting signs warn against trespassing and threats of potential radioactive contamination.

Once home to the world's largest plutonium-making operation, Hanford is now a sprawling 586-square-mile nuclear disaster zone.[6] The federal government recognizes Hanford as "one of the most contaminated places on Earth."[7] In 1942, the US Army Corps of Engineers, under the direction of Brigadier

General Leslie R. Groves, contracted the DuPont Company to procure a location to manufacture plutonium for the government's top-secret Manhattan Project. For several reasons, Hanford fit the bill. It had ample space, water, and electricity from the dams. Hanford was also nearly off the grid. Never mind that it contained a small population of 1,500 residents, mostly peasant farmers and Wanapum, Yakama, Umatilla, and Nez Perce people—tribes that still fished for Columbia River salmon, as their ancestors had for thousands of years. These Indigenous people, their cultures, and their livelihoods were seen as expendable.[8] The Wanapum tribe, along with their chief, Johnnie Buck, didn't give in easily. Unlike General Groves, Franklin Matthias, who directed the construction of Hanford, attempted to appease the Wanapum but failed, as the tribe was rightfully distrustful of the US military machine. The fall of 1943 was the first year the Wanapum were not allowed to fish at White Bluffs, one of the most scenic and sacred sites along this stretch of the Columbia River. While the tribe had survived the onslaught of white settlers and avoided being forced onto a reservation, they had no choice but to give up their traditional fishing rights. Matthias offered money, but Chief Buck refused. They didn't want money; they wanted to fish as they always had. It was about spiritual and cultural survival, something Matthias likely did not understand. Matthias allowed the tribe to be escorted in to fish, surpassing the strict background checks. But it wasn't a solution; it was a token, the last the tribe would receive before losing access to the land and river where they worshipped.[9]

"We lived three and a half miles out. Had thirty acres there. They offered us $1,700. . . . It cost $1,900 just to get the well in. We had overhead spray pipe, underground concrete pipe, plus the land, the purchase of the land," recalls Annette Heriford, whose family lost their farm in the Hanford land seizure:

Why, it was ridiculous! *Ridiculous!* Because no one could go any place. If they had said, "All right, if it is not worth anything, we will move you and we will give you thirty acres and we will put the same kind of well down. And you will have all your friends and your town right here." If they had wanted to do that and they could have found a place comparable to ours, then great. We would not have been as happy. We loved that Columbia River and the bluffs by it. That was a unique spot. It was beautiful.

General Groves quashed concerns by telling locals who were perplexed as to why the Army Corps wished to acquire their properties, "If I told you what the government is doing, I'd be court-martialed tomorrow." The War Powers Act of 1941 allowed the federal government to take the land and homes from residents, which it swiftly did. Many residents were only given thirty days to move out.[10]

This wasn't the first time area tribes were driven off their ancestral lands. Marcus and Narcissa Whitman, Protestant missionaries from Boston, established the Waiilatpu Mission along the nearby Walla Walla River in 1836. While it turned out to be prosperous for the evangelical Whitmans, it was not so for the Walla Walla and Cayuse. Like the fur traders before them, the fervent Christians brought along smallpox, which ravaged the tribes. Ten years after the mission was built, the Cayuse were fed up, rightfully blaming the missionaries for towing along infectious disease. On November 29, 1847, a group of Cayuse attacked and killed the Whitmans and twelve others after accusing them of poisoning two hundred Cayuse who were under their medical care. The incident sparked the Cayuse War, which lasted for eight years before the US government defeated the Cayuse. Settlers seized on the victory and used the Whitmans' deaths as justification for raiding Native camps and expanding their presence across the region. The event was a defining moment for the Oregon Territory.[11]

In 1855, as a result of the war, the Cayuse were forcibly moved to the Umatilla Reservation in present-day Oregon. The Walla Walla tribe later joined. The Yakama kept fighting the colonizers from the East but ultimately lost the Yakama War in a series of battles and were forced onto a reservation in what would later become southern Washington state. By 1858, most tribes in the Pacific Northwest had surrendered and became part of the federal reservation system. The Cayuse War is recognized by many historians as the catalyst for the US government's strong-armed treaty-making with area tribes. When World War II and the Manhattan Project arrived, Natives near Hanford were all too familiar with the federal government's long-standing policy of assimilation, annihilation, and relocation in the interest of US superiority.[12]

In March 1943, Hanford Engineer Works broke ground. People had been removed, even entire grave sites were dug up and relocated.[13] Nothing but US nuclear ambitions mattered. Two years earlier, University of California physicist Glenn T. Seaborg had produced the first plutonium 239 (Pu-239), which could be used in nuclear weapons. The federal Office of Scientific Research and Development (OSRD) had jumped on the discovery and moved quickly to produce the element on a much larger scale at Hanford, hoping to outpace the United States' enemies. With this mission in mind, General Groves ran a tight, authoritative enterprise. The entire operation was a closely held secret; all decisions had to be run by Groves. The staff numbered few, and most who worked on the remote site held little knowledge of the larger concept. While scientific and engineering concerns were raised about the feasibility of producing plutonium in mass quantities, Groves trudged ambitiously forward and soon the United States' noxious nuclear weapons industry was up and running. [14] Hanford, and the world, would never be the same.

"Considerations of maximum yield or durability did not govern the planning," the US Atomic Energy Commission (AEC) wrote in its 1949 Fifth Semiannual Report of the AEC.[15]

> Time was the governing factor: The single overriding necessity was to get pure uranium 235 and plutonium in a hurry. The builders knew that if these substances actually did release atomic energy in useful quantity, the concentrated efforts of scientists and technologists all over the world would probably be able to develop better processes and plants. Even if they succeeded, therefore, they believed that most of the giant structures they built were expendable.

This shortsighted philosophy that Hanford was "expendable" is largely why Hanford is in trouble today.

MAKING OF THE BOMB

Hanford and its people were sacrificed on the altar of US militarism as the nuclear arms race unofficially commenced in 1939, years before Seabord's plutonium production operation. In a letter to President Roosevelt, highly regarded physicists Albert Einstein and Leó Szilárd warned that "it may become possible to set up a nuclear chain reaction in a large mass of uranium, by which vast amounts of power and large quantities of new radium-like elements would be generated. Now it appears almost certain that this could be achieved in the immediate future."

"This new phenomenon," continued Einstein and Szilárd, "would also lead to the construction of bombs, and it is conceivable—though much less certain—that extremely powerful bombs of a new type may thus be constructed. A single bomb of this type, carried by boat and exploded in a port, might very well destroy the whole port together with some of the surrounding territory. However, such bombs might very well prove to be too heavy for transportation by air."[16]

Concerns were palpable that Nazi Germany, which was quickly advancing across Europe, would get its vicious hands on nuclear technology. "I think everyone was terrified that we were wrong (in our way of developing the bomb) and the Germans were ahead of us," recalled Manhattan Project physicist Leona Marshall Libby.

> That was a persistent and ever-present fear, fed, of course, by the fact that our leaders knew those people in Germany. They went to school with them. Our leaders were terrified, and that terror fed to us. If the Germans had got it before we did, I don't know what would have happened to the world. Something different. Germany led in the field of physics, in every respect, at the time war set in, when Hitler lowered the boom. It was a very frightening time.[17]

It may have been an alarming moment in history, but the alleged threat was enhanced by fear of the unknown, a fear that also characterized the Cold War to come. Nazi Germany never actually acquired the knowledge or technology to make a nuclear weapon. This was in part due to their removal of Jews from academia, including many physicists, which greatly weakened Germany's scientific community. The Nazis had created a brain drain of their own cruel design. Nevertheless, the United States continued to vigorously pursue a nuclear weapons program, believing it was in a race against time.

The US government quickly assembled what they believed to be the best and brightest scientists and engineers from universities and the private sector, then selected three US cities to carry out important bomb-making tasks. Hanford would construct nuclear reactors and produce plutonium. Oak Ridge, Tennessee would handle the uranium component. The bomb would be designed and built at facilities in Los Alamos, New Mexico. Hanford's first plutonium production was handled in a box-like structure known as the B Reactor. A first-of-its-kind facility, the B Reactor was designed by physicist Enrico Fermi and built by DuPont in 1943.

Here's how the early nuclear weapons worked. A "critical mass" of uranium or plutonium would cause a chain reaction and a massive explosion. This reaction, or "fission," which took place in the bomb's core, began when neutrons hit uranium or pluto-nium nuclei, splitting the atom, which in turn created a massive amount of energy, and ultimately a lethal atomic explosion.

The first nuclear bomb, informally called Gadget, a twen-ty-one-kiloton plutonium device, was detonated at the Trinity Site in Alamogordo, New Mexico, on July 16, 1945. Plutonium for Gadget was manufactured at Hanford. Kenneth Bainbridge, a professor of physics at Harvard, planned the test under the guidance of chemist George Kistiakowsky, who was the head of the Manhattan Project's E Division. The explosion was massive, its effects immediate. The resultant mushroom cloud spanned forty thousand feet and remnants of trinitite, a radioactive green glass, were strewn throughout a five-foot deep, three-hundred-foot-wide crater.[18] Ralph Carlisle Smith, who witnessed the blast from twenty miles away on Compania Hill, recalled:

> I was staring straight ahead with my open left eye covered by a welders' glass and my right eye remaining open and un-covered. Suddenly, my right eye was blinded by a light which appeared instantaneously all about without any build up of intensity. My left eye could see the ball of fire start up like a tremendous bubble or nob-like mushroom. I dropped the glass from my left eye almost immediately and watched the light climb upward. The light intensity fell rapidly hence did not blind my left eye but it was still amazingly bright. It turned yellow, then red, and then beautiful purple. At first,

it had a translucent character but shortly turned to a tinted or colored white smoke appearance. The ball of fire seemed to rise in something of toadstool effect. Later the column proceeded as a cylinder of white smoke; it seemed to move ponderously. A hole was punched through the clouds but two fog rings appeared well above the white smoke column. There was a spontaneous cheer from the observers. Dr. von Neumann said, "That was at least 5,000 tons and probably a lot more." My estimate of the width of the ball of fire was guessed to be one to two miles at that time. Someone said keep your mouth open and just then, about one and half to two minutes after the light flash, a sharp loud crack swept over us—it reverberated through the mountain like thunder.[19]

The majority of the radioactive fallout from the Gadget explosion occurred outside the restricted bombing zone on Chupadera Mesa, thirty miles from the blast. Diné (Navajo) and Apache peoples were the unwitting victims of the fallout. Winds carried a "white mist" that settled on the butte, blanketing a herd of cattle, scorching their backs with radioactive beta burns. The cows, eighty-eight in all, were purchased from local ranchers and transported to Los Alamos and Oak Ridge for testing and examination.

Residents of the area were not warned about the nuclear test, nor were they briefed on the health and environmental hazards that were sure to follow. Nobody was evacuated and no studies monitored the long-term health impacts of New Mexicans impacted by that first atom bomb explosion.[20] Now, so many decades later, the National Cancer Institute (NCI) is finally conducting a study to determine Gadget's impact on the Indigenous and general population of New Mexico, particularly on Hispanic and Mescalero Apache residents downwind from the test site. The Radiation Exposure Compensation Act of 1990, however, which might have otherwise provided compensation for victims of the blast, did not include residents of New Mexico.[21]

"This [NCI study] has been a long time in coming," Tina Cordova, a cancer survivor who grew up in Tularosa and heads the Tularosa Basin Downwinders' Consortium, told the *Santa Fe New Mexican* in 2015.[22] She believes her cancer and that of many others were a result of the Trinity bomb. "We were unwilling, unknowing and uncompensated participants in the world's largest science experiment," Cordova said. The more than two thousand nuclear weapons tests that followed around the world, from 1945-2017, disproportionately impacted Indigenous people from Australia to the United States. In Nevada, at the Air Force's infamous testing site, the Western Shoshone were the victims of an endless stream of radioactive fallout.[23] In the Pacific, Indigenous islanders on the Bikini and Enewetok atolls experienced the aftermath of the US military's extensive testing, where detonations occurred almost continuously from 1946-1996.[24]

It was the Trinity test that started it all. Largely seen as a success, Trinity was viewed as a feat of scientific ingenuity and US prowess. Preparations for striking Japan with a similar warhead were already underway. Two years earlier, in 1943, modifications were made to B-29s at Wright Field, in Ohio, to transport and drop atom bombs under the codename Silverplate, initiated by the Manhattan Project. Test runs of the altered B-29s proved successful, and following the Trinity test, President Harry Truman approved the planes to be readied with nuclear bombs for attacks on the Japanese cities of Hiroshima and Nagasaki. Two months after the Nazi surrender, Truman, while at the Potsdam Conference in Germany, was told that the Trinity test succeeded. Also at the Potsdam Conference were Britain's prime ministers Winston Churchill and Clement Attlee (who succeeded Churchill), as well as Joseph Stalin, the Soviet Union's General Secretary of the Communist Party. Here, Truman reportedly told Stalin the United

States "had a new weapon of unusual destructive force" and was planning to use it on Japan. While Truman was short on specifics, Stalin allegedly knew he was referring to a nuclear bomb, as German physicist Klaus Fuchs, who worked on the Manhattan Project, had shared information of the United States' nuclear ambitions with the Communists. Stalin responded to Truman that the United States should "make good use of this new addition to the Allied arsenal."[25]

THE EXPENDABLES

The United States' decision to drop nuclear bombs on Japan was not without precedent. In the winter of 1945, the United States firebombed both Dresden, Germany, killing forty-five thousand people, and Tokyo, Japan, killing more than three hundred thousand people. Some believe these estimates to be low. "I was on the island of Guam...in March of 1945. In that single night, we burned to death one hundred thousand Japanese civilians in Tokyo: men, women, and children," recalled Robert McNamara, who later served as secretary of defense under presidents Kennedy and Johnson.[26] In all, the United States firebombed sixty-seven Japanese cities over the course of that bloody year. While not all—particularly US secretary of war Henry Stimson—enjoyed the targeting of civilians, no complaints were officially raised within the US government about the firebombing's legal or ethical implications. Most officials believed these horrible bombings would help bring the war to an end, forcing the Japanese and Germans to surrender.[27]

Nonetheless, with UK approval, President Truman ordered a nuclear bomb to be dropped over Hiroshima on August 6, 1945, less than one month after the test run at Trinity. The United States alerted Japanese citizens, dropping leaflets that warned their towns would "fall to ashes." The bombing inflicted catastrophic damage. Temperatures on the ground topped 4,000°C. Birds dropped from the sky. Radioactive rain poured down on the city. The uranium bomb nicknamed "Little Boy," which exploded over Hiroshima destroyed 70 percent of the entire city. Nearly all of the city's medical staff were killed, and ultimately a staggering 140,000 deaths were recorded in the months and years that followed.[28]

The United States argued that Hiroshima and its military headquarters were legitimate targets, and conveyed little concern about the previous decision to firebomb tens of thousands of innocent Japanese civilians in Tokyo. Professor Alex Wallerstein argues that before the bombing Truman was unaware that Hiroshima was an actual city, and not simply a military outpost. In fact, Wallerstein notes, Truman was more intent on avoiding massive innocent casualties and was simply taking the lead from Stimson, albeit a misinformed one. "Truman's confusion on this issue," writes Wallerstein, "came out of his discussions with Secretary of War Henry Stimson about the relative merits of Kyoto versus Hiroshima as a target: Stimson emphasized the civilian nature of Kyoto and paired it against the military-status of Hiroshima, and Truman read more into the contrast than was actually true."[29]

"The Japanese began the war from the air at Pearl Harbor. They have been repaid many fold. And the end is not yet. With this bomb we have now added a new and revolutionary increase in destruction to supplement the growing power of our armed forces. In their present form, these bombs are now in production and even more powerful forms are in development," President Harry Truman read in a statement following the bombing of Hiroshima. "It is an atomic bomb. It is a harnessing of the basic power of the universe. The force from which the sun draws its power has been loosed against those who brought war to the Far East."[30]

The United States wasn't done yet. In the early morning hours of August 9, a B-29 named Box Car, outfitted with the plutonium bomb nicknamed Fat Man, took off from Tinian Airfield in the Mariana Islands, over 1,400 miles southeast of Nagasaki. Box Car was commanded by Major Charles W. Sweeney. The original target of the second bombing was not initially Nagasaki but a military cache located in Kokura. Weather, however, was not cooperating over Kokura. A haze obscured the plane's target and anti-aircraft fire proved frustrating, so Major Sweeney changed course and headed to the secondary target, of Nagasaki. Jacob Beser, an aircraft crewman, later recalled that they abandoned Kokura and headed to Nagasaki because "there was no sense dragging the bomb home or dropping it in the ocean."

As the plane neared Nagasaki, the visibility was equally as bad as over Kokura, but through a brief break in the clouds, Captain Kermit K. Beahan was able to spot the city's stadium. The plane circled back, and at 11:02 a.m. on August 9, 1945, the United States dropped the "Fat Man" bomb on Nagasaki. The bomb caused an explosion 40 percent larger than the Little Boy bombing of Hiroshima. The bomb's plutonium fuel was produced at Hanford.

"I have no regrets. I think we did right, and we couldn't have done it differently. Yeah, I know it has been suggested the second bomb, Nagasaki, was not necessary," said project physicist Leona Marshall Libby later, defending the bombing. "The guys who cry on shoulders. When you are in a war, to the death, I don't think you stand around and ask, 'Is it right?'"

The nuclear bombings of Hiroshima and Nagasaki were unlike anything the world had ever experienced. More than two hundred thousand people died in the fiery blasts and from acute radiation poisoning in the hours and days following the explosions. Bodies were vaporized, structures melted from extreme heat, and the radiation pulsated spherically from the bombs' hypocenters. Unlike the Trinity test in New Mexico, where the warhead exploded on the ground, both of the bombs dropped on Japan were detonated six hundred meters in the air above the cities. If there was any good news for the Japanese, this would be it. Had the bomb exploded on the ground the results would have been even more horrific.[31]

For survivors of the bombings, most of whom have now passed on, cancer rates remained astronomically higher than in populations unexposed to the same amount of radiation. According to the Radiation Effects Research Foundation, the risk of leukemia, or blood cancer, was 46 percent higher among bombing victims. For people in utero at the time, risk of physical impairment, such as small head size or mental disability, was even more significant.

Studies of the survivors later revealed what scientists had suspected even before the 1945 blasts—that radiation can mutate DNA and in turn cause different forms of cancer, blood cancer in particular. Among Hiroshima and Nagasaki victims, the rate of leukemia rose sharply in the 1950s. Their damaged cells were more susceptible to developing cancers. The Radiation Effects Research Foundation (RERF), a joint US and Japanese research effort that evolved from the 1946 Atomic Bomb Casualty Commission, has revealed startling findings in its lifespan study of ninety-four thousand bomb survivors, which followed their lives from 1958 to 1998. The more radiation a person received, the greater was their risk of developing cancer.[32] In fact, according to the RERF study, the relationship between radiation levels and cancer likelihood was linear. As radiation levels doubled, incidents of cancer doubled. Leukemia, however, proved to be exponentially correlated: as higher levels of radiation doubled, the risk of leukemia quadrupled.[33] Had the bombs exploded closer to the ground, scientists believe that higher radiation levels would have led to more cancers, and ultimately, more deaths.[34]

"I was three years old at the time of the [Nagasaki] bombing. I don't remember much, but I do recall that my surroundings turned blindingly white, like a million camera flashes going off at once. Then, pitch darkness," reflected bombing victim Yasujiro Tanaka.[35]

> I was buried alive under the house, I've been told. When my uncle finally found me and pulled my tiny three-year-old body out from under the debris, I was unconscious. My face was misshapen. He was certain that I was dead. Thankfully, I survived. But since that day, mysterious scabs began to form all over my body. I lost hearing in my left ear, probably due to the air blast. More than a decade after the bombing, my mother began to notice glass shards growing out of her skin—debris from the day of the bombing, presumably. My younger sister suffers from chronic muscle cramps to this day, on top of kidney issues that has her on dialysis three times a week. "What did I do to the Americans?" she would often say, "Why did they do this to me?"

A number of historians, including the late Howard Zinn, argue the nuclear bombing of Japan was not only criminal, it was unnecessary:

> The principal justification for obliterating Hiroshima and Nagasaki is that it "saved lives" because otherwise a planned US invasion of Japan would have been necessary, resulting in the deaths of tens of thousands, perhaps hundreds of thousands. Truman at one point used the figure "a half million lives," and Churchill "a million lives," but these were figures pulled out of the air to calm troubled consciences; even official projections for the number of casualties in an invasion did not go beyond 46,000. In fact, the bombs that fell on Hiroshima and Nagasaki did not forestall an invasion of Japan because no invasion was necessary. The Japa-

nese were on the verge of surrender, and American military leaders knew that. General Eisenhower, briefed by Secretary of War Henry Stimson on the imminent use of the bomb, told him that "Japan was already defeated and that dropping the bomb was completely unnecessary."[36]

"ATOM TOWN, USA"

Longtime residents of the region felt the wartime creation in Hanford. The nearby tri-cities in Washington—Pasco, Kennewick, and the new village of Richland, which was dubbed "Atom Town, USA"—all experienced population surges. Many of the residents of Richland embraced a strident form of patriotism, believing that the bomb they and their loved ones helped to build had ended the war. The town's paper proudly exclaimed, "PEACE! OUR BOMB CLINCHED IT!" The War Department applauded the Hanford employees; *Time* magazine and Portland's *Oregonian*, too, voiced appreciation for their efforts. The "peaceful" atom bomb was being celebrated across the country. For the moment, at least, Hanford and its citizens sat in the spotlight.[37] However, not all believed the wholesome veneer of Hanford, which was a direct result of General Grove's initial vision of the city, who thought it ought to resemble an army base that was "fenced, guarded, compact, gridded...with barracks-styled dorms and apartments centered around a few utilitarian commissaries." DuPont rejected the idea and Hanford became an early example of the type of suburban architecture that reshaped the postwar United States.[38]

The workers at Hanford, numbering around 5,500, were afraid their jobs would cease with Japan's fall and Nazi defeat. But in 1945, General Electric replaced DuPont as the lead contractor at Hanford, relieving fears that employees might lose employment. In 1947, the US government announced the work at Hanford would not only continue, but greatly expand. Henry Stimson had warned President Truman in 1945 that the United States ought to be cautious about sharing nuclear secrets with Stalin, but that if they did not, the Soviets too would rapidly seek to split the atom and create a nuclear warhead. In fact, Stimson argued, they were likely already on that path. Some historians and commentators claim Truman bombed Japan not to end the war but to scare off Stalin, whose military was moving toward invading Europe.[39]

While this may have played in the minds of Stimson and other military brass, the record to support this theory is not overly robust. In his seminal 1965 book *Atomic Diplomacy*, Gar Alperovitz argues that Truman and Stimson were not truthful in their accounts of the bombings and that the goal of bombing Japan was not to end the war but to put political pressure on the Soviets.[40] While this theory is captivating and well-reasoned, a hard look at the evidence raises important questions about its veracity. Most importantly, Stimson speculated shortly after the bombing that the Soviets' newfound knowledge of US nuclear weapon technology would only push them to aggressively develop their own nuclear capacity.

Stimson's analysis is difficult to reconcile with Alperovitz's, even if Truman did have Russia's reaction in mind when greenlighting the bomb. Dropping the bomb on Japan may have startled Stalin by propping up US power, but it did *not* deter Russia from pursuing its own nuclear arsenal. The bombing, of course, ultimately ended the pact between FDR and Stalin and started the Cold War. This exacerbated pressure on both sides to escalate the nuclear arms race and, with it, nuclear power. Disastrous impacts on Hanford and sites in Russia followed. In a September 11, 1945, letter to Truman, Stimson warned:

> I consider the problem of our satisfactory relations with
> Russia as not merely connected with but as virtually dom-

inated by the problem of the atomic bomb. Except for the problem of the control of the bomb, those relations, while vitally important, might not be immediately pressing. The establishment of relations of mutual confidence between her and us could afford to wait the slow progress of time. But with the discovery of the bomb they became immediately emergent. Those relations may be perhaps irretrievably embittered by the way in which we approach the solution of the bomb with Russia. For if we fail to approach them now and merely continue to negotiate with them, having this weapon rather ostentatiously on our hip, their suspicions and their distrust of our purposes and motives will increase. It will inspire them to greater efforts in an all-out effort to solve the problem.[41]

Stimson's prediction was prescient, and in 1949 the Soviets detonated their first nuclear warhead, all but clinching Hanford's status as a permanent military installation throughout the Cold War.[42]

During World War II, three nuclear reactors were built at Hanford. After the end of the war, nine more nuclear reactors were erected and an additional two weapons facilities were constructed, along with a total of 177 underground waste storage tanks, 149 of which are single shell and 28 double shell.[43] For the next two decades, Hanford was busy. The United States was attempting to keep pace with Soviet nuclear arms production, and Richland felt the strains of continued growth. The town endured water, electricity, and housing shortages. Newly planted lawns and summer heat created the perfect conditions for mosquitoes, and from 1947 to 1949, outbreaks consumed the growing city. Massive amounts of DDT were sprayed throughout Richland's streets to combat the insects, and residents were advised to cover their screen doors with the chemical, despite ominous scientific reports at the time that warned of DDT's dangers. None of these issues hampered the work at Hanford, however, and for nearly ten years, from 1956 to 1965, Hanford operated at peak capacity, producing sixty-three short tons of plutonium that fueled virtually all of the United States' nuclear arsenal. Richland had quickly become a government-dependent town.[44]

"We made friends very quickly. We have friends we have had for forty years who are closer than family. We came out here, and everybody was away from their families. You made friends in a hurry. The men were working anywhere from fourteen to eighteen hours a day, sometimes more than that, sometimes they didn't come home at all," recalled Vera Jo McCready, whose husband Mac worked at Hanford as a chemical engineer. The couple relocated to Richland from Alabama during World War II.[45] "So the women were left pretty much on their own. We had to do things together because we didn't get much gas in those days, so we shopped together. Because men didn't talk about their jobs, we could even get the husbands to come into the living room at parties and talk to the women."

While social life in Richland was active and vibrant, so too were Hanford's radioactive isotopes. At the time, Hanford's nuclear reactors were the biggest culprit of radiation. They needed constant cooling, requiring an estimated seventy-five thousand gallons of water from the Columbia River to be pumped in each minute, twenty-four hours a day, seven days a week. After treated water ran through the reactors' cooling systems, it was drained into retention basins, where, now radioactive, it sat for six long hours before it flowed back into the Columbia, virtually nonstop.[46] The water was still hot and raised temperatures in the river. In other instances, the reactors were "flushed," releasing radioactive contamination into the Columbia River. As with many of the furtive inner-workings at Hanford, information about these various episodes was withheld from the public until the 1980s and 1990s, even though radiation was discovered as far as two hundred miles downriver on the Oregon and Washington coasts, exposing an estimated two thousand people to dangerous doses.[47]

That wasn't the worst of it. The most significant radioactive events occurred between 1947 and 1951, when two hundred different radionuclides, including significant amounts of the most feared fission byproduct, iodine-131, went airborne during the process of separating plutonium and uranium, contaminating countless people and upward of seventy-five thousand square miles of land in Washington, Oregon, Idaho, Montana, and parts of British Columbia. Iodine-131 can accumulate in the thyroid glands of humans and other unfortunate animals, causing cancerous growths. In a secret military experiment known as the "Green Run," held over a two-day period in early December 1949, between seven thousand and twelve thousand curies of iodine-131 were released in an immense 200–by–40 mile plume that spread across the region. A single curie is thirty-seven billion atoms, and between 1944 and 1957, Hanford produced 725,000 curies[48] of iodine-131. By contrast, the accident at Three Mile Island released fifteen to twenty-four curies of iodine-131.[49]

It was called the Green Run for a reason. In the 1940s and 1950s, the normal timeframe for cooling uranium fuel was one hundred days (today, uranium is cooled for 180 days), which allowed iodine-131 to decay to slightly more moderate levels. But in the case of the Green Run, uranium fuel was cooled for a mere sixteen days, and remained "green." To make matters worse, filters that scrubbed the radioactive iodine before it entered the air were removed for the test.[50] Hanford allegedly carried out the Green Run so that the US Air Force could evaluate monitoring equipment for its covert Soviet intelligence program, which was initiated to detect and monitor the Soviets' advances in nuclear technology. Information on the test remained secret until 1986, when classified documents revealed the Air Force developed secret experiments in order to use their detection devices to evaluate the radioactive plume of iodine-131 and radioxenon (Xe-131) that was released into the air. But problems existed. The weather made the testing difficult, and radiation near the Hanford's T plant, where the Green Run occurred, was higher than anticipated as a result of heavy winds. A weather balloon was lost, and testing equipment failed. Even so, radioactive samples of animals, water, and local vegetation produced alarming results.[51] In a 1994 report by the Advisory Committee on Human Radiation Experiments, which was established by president Bill Clinton to investigate the government's various human radiation experiments, the special committee addressed Hanford's Green Run experiment:

> Measurements of radioactivity on vegetation produced readings that, while temporary, were as much as 400 times the then-"permissible permanent concentration" on vegetation thought to cause injury to livestock. The current level at which Washington state officials intervene to prevent possible injury to people through the food supply is not much higher than the then-permissible permanent concentration. Animal thyroid specimens showed contamination levels up to "about 80 times the maximum permissible limit of permanently maintained radioiodine concentration."[52]

The Green Run wasn't the first time Hanford officials purposely released dangerous amounts of radioactive iodine. Five years prior to the Green Run, the US Army Corps of Engineers conducted wartime research to determine how wind currents carried radiation. These tests, which first became public in 1987, were not solely designed to determine how radiation impacted the environment or the local population, who should have been evacuated. Instead, they were reportedly carried out to determine if their testing equipment worked accurately.[53]

The details of Green Run, which remain largely secret to this day under the guise of national security, have led some to believe the tests were not initiated to monitor equipment or radiation's impact on local ecology, but rather to test iodine-131 as an agent of radioactive warfare. Regardless of intention, little is known about what nefarious impacts these tests had on people downwind or on the Hanford employees handling the experiments. Nonetheless, one investigation, published in 1996, which looked into these tests' impact on women, showed that those who lived downwind from Hanford had a frighteningly high rate of hypothyroidism. These women were twice as likely to have experienced miscarriages compared those who did not develop hypothyroidism, alarming researchers. "It is difficult to think of any cohort of women anywhere with such a high percentage of hypothyroids, except for a thyroid clinic in a teaching center," the study's authors wrote. "This emphasizes the damage that most likely occurred from deliberate or accidental releases of radioactivity and its subsequent fallout."[54]

Another damning public health examination of the United States' long run of detonating atomic weapons in the Nevada desert, estimated that these tests were responsible for at least four hundred thousand deaths. Most of these individuals lived in surrounding states or as far away as the East Coast. Fallout from iodine-131, the study's author, Keith Meyers of the University of Arizona, noted, was carried away in high-altitude clouds which rained down on crops across the Upper Midwest. These crops were later consumed by cows, poisoning dairy supplies and eventually hundreds of thousands of unwitting people who drank the cows' tainted milk.[55] "Counterintuitively, the areas where fallout had the largest impact on the crude death rate was not in the region surrounding the test site, but rather in areas with moderate levels of radioactive fallout deposition in the interior of the country," said Meyers of his findings.[56]

In a study released in 2002 by the Centers for Disease Control and Prevention (CDC), which followed 3,440 people who were likely exposed to iodine-131 as children near Hanford, research determined there was no increase in the risk of thyroid cancer. "We used the best scientific methods available, and we did not find an increased risk of thyroid disease in study participants from exposure to Hanford's iodine-131," said Dr. Paul Garbe, who served as CDC's scientific adviser on the study. "If there is an increased risk of thyroid disease, it is too small to observe."[57]

Nonetheless, some residents near the Hanford site believe the constant barrage of radioactive pollution negatively impacted the health of their communities. In 1994, a feisty Hanford-area farmer named Tom Ballie showed the Advisory Committee on Human Radiation Experiments a map of the region and detailed what he called the "death mile," where he contended that "100 percent of those families that drank the water, drank the milk, ate the food, have one common denominator that binds us together, and that is thyroid problems, handicapped children or cancer."[58]

Ballie's "death mile" could have stretched from the Columbia River basin near Hanford all the way to the Pacific Ocean. From the site's inception up until the early 1970s, when Hanford was finally decommissioned, the Columbia River was considered the "most radioactive river in the United States."[59] While Hanford's nuclear plants aren't pumping today, and despite the fact that the site no longer produces fuel for nuclear bombs, radioactive waste still remains. Tons of it.

At many points during the operating years at Hanford, officials detected concerning amounts of contamination in the air and soil. They tested employees for exposure and worked to curtail the release of chemical and radioactive particles. Yet the public and even employees were not privy to the extent of the issues, some of which could have had fatal outcomes. Health physicists were worried early on of iodine-131's impact on workers and the surrounding communities. In fact, monitoring equipment that was utilized in 1945 became so contaminated it no longer functioned properly. As a result, scientists covertly tested the thyroid levels in farm animals and examined the extent to which iodine-131 made its way up the food chain.

"Great plumes of brown fumes blossomed above the concrete canyons [separations buildings], climbed thousands of feet into the air and drifted sideways as they cooled, blown by winds aloft," wrote physicist Leona Marshall Libby of the area's radioactive wildlife.[60] "The plumes cooled and descended on the desert where the iodine vapor stuck to the artemisia leaves: these leaves were eaten by rabbits, which in turn were eaten by the coyotes...the increasing radioactive content of...coyotes' thyroids were regularly monitored."

Only a handful of critics raised serious concerns about what this newfound plutonium obsession could do to the lands, ecology, and humans that lived near the operation. In a 1949 piece for the *Nation*, Richard L. Neuberger, who later would become a US senator for the state of Oregon, voiced concern, yet few, if any, were listening to his prescient words.

> Many details of the Hanford operation are Top Secret. But the great secret of all concerns the form in which plutonium-239 leaves Hanford. Innumerable gondola cars roll in behind Northern Pacific and Milwaukee locomotives. There is no perceptible movement outbound. Does this new radioactive element leave Hanford in a duffel bag, or a lead casket many feet thick?[61]

The Columbia River wasn't much better off than the lands around Hanford. A spike in radiation was recorded in the early 1950s, when contamination of fish in the Hanford Reach (the area of the Columbia River within Hanford's boundaries) reached an all-time high.[62] Levels of radioactivity were off the charts for waterfowl and river plankton as well. Bottom dwellers, like whitefish and sucker fish, appeared to be impacted the most. This worried scientists, who noted at the time that consuming even one pound of sucker fish would account for 20 percent of the permissible radioactive intake in humans.[63]

Hanford's groundwater also went nuclear. Over its lifespan, nuclear production discharged 450 billion gallons of radioactive liquids into the soil.[64] Today, two hundred square miles of aquifer beneath Hanford is contaminated, and fifty-three million gallons of radioactive and chemically hazardous waste remain stored in 177 leaky underground tanks that were built in the 1970s. In addition, Hanford has approximately twenty-five million cubic feet (750,000 cubic meters) of buried solid waste, spent nuclear fuel, and even leftover plutonium.[65]

The colossal legacy of Hanford, which now accounts for two-thirds of all high-level radioactive waste in the country, is fraught with calamity—a lingering atomic wreckage with little sign of being remediated anytime soon, if ever.[66] In the meantime, contractors hired by the DOE are making out like bandits at taxpayer expense, with virtually no significant public oversight. Remediation deadlines are consistently missed, upper management is continually in flux, and brave whistle-blowers have to risk their livelihoods just to be heard. It's also a precarious job for employees, and toxic accidents continue to plague cleanup efforts. There are many different scenarios that can play out at Hanford in the years ahead, the worst of which could leave a lasting impact as deadly as the nuclear bomb it helped to produce.

CHAPTER TWO

OF LEAKS AND LIES

A CATASTROPHE IN WAITING

The business of constructing more and more containers for
more and more objectionable material has already reached
the point both of extravagance and of concern.

—US Atomic Energy Commission, 1948

In 1987, Hanford's last operating nuclear reactor was finally
shuttered. In a sense, there was little need for the government
to keep the site up and running. The United States had amassed
a distressingly large nuclear arsenal of 21,393 warheads, and
the majority of the man-made plutonium fuel for these nukes
was created in Hanford facilities. Most plutonium is man-made
in nuclear reactors in a fissioning process, in which uranium atoms absorb neutrons.[1] By the mid 1980s, the Reagan administration was shifting US foreign policy and retooling Cold War
strategies.[2] Covert wars and coups d'etat continued to be the
United States' bread and butter, but fresh battles were being
waged on new fronts, and while nuclear weapons remained an
important aspect of US power, they were no longer essential to
the expansion of American dominance around the globe.

Throughout the 1980s, the United States was still locked in
bloody proxy wars aimed at combating the mythical commu-

nist threat, whether by supporting the mujahideen against the
Soviets in Afghanistan or by secretly backing the Contras in
their war on the Sandinistas in Nicaragua. The global nuclear
weapons furor had plateaued, or at least took on a new form
after Reagan expanded the global arms race during his first
term. In 1983, based on US propaganda that a Russian invasion
was imminent, Reagan announced the Strategic Defense Initiative (SDI): the first iteration of the anti-ballistic Star Wars
program that would ultimately cost taxpayers $30 billion.[3] And
while the program didn't directly produce nuclear weapons, the
threat it implied—that Russia had ballistic missiles aimed at the
United States—allowed the United States to ramp up its nuclear arsenal. The foe was no secret. Anti-Soviet fear permeated
this early Reagan era, when the US deployed three thousand
nuclear warheads in Reagan's "rearming" of the United States.
In 1981, Reagan even signed a presidential order declaring his
administration would carry on and expand the nuclear weapons policies of the Jimmy Carter White House.[4] After years of
sporadic and sometimes contentious negotiations, Ronald Reagan and the Soviet Union's Mikhail Gorbachev signed the Intermediate-Range Nuclear Forces Treaty in 1987. By 1990, the
United States cut its nuclear stockpile in half. The treaty may
have been more symbolic than tangible—the United States still
possessed more than enough nukes to destroy the planet. Yet
many considered the treaty a step in the right direction and a
pillar of arms control. The Intermediate-Range Nuclear Forces
Treaty lasted thirty years, until February 1, 2019, when president Donald Trump announced the United States would exit
the treaty.[5] Russia followed suit the next day. "This withdrawal
is a direct result of Russia's sustained and repeated violations of
the treaty over many years and multiple presidential adminis-
trations," accused defense secretary Dr. Mark T. Esper.[6] Gorbachev remarked that Trump's dismissal of the treaty was "not

the work of a great mind" and that "a new arms race has been announced."[7] Trump's move was largely initiated to heat up a new arms race with China. President Biden followed through on Trump's boisterous maneuver by supplying Australia with a fleet of nuclear-power submarines. This so-called AUKUS pact between the US, Britain, and Australia was launched as a direct reply to China's claim that they alone have sovereignty over the South China Sea, which holds at least 11 billion barrels of untapped oil and 190 trillion cubic feet of natural gas reserves.[8] [9]

During the advent of the Intermediate-Range Nuclear Forces Treaty, Hanford was also entering a new chapter. In February of 1986, nineteen thousand pages of documents were publicly released that detailed the radioactive and chemical turmoil that the United States' nuclear obsession had unleashed on the region since World War II. The news about Hanford's radioactive leaks and their effects went national. As a result, the state of Washington created the Hanford Historical Documents Review Committee, in which Native tribes including Umatilla, Yakama, and Nez Perce formed the Hanford Health Effects Review Panel. Locals, especially those living in and around Richland, felt a great sense of despair and powerlessness. For the first time, many learned the extent to which their government had covered up what they knew about Hanford's radioactivity and its potential impacts. Patriotism and the US war machine's obsession with nukes had come home to roost.[10] The evolving knowledge about radioactive dangers and the threat posed to workers was seeping into the consciousness of the greater Hanford community. "Their world has been knocked askew," wrote William Bequette, a retired editor who'd covered the region and its rural culture for decades. "Most are conservative, patriotic people who think of their jobs not just as a living but as a way to serve their country. . . . Now . . . they wonder if the trust they put in their supervisors and in officials in Washington DC, was misplaced."[11]

By 1990, even more damning information was gushing out of Washington. The DOE admitted that the radiation released from Hanford was more than enough to cause deadly illnesses and a variety of cancers. Energy secretary James D. Watkins, who was serving under president George H. W. Bush, tried to dismiss the alarming report by assuring the public that the nuclear ways of old were no longer, and the present-day DOE stewards of Hanford were not responsible for past mistakes. "[The current contamination] came about at a time when we knew little about the effects of radiation," said Watkins. "As years went along, we got a little smarter...I don't want you to relate it to what's going on today."[12]

While Watkins tried to allay concerns that Hanford was still dangerous, the reality was that Hanford would be a risk for centuries to come. In many ways, Hanford was now in an even more perilous spot than it had been in the 1940s and 1950s. No longer in the weapons development business, Hanford was entering an exhaustive and complex new phase, one that would require as much, if not more, ingenuity, and far more patience than it took to produce the first atom bomb that was detonated in the New Mexican desert in 1945. It was time to clean up, or at least figure out a way to manage, the immeasurable environmental turmoil that Hanford's nuclear proliferation had created.

In assessing both the damage caused by Hanford and the series of official responses to this damage, it is necessary to step back and look at the larger picture. For decades, the United States government had been aware of the perils of radioactive contamination, but took little action to prevent, protect, and contain its impacts during Hanford's atomic reign. By the time the site was finished as an atomic fuel production outpost, it had already set the stage for a slow nuclear catastrophe with impacts for thousands of years to come. This potential for destruction remained largely unknown to the US public. The numbers were staggering. In the immediate aftermath of the Hanford project, 430 million curies of man-made radioactivity remained, 185 million of which were in the form of discarded nuclear material. Additionally, sixty-five thousand metric tons of solid waste were still stored on site and a massive amount of radioactive chemical waste (220,000 metric tons) sat in aging tanks that would soon begin to leak.[13] To a layperson, this astronomical amount of radioactive material is difficult to comprehend. Like the dim reality of our changing climate, it is easier to banish the complicated reality from one's mind than to confront it.

Hanford was now a nuclear landfill, a radioactive cesspit laced with chemicals and particles that could destroy entire ecosystems and kill thousands of people. The numbers are frustratingly obscure; even scientists and engineers who spent their careers understanding this stuff were not certain how much radioactivity was released at Hanford during its four-decade run. Nonetheless, the task of cleaning it up, or at the very least ensuring it was safe, was now underway and would soon become a profitable enterprise—the likes of which had never been undertaken in human history.

TOP SECRET ACCIDENTS

The first sign of legitimate danger at Hanford, at least when it came to the US public's attention, occurred in June 1973, when a massive storage unit called 106-T at the complex's tank farm was confirmed to have leaked 115,000 gallons of boiling radioactive goop into the sandy soil surrounding its underground hull. An investigation by the contractor Atlantic Richfield tried to calm nerves by asserting the atomically charged liquid did not make it into the groundwater supply. "It was predicted that the leaked waste would be retained by the dry sediment above the water table," the report stated. "The greatest depth to which this liquid waste penetrated is about twenty-five meters below the ground surface, or about thirty-seven meters above the water table."[14] While the science indicated the contaminants did not leak into the groundwater or into the nearby Columbia River, the incident showed that another such accident, and one of an even greater magnitude, could happen at one of Hanford's other storage tanks.

What was perhaps most alarming about the 1973 event was that not a single person could say exactly how long 106-T had been leaking or what had caused the tank to crack in the first place. In fact, when administrators eventually realized what was going on, they weren't even sure what was *inside* 106-T. There was no panic. No major alert to workers, and not even a pithy press release warning the community about what administrators did or did not know. The secretive culture at Hanford was still alive and flourishing.

Workers had first noticed the problem on a Friday, June 8, 1973. But it wasn't until Saturday, June 9, that administrators began thumbing through their reports and read-outs in an attempt to uncover what was actually missing from 106-T. Even though pages and entire sections were nowhere to be found, the investigating team was able to piece together what they believed had occurred. For a full fifty-one days, an average of 2,100 gallons of gunk had seeped out of 106-T every twenty-four hours. In total, 151,000 gallons emptied into the soil, which included forty thousand curies of cesium-137, four curies of plutonium, fourteen curies of strontium-90 and other, slightly less toxic sludge. There had also been numerous leaks at Hanford in the early years. In 1958, fifteen different tanks leaked some

422,000 gallons of a similar nuclear waste by-product. Yet the 106-T was an entirely different animal. The 1973 accident was the largest single radioactive waste disaster in the history of Hanford, if not the United States, and unlike the incidents recorded in 1958, newspapers were finally covering it.

MOUNTING PUBLIC CONCERN

The Atomic Energy Commission (AEC), which oversaw overseeing operations in 1973, came under scrutiny in the press for the alleged mismanagement of Hanford's tank farm. "The scope of the problem is staggering," read a *Los Angeles Times* investigative piece. "It has been estimated, for example, that there is more radioactivity stored at the single Washington (Hanford) reservation than would be released during an entire nuclear war."[15]

The 106-T disaster also impacted public perception of the safety of the United States' nuclear technology. AEC commissioner Clarence E. Larson tried to downplay the accident and his agency's role in the mess, as well as the "implications that large masses of people are endangered." Larson, and a governmental report that followed, laid much of the blame on the contractor Atlantic Richfield and a few bad apples inside the AEC.

"The bungling attributed to Atlantic Richfield (which has declined to comment on the report) would be unbecoming for a municipal sewage plant, to say the least of the nation's main repository for nuclear waste," wrote nuke critic Robert Gillette in an August 1973 issue of *Science*, two months after the leak was discovered. He continued:

> The problem, according to the report, was that the operators who took the readings did not know how to interpret them; and a day shift supervisor in charge of half of Hanford's

tanks...let six weeks worth of charts and graphs pile up on his desk because of "the press of other duties" he said later, and never got around to reviewing them; and consequently a "process control" technician elsewhere at Hanford, who was supposed to be reviewing the tank readings for "long-term trends" received no data for more than a month. The technician...waited until 30 May to complain about the delays, but he nevertheless emerges as the hero in this dismal story. Fragmentary readings of fluid levels in 106-T arrived in his hands on Thursday 7 June, but it was enough to show that something was amiss. The technician put out the alarm, the supervisor confirmed the leak the next morning after checking his records and promptly resigned. All of this, the report says, led to the discovery that AEC officials had previously failed to notice or fully appreciate.[16]

It was the first time the public became starkly aware of how Hanford's tank farms were a tragedy in waiting, not only because the tanks were old and unfit to store massive amounts of toxic waste, but because the agency and the contractors assigned to monitor them had failed to do their job. But it wasn't just humans who had failed. The tanks themselves were unsettling and foreboding. One hundred and fifty of these gigantic underground silos were built on a dusty plateau just seven miles from the Columbia River and only a few feet below ground. Hanford's early history and conceptions around nuclear power, waste, and safety is imperative to understanding the disaster that lay ahead. A 1948 AEC report foresaw a future fraught with problems associated with these tanks, the way they were built, and their location:

> Hundreds of thousands of dollars have been spent and are currently being spent for providing holding tanks for so-called "hot wastes," for which no other method of disposal has yet been developed. This procedure...certainly provides no solution to a continuing and overwhelming problem.

The business of constructing more and more containers for more and more objectionable material has already reached the point both of extravagance and of concern.[17]

In other words, the tanks were a short-term fix to a problem with no long-term solution. They knew they couldn't just dump the waste into the Columbia River, so piping the stuff into hulking underground tanks seemed the obvious choice to the engineers of the 1940s. The waste was so hot it would boil, not for hours or days or even months, but for decades to come. Engineers hoped a better remedy would reveal itself down the road. Such are the pitfalls of nuclear waste, and over the years Hanford's reactors produced unfathomable amounts of this steaming radioactive soup.

When the AEC took control of Hanford after the end of World War II, they knew they had to do something to curtail a potential tank waste fiasco, so they developed a system that would keep the tank contents cool, designing contraptions to stir the waste so the hot gunk wouldn't settle and end up leaking out the bottom. This workaround was imperfect at best. The public first learned of the 1958 tank malfunction in 1968 after a secret Joint Committee on Atomic Energy report was released. But the government knew there had been plenty more. From 1958 to 1965, administrators recorded mishaps at nine different units, and these tanks would continue to spring leaks throughout the 1970s. Some leaks were small, but others were quite large: in total, upwards of 55,000 to 115,000 gallons of scalding atomic waste escaped, followed by the 106-T incident.[18] The tanks were also emptied on occasion to make room for new waste. Between 1946 and 1958, nearly 130 million gallons of waste had been discharged into the soil. Much of this waste went untreated, leaving behind an estimated 275,000 metric tons of chemicals and sixty thousand curies of radioactivity, a portion of which polluted local aquifers.[19]

In retrospect, the ongoing pattern of leaks, workarounds, and government secrecy ought to have been alarming to anyone who understood the risks. Hanford's storage tanks were not constructed to last forever, or even a fraction of the lifespan of their contents, and Hanford contractors were well aware of this fact. They knew all too well that an accident did not have to happen immediately. A leak could occur at any moment in the extensive life of the atomic waste the tanks were tasked with holding.

Let's put it all in perspective. An isotope of plutonium (Pu-239), for example, has a half-life of over twenty-four thousand years.[20] This means that after twenty-four thousand years, half of all the plutonium that leaks out of one of these shoddy tanks will still be as virulent as the day it was first released. Hanford had another big problem. They didn't have enough tanks to hold all the already existing waste, or the waste they would continue producing. Yet in 1959, despite the lack of storage, the AEC denied a request to build new storage units. It was not until 1964, after additional pleas, that the AEC finally gave the go-ahead to construct new tanks. Before these new tanks were finally approved, more and more waste was pumped into the older units, creating a host of problems, the most serious of which was that more nuke waste meant more heat and an increased risk of a serious accident. There were no new tanks to which to transfer existing waste had one of the tanks failed. This could have led to a disaster—a narrowly avoided catastrophic event.

By the mid-1960s, Hanford's lack of tank storage had become a serious conundrum. In the fall of 1963, a nine-year-old unit known as 105-A began to ooze radioactive sludge from a split seam, which stopped leaking when salt was added to its internal mixture. The AEC continued to utilize the tanks even after identifying the cause of the leak, because they didn't have any extra tanks to house its contents. They subsequently added more waste to 105-A, to a dangerous 10 percent over its recommended capacity. No single tank had ever been filled with so much radioactive effluent. In January 1965, as a result of too much waste, steam began to pour out of 105-A, and the ground surrounding the tank began to quake. It must have been a shocking development, but without new tank construction there was nothing to be done but wait and watch.

Fortunately, the rumbling wasn't catastrophic and 105-A held. A 1968 comptroller general report noted that only a small amount of radioactivity bubbled out and into the soil. 105-A wasn't the only case of a leaky tank at Hanford in the 1960s. A contractor report from 1967 disclosed that ten more tanks were leaking and fourteen others were struggling from "structural stress and corrosion." By the time the public learned about the problem with 106-T, twenty-five additional tanks were decommissioned by the AEC due to suspected leaking.[21]

Reports on the storage tanks' various issues had long been classified due to the secrecy of the Manhattan Project. One such report by the United States Geological Survey (USGS), completed in 1953 and not released for another twenty years, warned that Hanford would have major problems if a better solution wasn't found for the disposal of toxic processing materials. The study noted the tanks were a "potential hazard" and that their structural lifespan was not known. Hanford supervisors brushed aside such concerns. In 1959 Congressional testimony, Herbert M. Parker, who served as a manager of the tank farm, said he had no reason to believe the underground storage units would not hold up for many "decades" to come. When asked if there had ever been a problem in the past, Parker replied, "We are persuaded that none has ever leaked."[22]

It was nonsense, of course. A secret Government Accounting Office (GAO) report from 1968 revealed Parker had lied, and that for years officials had withheld information from the public about potentially disastrous issues with Hanford's tanks. The GAO report noted that at least 227,000 gallons of waste had bled into the soil from ten different units, the first of which, an alarming thirty-five thousand gallons, occurred six months prior to Parker's congressional testimony. It was a leak he most certainly knew about. While the AEC was in the habit of dismissing such incidents, they were also keen on ignoring unsavory advice from independent observers. Outside experts continually alerted the AEC that the tanks were not up to snuff. "Current analysis by the Illinois Institute of Technology (IIT) have revealed that the self-boiling tank structures are being stressed beyond accepted design limits," read one such report. IIT also put the life expectancy of the tanks at two decades, and in some cases, even less.[23] Yet the AEC, in the name of anticommunism, ignored these distress signals. Instead of being reevaluated, Hanford's processing plants ran nonstop, churning out thousands of gallons of atomic waste every single day to challenge the United States' Soviet nemesis. The waste had to go somewhere. As a result, a crisis as volatile as the scalding sludge itself was cooking at Hanford.

WIND, WATER, AND SHAKY GROUND

While leaks during this period had the potential to be fatal, administrators continued to downplay risks, particularly those posed to the area's freshwater supply. Hanford operation manager Thomas A. Nemzek told the *Los Angeles Times* in a 1973 interview that not only had none of the leaked waste made it into the groundwater, but that even if it did, it would take upward of one thousand years to reach the Columbia River, by which time its effects would be inconsequential. Essentially, Nemzek asserted, stop worrying so damn much. But not everyone bought Nemzek's dismissive rationale. A study by the National Academy of Sciences, the aforementioned comptroller general's report and other geological surveys all countered Nemzek's claim. These reports further noted that aside from the groundwater issue and depending on the scale of the leak, radioactive particles could go airborne, which would result in immediate and potentially nationwide impacts.[24]

Aside from radioactivity blowing in the wind, there was another big issue: Hanford sat on shaky ground. As early as 1955, the National Academy of Sciences' National Resource Council put together a committee, Geological Aspects of Radioactive Waste Disposal, to look into AEC operations. What they found was startling. The committee was not convinced that leaving radioactive waste to sit in the dirt was a particularly bright idea. When looking at two of the United States' nuclear weapon sites, Hanford and the National Reactor Testing Station (NRTS) in southeastern Idaho, the committee noted that "at both sites it seemed to be assumed that no water from the surface precipitation percolates downward to the water table, whereas there appears to be as yet no conclusive evidence that this is the case."

Like the tanks releasing waste into Hanford's soil, shallow underground pipes at Idaho's NRTS had released nuke waste into the ground, and as with Hanford, the AEC assured everyone that it wasn't worth the worry. In their echoes of Herbert M. Parker's congressional testimony, the AEC was either lying or belligerently naive. Later a 1970 report by the Federal Water Quality Administration proved as much, noting that a leak had indeed sprung from pipes at NRTS, and nuclear waste had made its way into Idaho's groundwater supplies. Another accident at NRTS, in 1972, discharged 18,600 gallons of "sodium-bearing waste" during a transfer from one holding tank to another. In this instance, an estimated 15,900 curies of strontium-90, a radioactive isotope, also leaked. As of 2006, the accident was still having a negative impact, and groundwater near the site exceeded drinking water standards for strontium-90 (twenty-eight-year half-life), iodine-129 (sixteen-million-year half-life), and technetium-99 (211,000-year half-life), along with other radioactive particles. To make things worse, the DOE's Idaho branch released a startling report in April 2006 warning that groundwater in the Snake River Plain would "exceed drinking water standards for strontium-90 until the year 2095." In addition, the DOE cautioned, soil that was used as backfill around NRTS's tank farm was so laced with cesium-137 that it posed a severe risk to workers as well as the environment.[25] Could the same happen with Hanford's tank waste?

While not publicly admitting these obvious, well-documented dangers, by 1973 the AEC recognized the long-term necessity of properly disposing of Hanford's tank waste. They initiated a program to turn the radioactive muck into a solid substance in as little as three years, and according to the AEC, the program appeared promising. The tanks would be emptied and the waste would be solidified and safely stored, not unlike filling up a liquid ice tray, placing it into the freezer, and forgetting about it. At least how the AEC portrayed it to a naive public. Yet there were two big hurdles. One was funding; the other was that converting the tanks' contents into a stable substance was a hell of a lot more difficult than making ice. In fact, doing so proved virtually impossible, which is why the tanks were filled up in the first place. By 1985, despite $7 billion spent over the previous ten years, no progress had been made in ridding the aging tanks of their contents.[26] Even so, the storage tank mess was just one of several atomic troubles facing the remote nuclear site. And concerns were slowly trickling into the public realm.

CHEMICAL TROUBLES

The reactors at Hanford produced not only heaps of radio-active garbage but also truckloads of nasty chemicals used in the reprocessing of spent fuel rods. The compounds were used to dissolve radioactive materials, and mephitic chemical baths were administered to purify the uranium that made its way into the atomic bomb. These processes left behind other toxins as well: magnesium, acidic waste, and lethal levels of mercury. Much of the waste byproducts from these chemicals, averaging thirty-four thousand tons (sixty-eight million pounds) per year during the 1970s and 1980s, were hauled off for disposal hundreds of miles from Hanford. But plenty was left behind, having leached into the ground from makeshift lagoons and outdoor trenches, and contaminating upward of six thousand acres. The volume of waste was probably larger, and the danger greater, than the sixty-eight-million annual pounds officially reported.[27]

By the mid-1980s, one hundred and twenty trenches, or "cribs," were filled with hundreds of millions of gallons of low-level radioactive fluid pumped in through perforated pipes. These gravel-filled trenches, Hanford operators argued, filtered the liquid before it reached delicate groundwater supplies. Since rainfall is minimal in the region, a mere seven inches a year, Hanford managers believed the lack of moisture would ensure that radioactive particles would never pose a danger. However, opponents, who included state and other federal agencies, countered that the trenches were absolutely a hazard, as the cribs sat only 250 feet above fresh aquifers that fed the Columbia River. The problem was not the amount of rainfall but the hundreds of millions of gallons of liquid piling up, which, opponents argued, would eventually drive the radioactivity downward toward the aquifers and ultimately into the Columbia. Excess waste pumped into these cribs had also created two groundwater mounds, one of which reached a peak of sixty feet in 1961. George Toombs, a well-regarded physicist at the Oregon Health Division who studied radioactivity in the Columbia, warned that a radioactive overflow from one of these small hills could destroy large sections of the river and many of its species. Yet like so many other warnings, Toombs's was shrugged off as doomsday alarmism by Hanford administrators.[28]

The majority of these gravel cribs were built in the so-called "200-Area" of Hanford. In one 1985 instance, a gigantic plume of radioactive hydrogen (tritium) expanded over one hundred square miles and seeped into the Columbia River. Hanford officials downplayed the risk, arguing the release of tritium wasn't enough to cause any real harm. Others, including Norman Buske, a consulting physicist who was hired by Greenpeace to look into the matter, challenged their methodology and reported that the plume posed a real threat to local groundwater supplies and ultimately the river itself. An even larger plume of nitrate emanated from another waste trench and made its way to an underground aquifer during the same period. Hanford managers brushed off this event as well, stating that water levels still met local drinking standards despite the soil's nitrate pollutants.[29]

In March 2017, a failure took place at one of Hanford's underground tunnels. It was a reminder that Hanford has many other potential problems besides tank waste hazards. The dirt-and-wood tunnel gave in, leaving a gaping four-hundred-square-foot hole. How surprising was the accident, which forced thousands of workers to find safety? Not very, according to a report uncovered by the Seattle-based advocacy group Hanford Challenge.

In 1991, Westinghouse Hanford Company had requested that Los Alamos Technical Associates, Inc. (LATA), evaluate the structural integrity of PUREX Storage Tunnel #1, where the 2017 collapse would occur. The 1991 study of the tunnel indicated a low probability of any degradation of the pressure-treated timber in the tunnel, the report noting that the "only structural degradation that is occurring is due to the continued exposure of the timbers to the high gamma radiation field in the tunnel."[30]

Although the 1991 the report stated the effect of this exposure was minor at the time, the strength of the timber walls in a 1980 LATA evaluation was only 65.4 percent of its original strength. The study recommended that another test be conducted in 2001 by the United States Forest Product Laboratory to check the integrity of the tunnel's wood beams. There is no evidence that any further tests were carried out in 2001 or at any other time since the 1991 recommendation.

"How can waste be left in a tunnel? Whose idea was that?" asks Rod Ewing, a Stanford University nuclear security researcher. "I've been to Hanford many, many times for conferences and things like that, and I don't recall anyone saying that there was waste in tunnels underground. I can't imagine why that would be the case."[31]

After the 2017 tunnel collapse, the DOE said there were no signs of a radioactive release and opted to fill the hole with fifty truckloads of dirt and a plastic cover. The question remains if this strategy will stop more collapses that could have far more dangerous impacts. According to Doug Shoop, manager of the DOE Richland Operations Office, the answer is no. "There is potential for more collapse," says Shoop.[32]

A GAO report released in January 2020, which inspected the tunnel collapse and the DOE's response, scolded the agency for not doing enough to prevent failures from occurring. The GAO accused the DOE of avoiding finding out what had caused the collapse to begin with.[33] The report indicated that if the DOE had performed a thorough analysis, the tunnel collapse might have been prevented. "DOE would have had greater assurance that another, similar event will not take place at Hanford," the GAO said. Additionally, the report noted, parts of the Hanford reservation had not been inspected in over fifty years. How many other problems, potentially deadly ones, are waiting?

The DOE responded to the GAO report indicating that by the end of 2020 they would take up the GAO's recommendations and investigate other potential issues. While tank waste is often the focus at Hanford, another facility at the site, called the Waste Encapsulation Storage Facility (WESF), holds nearly two thousand capsules full of radioactive cesium and strontium, floating in liquid pools. There are fears they could break open during a seismic event, releasing a cloud of radioactivity that could blanket the entire region. The plan (delayed due to loss of funding under the Trump administration) is to relocate these capsules into dry storage by 2025. Critics say that's too long to wait and that the technology exists now to move them out of WESF. But the timeframe has not been altered despite concerns.[34] Like other safety concerns at Hanford, problems aren't often addressed until after the fact. The tunnel collapse cost $10 million to repair.[35] These types of mistakes are part of the greater problem facing the future of Hanford: the work that needs to be done is profitable. Accidents, too, even catastrophic ones, are profitable, and very few people are keeping tabs on the government, its contractors, and the workforce carrying out these precarious tasks. Largely because of its location, as well as the government's reluctance and inability to grapple with the enormity of the problem, Hanford remains the most complex environmental mess in the United States. Decades of lies, mismanagement, and blatant cover-ups have forged a secretive culture that continues to monopolize the ongoing work at Hanford, so much so that we might not know an accident is coming until it's far too late.

Much of the damage left behind after operations ceased at Hanford will never be reversed. The question is, can it be contained so as to not pose a danger in the future? Can safety improve for workers? Could all that tank waste (525 million gallons), all that toxic buried solid waste (25 million cubic feet), all the leaked and released waste (over 300,000 short tons), and all that discharged liquid (450 billion gallons) ravage the entire region, if not the country, if an accident occurred?

One incident in 1957, in present-day Russia, sheds light on such a frightening scenario.[36]

RUSSIA'S FORGOTTEN NUCLEAR DISASTER

It was a warm fall day on September 29, 1957, not unlike any other in the deep Russian interior. Residents in the Chelyabinsk region cared for their crops of wheat and potatoes; others herded cattle. Women hung out their family's clothes to dry as the winds picked up before the sun descended. In the distance, along the ridge in the southern sky, streams of dark colors began to appear. The town paper would speculate that the natural polar lights were responsible for the odd aura along the horizon. But there was a problem: the strange hues were not where the Northern Lights typically appeared. Those lights appeared north, not south of Chelyabinsk—plus, the Northern Lights were shades of blue and green, not gray and black. Something was off, but there was no panic in Chelyabinsk. In the Southern Urals, where Chelyabinsk was located, the local strain of late-1950s culture was not unlike that in the rural farming communities of the American Midwest: people were hardworking, churchgoing, family-oriented, patriotic, and tough. Their lives, however, were about to change forever.[37]

Government workers descended on the small towns in and around Chelyabinsk, twenty of which were soon evacuated. Around ten thousand people, mostly peasants, were forced out, leaving their pets and possessions behind. Farmers were instructed to slaughter their cows, destroy fertile farmland, and kill off their crops. Their livelihoods and way of life were destroyed, and no reason was given as to why they had to take such rapid drastic measures. Little did they know that a nuclear accident, the largest in history, had taken place at Hanford's sister facility in Russia, known as Mayak Chemical Combine.[38]

Conceived during the same period as Hanford, Mayak was constructed in 1946 and helped procure the Soviets' first atomic bomb, in 1949, under Stalin. Like virtually all of Russia's nuclear projects during the Soviet era, and just like the United States' Manhattan Project, Mayak was built and operated in total secret and with outright disregard for local communities and ecology. As one of the Soviets' covert "plutonium cities," Mayak became known as Chelyabinsk-40, a sort of dehumanizing code name that would soon become synonymous with disaster.[39]

"Starting in the late 1940s, the Russians released a great deal of radioactive waste into the waterways near Mayak, including lakes, streams, ponds, and reservoirs," recalls Don Bradley, author of *Behind the Nuclear Curtain: Radioactive Waste Management in the Former Soviet Union*. "For many years, radioactive effluent at Mayak was released directly into the Techa River, a major source of water for twenty-four villages along its banks." Every one of these villages, Bradley notes, no longer exist. All residents were evacuated years ago.

Today, Mayak no longer makes plutonium, but the facility is still operational and serves as a reprocessing site for spent nuclear fuel. The practice of reprocessing spent fuel was banned in the United States in 1977 by president Jimmy Carter. His administration believed doing away with spent fuel reprocessing was an important step in reducing nuclear weapons proliferation.[40] Even though Mayak isn't active as a production site, from the radioactive waste all around it, you'd think that it's still churning out nuclear fuel.

The body of water that received the most contamination from Mayak's nuclear fuel production was Lake Karachay. "Contamination [in Chelyabinsk] is perhaps the highest in the world, and the most acute problem in that region is at Lake Karachay," Thomas Nilsen, a researcher at the Bellona Foundation, an environmental organization headquartered in Oslo, Norway, said in 2001, fifteen years after the accident at Chernobyl, ten years before the Fukushima meltdown. He continued: "The Soviets started dumping waste from reprocessed plutonium into Karachay in the early 1950s, and extreme levels of radiation are still being monitored there."[41]

In fact, an isolated corner of the lake was at one time so chock-full of radioactive particles that human survival after a mere thirty minutes of exposure was fifty-fifty. Over 120 million curies of radioactive waste polluted the body of water. In the 1990s, Don Bradley, along with other researchers, visited one of the least polluted areas of the lake. "We drove out [to]. . . the lake with a guy holding a Geiger counter and a watch," recounted Bradley. "After ninety seconds, we came back. In that brief time, we received the equivalent dose of radiation of an airplane flight from Moscow to New York."[42]

However, the danger does not just exist in the lake itself. If levels are low, the lake has the potential to dry up during the hotter summer months, leaving open the possibility that the wind could carry radioactive dust across the region. This happened in 1967 when low snowfall resulted in a drastic decline in Lake Karachay's water levels, producing something of a nuclear summer. Wind currents blew particles from the toxic lake bed across an 1,800 square mile stretch of Chelyabinsk, contaminating upward of a half a million unwitting people. To this day, little is known about what impact the windblown particles had on the health of people or the land. In recent years, workers have placed large concrete blocks and stones on the lakebed to keep the dust at bay. There's no easy solution, of course, and this rudimentary fix could spawn another problem. "The stones help prevent the dust, but the weight also presses the sediments down and moves them closer to the groundwater," says Thomas Nilsen. "It's a catch-22."[43]

Over a ten-year period from 1948 to 1958, over 17,245 Mayak workers were exposed to radiation overdoses. Dumping of radioactive waste in nearby rivers was also responsible for a number of nuke-related illnesses downstream, where drinking water and agricultural production depended on irrigation.[44]

While residents were aware that the secret site of Mayak was a problem, they had no idea what had caused those mysterious lights in the sky on that fall afternoon in 1957. The secret was that something had gone terribly wrong at Mayak. Like the tank waste at Hanford, Mayak instituted a cooling system early on that continually kept its hot nuclear waste from reaching a critical point. But the waste in a holding cistern buried twenty feet underground began to heat up fast. The system had failed, but nobody knew what was happening until it was far too late. As the radioactive slop reached 350 degrees Celsius, its 160-ton concrete lid began to tremble, and finally blew. The cistern and the eighty tons of boiling gunk inside exploded in a volcanic eruption filled with radioactive steam and soot a half mile into the air. The black cloud darkened the sky, spreading twenty million curies of blistering atomic particles across fifty-two thousand square kilometers, roughly the size of West Virginia, and contaminating the homes of an estimated 270,000 people. Later, the accident at Mayak became known as the Kyshtym disaster, after the name of the closest town to the blast. In the immediate aftermath, the first wave of forced evacuation encompassed nearly ten thousand people. It nevertheless took upwards of two years for other evacuations to be carried out in nearby towns that had also been exposed to the radioactive fallout. [45]

The blast was measured as a Level 6 disaster on the International Nuclear Event Scale, placing the Kyshtym disaster behind Chernobyl and Fukushima (both Level 7s) as the third-most significant nuclear disaster ever. It is certainly the least well known. At the time, just as the United States government kept the inner workings of Hanford shrouded in secrecy, the Soviet government kept Mayak under wraps. Mayak, according to many Soviet maps, did not even exist.

It wasn't until 1976, when dissident scientist Zhores A. Medvedev wrote an article for the British journal *New Scientist*, that the Western world was made aware of what happened.

> For many years nuclear reactor waste had been buried in a deserted area a few dozen miles from the Urals town of Blagovehsnesk. The waste was not buried very deep. Nuclear scientists had often warned about the dangers involved in this primitive method of waste disposal, but nobody listened. Suddenly there was an enormous explosion. The nuclear reactions had led to overheating in the burial grounds. The explosion poured radioactive materials high into the sky. It was just the wrong weather for such a tragedy. Strong winds blew the radioactive clouds hundreds of miles away.
>
> Tens of thousands of people were affected, hundreds dying, though the real figures have never been made public. Many villages and towns were only ordered to evacuate when the symptoms of radiation sickness were already apparent. The irradiated population was distributed over many clinics. But no one really knew how to treat the

different stages of radiation sickness, how to measure the radiation dose received by the patients and their offspring. Radiation genetics and radiology could have provided the answer, but neither of them was available.[46]

Not all believed Medvedev's account. Sir John Hill, chairman of Britain's Atomic Energy Authority, called the report "rubbish" and "a figment of the imagination."[47] Hill's blustery denial was of course motivated by the United States' and Britain's efforts to cover up the dangers of their own nuclear programs. However, Medvedev's story was later confirmed by ex-Soviet physicist Leo Tumerman, who stated he had seen firsthand the devastation of Kyshtym only a couple of years after the incident. "The area was filled with radiation," admitted Tumerman. "And you couldn't drink the water or eat the fish." Tumerman added that "All the people with whom I spoke, scientists as well as laymen—had no doubt that the blame lay with Soviet officials who were negligent and careless in storing nuclear wastes."[48]

One anonymous witness wrote of what happened immediately following the blast. "Very quickly all the leaves curled up and fell off the trees." The observer also described a gruesome scene at a local hospital. "Some of the [victims] were bandaged and some were not. We could see the skin on their faces, hands and other exposed parts of the body to be sloughing off. These victims of the blast were brought into the hospital during the night. It was a horrible sight."[49]

The explosion was indeed horrific, but radiation doesn't always have an immediate impact. It can take weeks, months, or even years to make itself known. The fallout from the Mayak explosion landed throughout the region, most of which descended on an area four miles wide and thirty miles long. Streams, lakes, and acres of farmland were blanketed with radioactive soot. In villages closest to Kyshtym, men jumped in space-suit-like garments from military helicopters, instructing those tending to the fields to continue to dig out their crops. Entire families worked without proper safety gear. Not even shoes or protective masks were provided. They were told to dump what they had harvested into holes that had been dug by bulldozers. Throughout that fall, these families harvested and stacked wheat and hay into large piles, which were then set on fire. In other villages outside the immediate blast-zone, life appeared normal, until investigators began to look a bit more closely.[50]

Another anonymous eyewitness, who surveyed the area shortly after the blast, discovered a ravaged scene. "[We] crossed a strange, uninhabited, and unframed area. Highway signs along the way warned drivers not to stop for the next twenty to thirty kilometers because of radiation. The land was empty. There were no villages, no towns, no people, no cultivated land; only chimneys of destroyed houses remained."[51]

In one village, a full week after the accident, monitors discovered something startling. Children there were literally steaming with radiation. S. F. Osotin, who had been a member of the team that carried out those initial findings, recalled that a colleague placed a Geiger counter up to one child's belly and got a reading of forty to fifty microroentgens per second. They couldn't believe what they were witnessing. Cows that munched on atomically charged grass were visibly sick, bleeding at the mouth. Soldiers shot them on sight. Chickens, too, were loaded up with atomic particles but were still being eaten by locals because they had no idea what was going on. Other unwitting villages had astonishingly high levels of radiation as well. One such town, Berdianish, produced readings of 350 to 400 microroentgens per second—amounts that will kill you after four weeks of exposure.[52]

Though kept a secret by the Soviets, the Kyshtym nuclear accident was discovered by the CIA a few years after the fact through a network of spies and on-the-ground informants, along with aerial photographs of the wreckage. In May 1960, U-2 spy pilot Francis Gary Powers was shot down by Soviet Air Defense Forces as he was attempting to capture high-altitude photographs of the devastation at the Mayak site. Powers was captured and sentenced to three years for espionage, and in 1962 was exchanged for Soviet officer Rudolf Abel.[53]

It wasn't until 1978, after the Critical Mass Energy Project acquired fourteen heavily redacted documents, that the CIA admitted they had known about the Mayak disaster all along. Like the Soviets, the United States government kept what they had learned a secret and did not share what they knew with the public—not only to protect their sources but also, critics argued, in order to avoid raising concern about the United States' own nuclear program, and in particular operations at Hanford.[54]

"Absent any other reason for withholding information from the public," nuclear critic Ralph Nader said in a 1978 interview, "one possible motivation could have been the reluctance of the CIA to highlight a nuclear accident in the USSR that could cause concern among people living near nuclear facilities in the United States."[55]

According to one estimate by the Soviet Health Ministry in Chelyabinsk, the ultimate death toll caused by the Mayak explosion was 8,015 people over a thirty-two-year period. The long-term impacts of the singular event are difficult to quantify, as the facility, much like Hanford, released an immeasurable amount of radiation for over three decades.

The Mayak disaster of 1957, while covered up by both the Soviets abroad and the US government at home, should have raised serious alarms about nuclear safety and the risks associated with radioactive contamination. However, being truthful about the danger associated with producing atomic bombs and storing radioactive waste would have also meant having to confront the reality that Hanford, along with other nuclear sites around the country, was putting local populations and environments in serious peril. No doubt the people of Richland, Washington, would have had to come to terms with the fact that such an accident could just as easily happen in their own backyard. Keeping the war machine running meant putting a positive spin on nuclear technology, from weapons to nuclear energy. In a sense, US power was based on the myth that there was little downside to nuclear proliferation, only endless potential. The mythical capabilities of atomic energy continue to permeate debates today about combating climate change and challenging our fossil fuel addiction. In the meantime, there's still a very real threat facing the United States, and it's bubbling in Hanford's ancient tanks—tanks just like the one that blew at Mayak over sixty years ago.

A SCIENTIST IN DISTRESS

In the late 1980s and early 1990s, two US teams visited Russia to study Mayak, focusing on the 1957 accident as well as on waste impacts on underground aquifers. Dr. Donald Alexander, a retired high-level DOE physical chemist who worked at Hanford, was a member of the 1990 delegation. At the time, Alexander was the director of the International Technology Transfer program for the Office of Environmental Management in Washington, DC.

"The mission I led to the former Soviet Union was the second mission there under the sponsorship of the newly formed DOE Office of Environmental Management (EM)," said Alexander:

EM is the same office that runs the cleanup work at Hanford. The first mission consisted of a combined scientific and management team. In 1990 our mission was the first fully technical team of environmental scientists from the DOE and the DOE National Laboratories. We spent a lot of time with the Russians discussing deep well injection issues that had arisen at their site. Apparently, they had deliberately injected nuclear waste down deep boreholes into underground aquifers. We had considerable experience [in this field].

In addition to sharing this information with the Russians, Alexander learned their counterparts had also been collecting health data on the 1957 event. Alexander's team successfully negotiated for the transfer of the data collected by the Soviets on the health effects of Mayak's radioactive release and established a program that allowed Russian and US scientists to share nuclear cleanup technologies and research.

"I was determined to negotiate for the health data since we do not experiment with humans in the United States and had no such data," adds Alexander. "We did not examine the health effects data while we were at Mayak but we were shown films of their health studies. Our negotiations for the health data were successful and the data was delivered to the United States."

Alexander's research in Russia caused him to worry about tank safety issues at Hanford, in particular the potential for a hydrogen explosion. In 1993, a "burping" tank at Hanford was emitting large amounts of hydrogen until it was stabilized by an innovative mixer pump. "This hydrogen, if ignited, could have led to a tank explosion with consequences similar to that of Mayak's," warned Alexander. "There is no way of guaranteeing that such a gas release will never happen again even in the newly constructed Waste Treatment facilities."

It's not just Alexander who became concerned about a Mayak-like accident at Hanford. Even the Oregon Department of Energy noted that the tanks are a ticking time bomb: "A fire or other accident involving Hanford's contaminated facilities or underground waste tanks could cause an airborne release of radioactive materials," they wrote in 2007.[56] The Defense Nuclear Facilities Safety Board also believes the tanks are ripe for an accident. "All the double-shell tanks contain waste that continuously generates some flammable gas," the board said in 2013 and has reiterated the same sentiment over the years. "This gas will eventually reach flammable conditions if adequate ventilation is not provided."[57]

This potential buildup of hydrogen is why Alexander is so concerned about a possible explosion in the future that could leave much of the region under a cloud of radioactive smoke and debris.

Today, as Hanford faces the daunting task of ridding the tanks of their toxic waste, an accident cannot be ruled out. Alexander also points out that the DOE is not equipped to manage this massive undertaking. "One of the main problems at Hanford is that DOE is understaffed and overtasked," Alexander told me. "As such, we cannot conduct in-depth reviews of each of the individual systems in the facilities. Therefore there is a high likelihood that several systems will be found to be inoperable or not perform to expectations."

If these systems don't perform, the risk of an immeasurable nuclear accident could ravage the Pacific Northwest, killing thousands, just as Mayak did in the Soviet Union. It's difficult to fathom what kind of turmoil a comparable explosion would inflict. The fallout, no doubt, would spread far and wide. During the massive fires of summer 2021, smoke from Oregon and California reached the East Coast, blanketing Chicago, New York City, and other cities in a dark, murky haze.[58] It was much the same when Washington State's Mount Saint Helens blew on March 27, 1980, volcanic ash spreading north to Canada and east across the United States. Air pollution monitors in northeastern United States cities detected fine ash particulates.[59] I vividly recall my mother instructing my brothers and me to stay indoors in Billings, Montana, as our front yard was blanketed in a grey soot, as if a giant ashtray had been dumped on our lawn. This heavy ash devastated entire streams in Oregon and Washington, killing off salmon hatchlings. It laid waste to forests. Many of these rivers and wild areas have rebounded, but what if they'd been consumed in scalding atomic debris and not volcanic minerals?

A Hanford tank eruption would no doubt create a similar crisis, but instead of ash, radioactive particles would fly across the region. The Columbia River, the lifeblood of more than ten thousand farmers and dozens of commercial fisheries in the Pacific Northwest, would certainly be contaminated. These industries, much like the agricultural communities around Mayak in the 1950s, would be unlikely to survive such a horrific event. Then there's the toll on people. Depending on wind patterns, an atomic plume would immediately impact millions of residents across multiple states. Places like Walla Walla, Washington, and Boise, Idaho, would be forever changed. Even if they weren't immediately impacted, no family would choose to raise a family in a city that boasted high levels of radioactivity. Towns close to Hanford, like Richland, would be forced to evacuate, becoming ghost towns overnight. The entire economy of the Pacific Northwest would be crushed, in turn triggering a market crash that would spread across the globe.

Aside from the economic turmoil, a radioactively charged explosion would be unlike anything the United States has ever experienced, and it would create environmental challenges far greater than the fall of the Twin Towers on 9/11, the accident at Three Mile Island, or the Deepwater Horizon oil spill—combined. People would die. Ecosystems would be devastated. The environment, especially the Pacific Northwest, would be forever altered. It's a dire but entirely realistic scenario that nobody wants to see unfold.

Next page: Inside the B Reactor, © Mark Ruwedel 1992–93

CHAPTER THREE:

THE PERMANENT DISASTER ECONOMY

Bechtel, by all accounts and purposes, has done an absolutely miserable job.

—Tom Carpenter of Hanford Challenge

If you only needed to know two things about what Hanford is today, they would be these: first, it's the most toxic place in Western Hemisphere, and second, it's the most expensive environmental cleanup in world history.[1] The latter is the result of a free-market approach to the cleanup. The former is a byproduct of the Cold War and the United States' addiction to the deadly weapons industry. In every aspect, Hanford is a quintessential US project. It's tough. It's dangerous. It's built on stolen lands. It's also vitally important to understand that the issues plaguing Hanford are not solely the result of a few bad apples. The various problems are also not the result of bad science or a lack of know-how among staff at the DOE. Instead, the troubles engulfing this corner of Washington State are wholly systemic in nature, entombed in a profit-driven model that more often than not creates as many fiascos as it solves. In other words, Hanford is a solid case proving that capitalism, and an almost religious devotion to

private industry contracts, is *not* the best remedy to environmental disasters. Hanford's calamity was also exacerbated by
the Cold War's inter-imperial rivalry between the Soviets
and the US, a dynamic that is playing out in a similar fashion
between the US and China today.

Government contracting to private companies, also known
as the "federal procurement system," was shaped and solidified
by the United States' growing military apparatus. During the
Revolutionary War, the Continental Congress streamlined
the government's contracting process so that supplies would
quickly reach the Continental Army. The government at the
time was intent not to rely on foreign countries to provide the
United States with war goods and materials, believing it was a
potential liability. In other words, it was crucial to the budding
empire that its weapons were manufactured on US soil and not
by its adversaries across the pond. By 1775, the government in
Washington appointed the country's first Quartermaster General and Commissary General, who together worked to "buy,
store, transport, and distribute needed goods" for the army.
These roles quickly evolved, and the system by which the US
government provided goods to its servicemen expanded. By
1789, the Departments of War and Treasury were founded,
and by 1798, the US War and Navy Departments became authorized to make all purchases from private industry directly,
where the lowest bidder was more often than not the recipient
of these government contracts.[2]

Lack of accountability with government contracts is not
new to the gargantuan Hanford cleanup. It's a centuries-old
problem. Janet A. McDonnell writes, in "A History of Defense Contract Administration," that during the War of 1812
there was a total lack of accountability when it came to the
government's procurement process. While some conditions
improved by 1860, the Civil War brought more chaos and

scandal. The war had expanded at such a rapid clip that supply officers in the field had to keep up by purchasing goods on the open market. Congress, in an attempt to rein in misconduct and government waste, enacted legislation to curb this abuse, but the efforts were futile as there was little to no enforcement of the new law.[3]

But while the government purchased many of its goods and services from vendors, it also ran weapons production sites. Harpers Ferry Armory in Virginia was one such government-owned gun factory, which was raided by abolitionist John Brown and his party of twenty-two in October 1859 in an attempt to spark a slave revolt.[4] Brown was defeated and later executed, and the United States weapons machine ramped up.

Very early on, procuring government contracts while building up US military power was a lucrative business. From the Civil War to World War I, the largest deals were handed out to the lowest bidder in what was deemed a competitive open and free marketplace. In other words, capitalism was intricately intertwined with the military. During this period, it was the navy that proved the most adept at allocating taxpayer dollars. From shipyard construction to gunboats and expensive battleships, virtually every aspect of the country's naval fleet was made by private companies and at taxpayer expense. The whole complicated operation, which had very little oversight, was a disastrous yet profitable mess.

This traditional government procurement was not unique, as it had existed in Europe for centuries. Yet it took the US government and its free market ethos to make the bidding a competitive, profit-dependent process. The onset of World War I only accelerated government contracting. Laws were eventually passed allowing the US government to unilaterally end agreements once the war ceased, but even canceled contracts left taxpayers on the hook for ensuring the companies would see the remainder of their contracts paid in full. In other words, the system was rigged from the start, and taxpayers paid the price.

The public's awareness of the free market's death grip on the US Armed Forces became a topic of national discussion on January 18, 1961, when president Dwight D. Eisenhower called attention to the "conjunction of an immense military establishment and a large arms industry."[5] It was during the creation of the Hanford project that the military-industrial complex, as Eisenhower put it, officially commenced. By the time of Eisenhower's famous public address, nearly twenty years had passed since the United States dropped nuclear bombs on Japan. And while the seeds had been planted during the fight against Britain and later during the Civil War, it was the United States' commitment to World War II that turned this for-profit military enterprise into a robust economy unlike anything that had existed before it. In 1941, the War Department, with Congress's blessing, allocated $36 billion to fight the war. It was more than the army and navy had spent on the entire World War I, a staggering amount, as the US would end up spending $4.1 trillion in today's dollars on its war efforts. "If you are going to try to go to war, or to prepare for war, in a capitalistic country, you have got to let business make money out of the process or business won't work," said secretary of war Henry Stimson.[6] By all accounts, it was a blood-soaked, greed-based system and still is. Capitalism and war go hand in hand, and nothing encapsulated this flourishing wartime economy and the budding military-industrial complex more than the creation of Hanford.

BIRTH OF THE WAR ECONOMY

US commitment to World War II was without precedent. No country in history had spent more on fattening up its military. Dubbed the "arsenal of democracy," the government's spending made up 40 percent of the nation's gross domestic product (GDP).[7] The war forever altered the the US military. In 1940, the country's defense budget was $1.9 billion; by 1945, military spending had ballooned to $59.8 billion. During the same period, no other country even came close.[8] The United States spent double that of Germany and over ten times what Japan had allocated to the war. Signs of this radical shift could be seen everywhere as the United States' "permanent war economy" settled in.

"The term 'permanent war economy' is attributed to Charles Wilson, CEO of GE, who warned at the end of World War II that the US must not return to a civilian economy, but must keep to a 'permanent war economy' of the kind that was so successful during the war: a semi-command economy, run mostly by corporate executives, geared to military production," explains Noam Chomsky. "After World War II, most economists and business leaders expected that the economy would sink back to depression without massive government intervention of the kind that, during the war years, finally overcame the Great Depression. The New Deal had softened the edges, but not much more . . . the 'permanent war economy' has an economic as well as a purely military function."[9]

World War II was a big money maker, and the impact of the exploding economy was felt across all sectors of society. More women entered the workforce than ever before; in fact, 65 percent of the aviation sector, a total of 310,000 workers, were women. The now famous image of "Rosie the Riveter" was born out of this drastic shift. Based loosely on a real-life military munitions worker, the overtly patriotic Rosie the Riveter propaganda campaign was conjured in an attempt to inspire more women to pitch in. Job sectors that were typically male dominated opened up and the government stepped in to help out women who were leaving their roles as homemakers for the first time. In 1940, the federal government passed the Lanham Act, which provided grants for childcare and other community services in areas where women were employed in the defense industry. In 1942, under the prodding of his wife Eleanor, president Franklin D. Roosevelt ushered through the Community Facilities Act, creating the first government-backed childcare centers. In total, seventeen million jobs were created through the war economy, ultimately lifting the country out of the Great Depression.[10]

Industry output also grew at a pace never seen before in US history. One-third of the entire US economy was devoted to the war effort. Wages rose. Corporate taxes increased, as did corporate profits. Manufacturing saw one of the largest boons, with salaries jumping by 50 percent. Union ranks filled. Black people entered sectors of the workforce for the first time and employment was higher than ever. Though these gains weren't equally spread throughout society, they translated to high support for the war even as deaths of US troops mounted abroad. Many economists and historians believe that without the government's full commitment to World War II, the New Deal programs would not have been as long-lasting or significant. As Doris Goodman explains in *The American Prospect,*

> Despite the New Deal, even President Roosevelt had been constrained from intervening massively enough to stimulate a full recovery. By 1938 he had lost his working majority in Congress, and a conservative coalition was back, stifling the New Deal programs. When the economy had begun to bounce back, FDR pulled back on government spending to balance the budget, which contributed to the

recession of 1938. The war was like a wave coming over that conservative coalition; the old ideological constraints collapsed and government outlays powered a recovery.[11]

It wasn't just the fact that the war improved upon the economic efforts of the New Deal, notes Goodman, it also was the first time the US government was the main purchaser of US goods produced by US workers. It was a truly astounding change. One-half of every single good manufactured in the United States was later purchased, or contracted to be made in the first place, by the US government, which quickly became deeply intertwined with labor, a concept never before experienced in the US economy.[12] Sadly, this expansion and transformation of economic life materialized due to the United States' commitment to World War II and not from a grand socialist experiment.

Government and private capital had never before experienced such a tumultuous relationship. The government seized control of corporations. In 1944, FDR took control of Montgomery Ward after a thundering labor dispute. It was the fourth year of the war, and there was no end in sight. Companies like Montgomery Ward had been producing items that the government deemed war essentials. Two years prior, the National War Labor Board was created to deal with labor disputes during the period, along with other issues that arose from this drastic economic reconfiguration. In the case of Montgomery Ward, which was one of the largest department stores in the country, they were forced to make items like clothing, auto parts, and farm equipment.

Montgomery Ward's chairman Sewell Avery had other plans. Avery didn't care for the government telling him what his company ought to produce, and he wasn't going to sit by and let the United Retail, Wholesale, and Department Store Union dictate the terms of his company's production through an organized strike. Avery went livid, infamously yelling "To hell with the government!" at a lawyer who was attempting to calm his nerves about the government's intrusion. "I want none of your damned advice," he bemoaned.[13]

In a photo that has now become a hallmark of the capitalist dismay at federal dictates during World War II, Avery can be seen carried from his office by two National Guardsman in a seated position, in his black suit and tie, arms crossed with a smirk on his face. FDR was as upset at Avery's grandstanding as Avery was with FDR. But FDR, with the force of his government behind him, gained the upper hand, and ordered Henry Stimson to take over Montgomery Ward's offices and warehouse plants in Michigan, California, Illinois, New York, Colorado, and Oregon, a move prompted by the pending union strike and Avery's perceived threat to the US war machine. If Avery and the union couldn't come to an agreement, Roosevelt would quash the conflict to keep the war engine running—not because FDR was a friend of labor, but because of his thirst for victory. He happily ordered the National Guard to break up the strike, which ended on the eve of the seizure. FDR's infamous no-strike pledges were in place to block these types of labor uprisings.[14] "The Government of the United States cannot and will not tolerate any interference with war production in this critical hour," said FDR following the seizure. In May 1944, Commerce Secretary Jesse Jones gave Avery back control of his company.

It's a fascinating tale. It is also instructive as to how the economy of World War II completely, if only temporarily, reshaped US industry. Some on the right look at this era and see the private sector as the true engine of ingenuity. Others on the left view the economics of World War II as solely a destructive, evil force. It was more complex and nuanced, argues left historian Mark R. Wilson in his 2016 book, *Destructive Creation: American Business and the Winning of World War II:*

Had the labor movement been less divided and had the Roosevelt administration been more unified and disciplined when it came to public relations, more Americans might have heard messages that touted the crucial contributions of public institutions—military as well as civilian—to the nation's victory in the war of production. But during World War II, the business community was more unified and energetic than its ostensible rivals. Although this unity waxed and waned over the years since 1945, American business leaders and their allies have mostly continued to prevail over trade unionists and left-leaning policymakers in struggles over ideas, language, and power. Decades of mainstream political discourse denigrating government, along with widespread reticence about the contributions of military and civilian governmental authorities, have almost certainly damaged public welfare and the ability of Americans to engage in constructive citizenship. . . . If American policymakers had applied the lessons of World War II mobilization to the toughest challenges of the later twentieth century, people around the world would be better off today.[15]

FISSION OR BUST

Nothing embodies the government's commitment to World War II more than the Manhattan Project. In January 1939, news quickly spread that nuclear fission had been achieved in Berlin under the steady hands of German chemists Otto Hahn and Fritz Strassmann. The following year, FDR raced to set up the Advisory Committee on Uranium, which ultimately found that nuclear fission "would provide a possible source of bombs with a destructiveness vastly greater than anything now known."[16] It was a preliminary assessment, but the atomic wheels were in motion.

In early 1940, research experiments were proceeding in university labs around the country. In Britain the story was the same, and the science was progressing swiftly. The Frisch–Peierls memorandum, prepared by German-Jewish physicists Otto Frisch and Rudolf Peierls, dropped in March 1940 and prompted a sort of nuclear revolution in the United Kingdom, which was already at war with Germany. The document contained the first calculations of what it would take to create a functioning and deadly nuclear warhead. The game-changing document was produced by the British government's MAUD Committee, a scientific working group that acted as a precursor to the US's clandestine Manhattan Project. Urgency mounted in Britain and the United States as concern grew that Germany was on the same path to creating a bomb. Following Japan's Pearl Harbor attack on December 7, 1941, FDR was ready to put the full support of the United States government behind this budding nuclear science. By June 1942, the Manhattan Project was officially up and running.[17]

The Manhattan Project was not developed out of thin air; it was a culmination of ongoing research. Government committees—the S-1 Committee in particular, which was born out of the Advisory Committee on Uranium—had been reviewing and conducting research in labs across the country. But there was something palpably different about this new phase of nuclear development in the United States. The United States would no longer dabble on the fringes of this new, earth-shattering technology. Instead, it would be at its forefront, directing not only its best scientific minds but also nearly endless resources to the endeavor.[18]

The Manhattan Project, named for its central location at 270 Broadway in New York, evolved from a research phase of nuclear development to testing and construction. The US

Army, under the guidance of Major General Thomas M. Robbins and Colonel Leslie Groves, would collaborate with the Corps of Engineers Construction Division to select sites across the country suitable for specific aspects of the project. Over fifty-six thousand acres were seized under eminent domain in Oak Ridge, Tennessee, and would be used to enrich uranium for a nuclear bomb. Some fifty-four thousand acres in Los Alamos, New Mexico, home to Project Y, were chosen due to their remote location, and were used by University of California researchers and engineers to design and build an atomic bomb. In Washington, Hanford's forty-thousand acres were picked for their remoteness and access to water for the similar job of producing plutonium, which was undertaken by DuPont.[19] Bechtel, the largest contractor at Hanford, was also involved in the early years of the Manhattan Project, constructing buildings at Hanford and later at Los Alamos.[20]

There was concern that Oak Ridge was located too close to Knoxville and was at risk of killing Americans if there was an explosive accident. As a result, Hanford was chosen as an additional location for the nation's plutonium production. Lastly, a scientific laboratory was erected at the University of Chicago and later relocated to Red Gates Woods in Cook County, Illinois, where the world's first nuclear reactor was built, in May 1944.[21] Even at the Manhattan Project's inception, there was concern that something could go wrong, endangering the lives of US citizens in the government's quest to perfect this novel nuclear technology.

The Manhattan Project, like other aspects of the insidious US war enterprise, cost taxpayers a bundle. In August 1998, the US Nuclear Weapons Cost Study Project, conducted by the Brookings Arms Control Initiative, found that between

1942 and 1945 the United States spent $21.5 billion on nuclear arms development.[22]

The entire war cost the country $3.3 trillion. On average, each nuclear bomb used in the war cost $5 billion to develop. The United States produced four and detonated three: Gadget (New Mexico test), Little Boy (Hiroshima) and Fat Man (Nagasaki). Bomb number four, which was made and at the ready, was never utilized. Oak Ridge was the most expensive site built during the Manhattan Project's heyday, with Hanford and Los Alamos trailing behind.

The United States only escalated its allocation of tax dollars toward building its nuclear arsenal after the war ended. From 1945 to 1990, the United States went all in, developing over seventy thousand nuclear bombs and warheads during the Cold War. It was a booming business, and Hanford was operating at full throttle. In total, the site produced 103.5 metric tons of plutonium. Meanwhile, sites in Kentucky, Ohio, and Tennessee produced 745.3 metric tons of uranium. The government also had to test the goods. In all, 1,030 nuclear arms tests were conducted by the US military and its contractors, 215 in the air and 815 underground from 1945 to September 1992. The accounting is stunning. Nuclear weapons made up almost 30 percent of all military spending from 1940 to 1996, $5.5 trillion of an $18.7 trillion total.[23]

RADIOACTIVE AFTERMATH

Despite the trillions of dollars that poured into nuclear weapons development, the United States did very little to prepare for their aftermath. Not the aftermath of dropping nuclear bombs on innocent civilians in Japan but the aftermath of producing these nukes with their inevitable byproduct, radioactive waste. At Hanford, the quest to make nuclear fuel outpaced any plans to keep the waste safe from humans and the fragile environment around the site. It's no wonder that as nuclear production began to slow, a new industry, that of a massive cleanup project, took shape. The economy of Richland had for over forty years depended on consistent government contracts to keep the nuclear site running.[24]

The Tri-Party Agreement represented a new era at Hanford. Signed in 1989 by the Environmental Protection Agency, the DOE, and the Washington State Department of Ecology, it set a well-intentioned template for the remediation of the site. In short, it was an attempt to keep the DOE honest in its dealings with private contractors, ensuring contractors followed environmental laws and cleanup deadlines. However, big milestones over this more-than-thirty-year project are still far from being achieved. There has been progress in cleaning up some polluted groundwater, for example, in an area that once spanned 120 square miles, which is now down to sixty. Washington State, using cutting-edge forensic science, helped the DOE identify the most at-risk leaky tanks. There have been other successes but nowhere near what was initially promised.[25]

"That led to a huge shift in how the Department of Energy looked at the more imminent danger of the tank farms, because it wasn't just these things that were going to hold up…that no, they were already impacting groundwater," says Suzanne Dahl, a hydrogeologist with Washington's Department of Ecology.

The challenges of how to clean up Hanford are not only scientific. They are structural, too, and some argue that the project's longstanding system is a hindrance rather than a help to remediation. The DOE's reliance on private contractors to get the job done, the immense profit incentive for these large companies to rush to meet deadlines, the lack of government expertise and oversight, and the secrecy often surrounding the cleanup all create more problems than they fix.

Take the case of tank waste. For thirty years, scientists, some
employed by the DOE and most by various contractors, have
attempted to figure out how best to deal with all the waste
sitting there in underground tanks. They still aren't sure how
best to do it. There have been lots of promises but very little
progress. As of 2020, the plan is to have the tanks cleaned
by 2080, at a cost of $550 billion.[26] Even with a deadline so
far in the future, nobody working on the project and no contractor carrying out the work can say for sure if this will ever
be achieved. Nor can they promise that the price to taxpayers
won't continue to balloon. Hanford has become the epitome of
the US government's permanent war economy—in this case,
not by making weapons but by cleaning up the aftermath of
their production. The problem, of course, is that they aren't
cleaning it up at all.

THE BECHTEL BOONDOGGLE

Nothing embodies the magnitude of these bumbling failures
at Hanford more than the Waste Treatment Plant (WTP),
commonly known as the vitrification or "vit" plant. The plant's
construction began in 2002 and was to be completed by 2011.
That didn't happen, and now, after numerous deadline exten-
sions and cost increases, the earliest that WTP may be fully
operational is 2036, and even that is unlikely given the current
state of affairs. At the heart of this evolving problem, according
to various Hanford observers, former workers, and activists, is
WTP's chief contractor, Bechtel, and the DOE's inability to
manage the company.

By any honest accounting, Bechtel has failed on numerous
occasions yet continues to operate with little public scrutiny. It
is the benefactor of a federal contracting bonanza that keeps
the floodgates of taxpayer funding open. Bechtel's WTP con-

tract, like many of those doled out at Hanford and devised by Bechtel in its previous government contracts, is what is known in contractor parlance as "cost and schedule performance based." It's an arrangement that all but guarantees a profit, no matter if the job is done right or not at all. Such contracts, now standard in the defense world, reward contractors like Bechtel for "meeting milestones" within their proposed budget—in some instances, even if plans and construction turn out to be critically flawed. Despite blatant mistakes, including those made during the first three years of building the WTP with seismic deficiencies, Bechtel boasted in 2004 that they had received 100 percent of the available milestone fees available to the company through their Hanford contract with DOE. That was cash in their pocket for meeting deadlines, not necessarily for getting the job done right.

Since 2000, Bechtel has held the rights to build WTP. The plant, like Bechtel's Hanford contract, is gargantuan. The equivalent of constructing two full-scale nuclear power plants, WTP is to one day span sixty-five acres and include four major nuclear facilities: Pre-treatment, Low-Activity Waste Vitrification, High-Level Waste Vitrification, and the Analytical Laboratory.[27] It's currently the largest single construction operation taking place anywhere in the United States. Not only is the proposed WTP immense, it also comes with a staggering price tag of $41 billion, funded solely by the public trust, part of which comes out of the annual DOE budget.[28]

Before Bechtel, the DOE's WTP contract was with British Nuclear Fuel Ltd (BNFL). But in May 2000, after the company estimated they would spend more than $14 billion—despite an earlier cost estimate of $7 billion—the DOE ended the contract. Bechtel was then awarded the job through a competitive contract bid, receiving a $4.3 billion deal when it assured the DOE it could do the work for less than BNFL's price tag.

Since then, however, the company's cost estimates, start dates, and deadlines have changed frequently. Bechtel has also swapped project presidents on many occasions. In 2010, the company installed Frank Russo as director, replacing him in 2013 with Margaret McCullough. Then, McCullough was replaced in 2017 by Brian Reilly. Reilly, who only stayed on the job for a year, was dumped for Valerie McCain, who was still on the job midway through 2021.[29]

Once operable, WTP is intended to turn the millions of gallons of radioactive sediment currently in Hanford's waste tanks into glass rods by combining the toxic gunk with glass-forming material at a blistering 2,100 degrees Fahrenheit in a process called vitrification. Originally, the facility was to begin turning Hanford's radioactive materials into glass by 2011, with all vitrification completed by 2028. But in 2007, Bechtel pushed up their original cost estimates to $12.2 billion and their deadlines to start the vitrification process to 2019. The $12.2 billion price tag didn't last long. Vitrification didn't start in 2019; in fact, by 2020, the cost of WTP went up to $41 billion. The start date, too, continually shifts. Even by the rosiest estimates, the job won't be finished until 2047.[30] The timeline and cost projections have constantly changed because of poor management decisions and a rush to fast-track completion, say critics, as was the case with the redesign of WTP based on its seismic preparedness.

"Bechtel, by all accounts and purposes, has done an absolutely miserable job," says Hanford Challenge director Tom Carpenter. "They [the DOE] simply don't have enough [personnel] to deal with all the technical challenges, so Bechtel is getting away with whatever they want out there." Importantly, Bechtel has hundreds of engineers and scientists on the project. Far fewer at Hanford are those employed by the DOE.

Furthermore, an internal DOE document published August 2011 by the Construction Project Review (CPR) stated that Bechtel's $12.2 billion estimate at the time, which increased in 2007 after the DOE revised their WTP goals, would climb yet again, which it did, and now sits at a staggering $41 billion.[31] These increases are directly related to the DOE's inability to manage Bechtel, and as a result, the cleanup could run out of money.

Either Bechtel drastically underestimated the cost to build the WTP, or they blatantly misled the DOE when they said they could complete the project for $12.263 billion.

Aside from its ongoing tribulations at Hanford, Bechtel has a string of bungled jobs under its belt, some of which have been deadly. In 2006, an underground highway constructed by Bechtel during Boston's "Big Dig" collapsed, killing a thirty-nine-year old woman when twenty-six tons of rubble fell onto her vehicle. An investigation by the National Transportation Safety Board (NTSB) into the incident found Bechtel and its subcontractors at fault, pointing out that the company should have known the epoxy glue they used to hold bolts into ceiling panels would eventually fail. NTSB found that the tragedy was preventable and Bechtel had been negligent. The deadly incident followed years of budget increases, deadline lapses, and complaints that construction of the labyrinthine road system beneath Boston's historic district was of poor quality. In a settlement with the State of Massachusetts, Bechtel agreed to pay $357.1 million in damages, which excused them from any criminal wrongdoing.[32]

Of course, this was not the first time Bechtel lengthened a government contract, failed to deliver, increased their budget, or royally botched a publicly funded project: in March 2006, the Special Inspector General for Iraq Reconstruction (SIGIR), an oversight group set up by Congress to keep an eye on government contracts in Iraq, found that Bechtel was mismanaging a hospital build that was way over budget.

In mid-October 2004, Bechtel won the contract to build a children's cancer hospital in Iraq for $50 million, promising to complete the construction by late December 2005. However, SIGIR's report found that Bechtel likely wouldn't finish work on the hospital until at least July 2007, with a final price tag of $169.5 million. After SIGIR's report on Bechtel's gross mismanagement, the government canceled the company's contract for the hospital. Another contractor later completed the hospital construction in 2010.

This incident wasn't unique. The SIGIR report also found that fewer than half of Bechtel's projects had met their original objectives. Additionally, the majority of Bechtel's Iraq projects were canceled, reduced in scope, or never completed at all.[33] After Bechtel's botched reconstruction efforts in Iraq, a number of engineers and scientists began to wonder why Bechtel wasn't coming under similar congressional scrutiny for its even larger deal to build the WTP. This is not to say there are not well intentioned and bright people working at Hanford. The problem is that they are often tied up in a bureaucratic, profit-driven nightmare. This is also not to say the DOE doesn't know Bechtel is a never-ending problem. In 2018, the department released a letter lambasting the company for quality and design problems resulting in "potentially unrecoverable quality issues" and "a lack of corrective actions" in regard to the company's work on WTP. Bechtel was doing shoddy work and the DOE called them on it.[34]

"This could be a showstopper. We applaud [the] new DOE leadership for finally holding the contractor's feet to the fire on this critical issue of quality assurance, but I'm more interested in what happens next. For DOE to fix this, it must enforce a rigorous nuclear safety culture and put a new contractor in place that takes nuclear quality assurance seriously," said Carpenter.

Yet, like so many other issues with Bechtel's handling of WTP, this was not the game-changing event it should have been. This wasn't even the first time Bechtel was called out for failing to do their job. In 2012, DOE official Gary Brunson released a memo listing thirty-four reasons "Bechtel National Inc. is not competent to complete their role as the Design Authority for the WTP, and it is questionable that BNI can provide a contract-compliant design as Design Agent."[35]

"The leaked memo puts the Waste Treatment Plant's woes into sharp relief," said Carpenter at the time, whose organization got ahold of the document. "This memo details exhaustive and disturbing evidence of why Bechtel should be terminated from this project and subject to an independent investigation."

Then there is the case of a massive Bechtel rip-off at Hanford. It was a multimillion dollar fraud at the expense of the US taxpayer and on the world's biggest, most expensive environmental cleanup. Yet almost nobody has heard of it. In September 2020, Bechtel and AECOM Energy & Construction Inc. agreed to pay the federal government almost $58 million in fines. From 2009 to 2019, Bechtel and AECOM were overcharging the government for "unreasonable and unallowable idle time" of its workers. Four whistleblowers in 2016 exposed the scheme, for which the companies paid a fine of $125 million after they "knowingly violated quality standards at Hanford and used substandard materials."[36] This hefty bill, however, wasn't enough to deter these Bechtel crooks, and they continued to rip off taxpayers for three more years, never having to publicly admit guilt.

"It is stunning that, for nearly a decade, Bechtel and AECOM chose to line their corporate pockets by diverting important taxpayer funds from this critically essential effort," said assistant US attorney Joseph Harrington following the settlement.

In 2019, the DOE Office of Inspector General down-graded the company's Contractor Performance Assessment Ratings for the 2018–early 2019 period, citing ongoing investigations Bechtel was facing, moving the company from "satisfactory" to "marginal." Even so, Bechtel is on the Hanford job and still moving deadline goalposts while pocketing a mountain of cash. Their contracts with the DOE continue to be renewed.[37]

THE FIX IS IN

So how does Bechtel get away with it? From 2019 to 2020, the company spent $1.8 million on lobbying efforts in Washington, DC, and they were keen to cover their bases on both sides of the aisle. Both Republicans and Democrats were on the receiving end: $32,734 to Trump, $51,795 to Biden and even a little $10,943 donation to Bernie Sanders. They also covered their assets locally, writing a $14,050 check to Republican Dan Newhouse, a US representative serving the tri-city area of Washington State, where Hanford is located. Additionally, Bechtel ponied up $10,051 for US Representative Jaime Herrera Beutler, whose district encompasses the majority of southwest Washington State along the Columbia River. In the case of its donations to Representatives Newhouse, they seem to be paying off handsomely, and he keeps his mouth shut about Bechtel's numerous flops. When he received Biden's secretary of energy Jennifer Granholm at the Hanford site, he conveniently didn't mention the role contractors play, or any of the troubles Bechtel has had in recent years.[38]

"Hanford cleanup represents one of the most significant liabilities across the federal government, and it is vital that all partners in this important cleanup mission, including the federal government, congressional delegation, the state of Washington and local communities, work together in a concerted and responsible manner for the health and safety of communities," said Newhouse.

Newhouse, like Bechtel, has become an ardent supporter of former US president Donald Trump's reclassification of much of Hanford's nuclear waste as "low-level." This opens up the possibility that much of the waste sitting in Hanford's tanks will never actually be treated. In the end, this is exactly what Bechtel desires. Such a reclassification would allow the federal government and its contractors to forget about cleaning up the majority of Hanford's tank waste. This new "Class C low-level radioactive waste" designation would retool the entire cleanup, letting Bechtel off the hook for failing to properly build the long-overdue Waste Treatment Plant. Currently, Bechtel believes it will have no problem dealing with the existing low-level waste, but the higher-level waste, the stuff Trump moved to declassify, is a different story.

"They've invested billions of dollars into these facilities, and if they were to change course on what constitutes 'high-level waste' and how it should be treated . . . it's a huge concern for taxpayer dollars," wrote Alex Smith, nuclear waste program manager for Washington's Department of Ecology, in a 2019 letter to DOE.[39]

There's no question that Representative Newhouse, in his support for reclassification of Hanford's high-level waste, is not on the side of those seeking accountability from Bechtel and a safer and cleaner environment in the Pacific Northwest. In a 2021 letter, the Yakama Nation, Washington State, Columbia Riverkeeper, Hanford Challenge, and the Natural Resources Defense Council implored the new Biden administration to drop the Trump plan:[40]

> We write today on a matter of extraordinary concern. Dur-
> ing the previous administration, the Department adopted
> a High-Level Radioactive Waste interpretive rule, pub-
> lished in the Federal Register on June 10, 2019. 84 Fed.
> Reg. 26,835 (June 10, 2019). We believe this rule lays the
> groundwork for the Department to abandon significant
> amounts of radioactive waste in Washington State precip-
> itously close to the Columbia River, which is the lifeblood
> of the Pacific Northwest, creating a long-term risk of harm
> to the residents of the Pacific Northwest and the natural
> resources critical to the region.

Bechtel's lobbying and campaign contributions may influence not only Washington State politicians, but also the Biden administration as it considers whether to abandon or adopt Trump's low-level waste designation. Such is the game played by pernicious corporations and a militarized government that would rather produce weapons than act in the best interest of its citizens and the environment. The company's influence goes deep, of course, evidenced by its integral role in US imperialist projects in the Middle East and elsewhere. In addition to its botched projects in war-torn Iraq, Bechtel has followed US military operations, covert and otherwise, from Yemen to Syria, Iran, Palestine, Lebanon, and Libya. In the case of Syria, it's accused of playing a significant role in the CIA-backed coup of 1949, while also providing its services to the CIA's Operation Ajax, which orchestrated the 1953 Iranian coup. Bechtel turned a profit in the ensuing years by using covert information provided by its contacts within the US intelligence establishment. Wherever the CIA carried out its agenda, Bechtel often trailed closely behind, raking in the spoils.[41] When it wasn't cashing in on the wreckage of the US government abroad, the company was busy on the home front, working on country's secretive nuclear program and the infrastructure that was required to maintain it. The relationship between Bechtel and its government benefactors has been a deep and bloody one.[42]

By 2013, Bechtel had become the fourth-largest privately held company in the United States, and with that rise came the power to influence Washington at will. If you thought this dynamic might change with Joe Biden's election, think again. Bechtel plans to benefit handsomely from Biden's infrastructure plan, for which the company lobbied publicly.

"It's even more important now to ensure a rapid economic recovery," said Brendan Bechtel, chairman and CEO of Bechtel. "The administration and members of both parties should work together to promote jobs and economic growth by making long overdue investments in our nation's aging physical infrastructure, and we urge them to do so through a bipartisan, regular orderly process."

In an interview with Brendan Bechtel in 2021, Biden's secretary of transportation, Pete Buttigieg, ensured that the company would see its fair share of profits from the infrastructure bill. "There's an enormous need here and with that comes an enormous opportunity," said Buttigieg. "If we get this right everybody is going to be better off. This is about making sure that America wins the era that we're living in."[43]

"The Bechtel story is most important for how the company embodied the rise of a corporate capitalism forged in the American West that over the decades took the world by storm —a capitalism much more in line with cronyism than free market ideology," writes journalist and author Sally Denton in *The Profiteers: Bechtel and the Men Who Built the World.* "Bechtel pioneered the revolving door system that now pervades both US politics and the American economic system—a door that came to shape foreign policy not always in the interest of the nation and its citizens, but for the interests of multinational corporations."[44]

In fact, Bechtel's influence in Washington has become more
of a conveyor belt than a revolving door. Former defense secretary Caspar W. Weinberger, who served in the Nixon and
Reagan cabinets and was deeply involved in the Iran-Contra
scandal, is a former vice president of Bechtel.[45] Daniel Chao,
previously president of Bechtel China, was an advisor of the
United States' Export-Import Bank, a federal government
business that "assists in financing and facilitating US exports
of goods and services."[46] Jack Sheehan, a retired Marine Corps
general and former supreme allied commander for NATO,
later cashed in at Bechtel as senior vice president for Europe,
Africa, Middle East, and Southwest Asia. Ross J. Connelly, a
former executive vice president for Bechtel, was appointed by
president George W. Bush to serve on the Board of the Overseas Private Investment Corporation, a US-backed finance and
development institution that directly helps US corporations
like Bechtel with overseas ventures.[47] Donald Rumsfeld, acting as an unauthorized lobbyist for Bechtel, pressed Saddam
Hussein in 1983 to allow the company to build an oil pipeline
to Jordan.[48] The list goes on and on.

Bechtel's frequent troubles at Hanford stem from the romantic embrace between these powerful capitalist interests and
their friends inside the US government—a long-standing relationship that fosters impunity. Thus, despite the overwhelming
evidence Bechtel is failing at its duties at Hanford, there's no
indication its contracts will be torn to shreds any time soon. On
the contrary, Bechtel will most certainly sign lucrative deals in
the years ahead for an array of government-funded exploits. The
permanent war economy, from Hanford to the Middle East, is
not about to fall into a recession anytime soon, especially now
that the United States has its sights on China and is intensifying
a new arms race in the Indo-Pacific region.[49]

The nuclearization of World War II—from the impact "the bomb" had on the land to the profit-driven fraud of the Hanford cleanup—is still being felt. Fortunately, a few brave workers are blowing the whistle on the whole damn travesty.

100 D and DR Areas

White Bluffs, © Mark Ruwedel 1992–93

Hanford Town Site

A Nez Percé Meeting Place, © Mark Ruwedel 1992–93

100 KW and KE Areas (Breaking Camp, Early Morning)
© Mark Ruwedel 1992–93

CHAPTER FOUR

THIS DAMN PLACE WILL DESTROY YOU

HOW HANFORD WORKERS RISK THEIR LIVES EVERY SINGLE DAY

> To see a person who loves to learn and make his brain work get reduced to this, it's heartbreaking. It's totally heartbreaking to see a person's brain get wasted like that.
>
> — Bertolla Bugarin, wife of
> former Hanford worker, Abe Garza

If you thought breathing in microscopic drops of COVID-19 was bad for your lungs, try inhaling a little of the vapor emanating from the exhaust pipes of Hanford's burping waste tanks. For years, workers at Hanford received mixed messages about whether or not they should wear respirators while working in areas that could potentially expose them to noxious, even radioactive fumes. This was despite ample evidence that dangerous incidents were commonplace. In July 2021, Washington State released a survey of 1,600 Hanford workers, past and present, of which 57 percent admitted they had experienced a dangerous exposure event at some point while on the job, and 32 percent stated they had long-term exposure to noxious vapors.[1]

Abe Garza, who worked as an instrument technician for over thirty years, is one of Hanford's many worker victims. Over the years, hundreds of Hanford contractors have breathed in these foul invisible fumes. Garza can't even count how many times he inhaled toxic gases during his tenure at the nuclear site, but it was enough to cause him lifelong problems: headaches, nosebleeds, and the inability to smell the onions his wife chops up. At times, he even passes out from an uncontrollable cough. More significantly, Garza has brain damage, and his lungs are permanently scarred, which makes it hard to breathe, hence the perpetual cough.[2] Such is the price for working around Hanford's tank farm for three decades, but does it have to be?

On August 15, 2014, Garza was rushed to the ER. He could hardly take a breath; his chest felt as if it was collapsing. The day before he had been exposed to vapors while on duty at Hanford's tank farms. He wheezed on his drive home from work, his head was killing, his nose kept gushing blood, and he had a persistent, odd metallic taste in his mouth. He was sick and quickly getting worse. It turned out to be his last day at Hanford.[3]

Hanford officials dismissed the idea that Garza was hurt on the job, and his managers dismissed the idea that he or others inhaled anything that could have caused a minor headache, let alone a serious health problem. In the spring of 2016, two years after Garza's final day at Hanford, fifty-one workers reported falling ill, claiming they too had inhaled dangerous vapors. Washington River Protection Solution (WRPS), the Hanford contractor in charge of the site's tank waste, downplayed any potential health hazard risks. Then, nine sick workers left the job site, complaining they'd too been exposed to vapors. WRPS was forced to respond; its public statement claimed that internal tests showed that the workers couldn't possibly have gotten sick on the job from inhaling vapors.[4] "Air samples taken yesterday in two areas where odors were reported indicated chemical concentrations well below regulatory standards," said WRPS spokesperson Rob Roxburgh.

This sort of tepid, dismissive response by WRPS wasn't new. They were conducting tests, after all. It was the same bullshit Hanford officials spouted for years. Management at Hanford consistently downplayed the threat of chemical exposure. It appeared to be a crucial aspect of their job. Respirators weren't always mandatory and safety precautions were often flouted on the job site. Garza and others confirm that nowhere in their work-safety manuals, or hours of training videos, had they come across anything about the threat of chemical vapor exposure.

"I've never heard anybody say anything about that," recalled Garza. "When they tell you what's safe you would think that that's [the truth]."

A June 2016 investigation by Seattle's KING-5 news revealed that Hanford officials were absolutely lying about their own internal sampling of the tank vapor emissions. On numerous occasions, readings were well above safe levels, but these startling numbers were never released to the public or even passed along to the unwitting Hanford employees. According to the KING-5 investigation:

> Dozens of readings over the years show measurements far above acceptable levels. Some examples include: mercury, which can cause brain damage, measured in 2009 at 473 percent above occupational limits. Also in 2009, furan, a carcinogen, measured at 3145 percent above occupational limits. Ammonia, which can cause glaucoma and lung damage, was measured at more than 1800 percent above the limit. A known cancer-causing chemical called nitrosodimethylamine was recorded at 13,000 percent above the legal limits in 2005.

And on October 21, 2015, in what is known as the C-Farm of underground tanks, routine sampling found emissions "above (the) action level," which prompted managers to "ac-

cess restrictions" they deemed as necessary "to prevent worker exposure to an uncharacterized chemical hazard."[5]

The scheme was deceptive and deliberate. That was Garza's
takeaway, at least. At the time he was employed at Hanford,
health and safety measures like wearing personal protective
equipment were up to the employee. Without proper risk assessments, however, how could workers make that judgment?

"I'm most mad about Hanford lying to the employees that it
is not dangerous out there. And that they are safe. That's what I
am most mad about," said Garza's wife, Bertolla Bugarin, who
wasn't shy about expressing her anger. "It's a lie. It's impossible for that to be. It's scientifically impossible to have normal
levels all the time. You're in the most toxic site in the United
States. It's almost an insult to anybody with [any] intelligence."

While over 1,800 chemicals are known to exist at Hanford, a
handful are proven to be the most destructive: dimethylmercury,
benzene, carbon tetrachloride, and n-nitrosodimethylamine
(NDMA), along with several others.[6] Surprisingly, it wasn't until 2004 that dimethylmercury was discovered on the grounds
at Hanford. Perhaps the most toxic chemical emanating from
the underground tanks, dimethylmercury can enter the human
body through ingestion, inhalation, or even a splash to the
skin. So why had it taken so long to discover that the chemical
was floating around Hanford? There is a simple answer: contractors and the government had never thought to test for it, or
worse, didn't care to until it was discovered at another DOE
site. Down in South Carolina, dimethylmercury was found to
be present in the waters of the Savannah River, leaking from
a nearby DOE-operated nuclear site. CH2M Hill Hanford, a
full-service engineering and construction company, took note
and decided to conduct their own tests to see if the same toxin
was leaking out of Hanford. What they found was startling.[7]

"Approximately seven C-Farm tanks have indications of headspace or breather filter data in excess of the mercury vapor TLV's (Threshold Limit Values) If all this mercury was present as dimethylmercury (unlikely, but conservative): a total of nine C-farm tanks would exceed the dimethylmercury vapor TLVs," wrote Jim Honeyman of CH2M Hill.

The testing group sampled twelve tanks at the site's C-Farm. In all, fourteen samples were taken from inside the tanks and around their aboveground filters, and dimethylmercury was detected. No doubt, had they tested for dimethylmercury years prior, they would have discovered it was present. It had been there for a long time.[8]

"This chemical is so rare and unusual, we're concerned they found any, and it was found at a time when no work was being done in the tank farm," insisted Tom Carpenter, who at the time was director of the Government Accountability Project's nuclear oversight campaign. "This is lethal at very low levels."

That left Carpenter and others to wonder how many workers had been exposed over the years without their awareness. But while Carpenter was alarmed, the contractors at Hanford weren't the least bit interested in investigating the problem further. When CH2M Hill handed over their contract to WRPS in 2008, dimethylmercury was not on the list of chemicals that required consistent tracking and the DOE didn't force the issue. Consequently, dimethylmercury was not further monitored as a potential hazard to human health. From a work safety and public health perspective, it was a deeply dangerous omission.

WORSE THAN BAD

On a warm August day in 1996, professor Karen Wetterhahn at Dartmouth College was in her Hanover, New Hampshire lab conducting tests when a few tiny drops of dimethylmercury fell onto her gloved hand.[9] She immediately followed protocol, removed her gloves and flushed her hands in a nearby sink. But it was too late. She was poisoned. Over the following months, Wetterhahn experienced excruciating symptoms: severe weight loss, immobilizing abdominal pain, and neurological decay. She was quickly deteriorating. Soon, Wetterhahn ended up in a vegetative state. In June of 1997, ten months after the initial accident at the lab, her unconscious body was taken off life support. Her death sent shock waves through the chemistry community as well as regulatory agencies in Washington, DC. The death of Karen Wetterhahn, who was extremely well-regarded in her field, wasn't a freak accident. She had taken all the proper precautions and still did not survive. The case was well-documented. Therefore, the detection of dimethylmercury at Hanford ought to have caused a complete re-evaluation of safety measures at the site. At the very least, the toxic substance should never have been taken off the list of routinely monitored chemicals.[10]

"Dimethylmercury is probably one of the most insidious, most dangerous compounds that could be in the breathing environment anywhere," said Dr. Marco Kaltofen, a nuclear research engineer and a Hanford expert.[11] "Any responsible employer is going to be looking for dimethylmercury if they have a suspicion it might be present. We have more than a suspicion. We've got years of test data that show that it's in the tanks; that it's in the air."

Clearly, WRPS had not been a responsible employer and the DOE failed to provide adequate oversight. When Seattle's KING-5 News first investigated Hanford management's negligence, WRPS failed to respond. Now, at last, WRPS is now required to monitor dimethylmercury: in 2015, they found that the chemical vapor exceeded state "permit limits." Surprisingly, WRPS wasn't keeping track of dimethylmercury in order to protect workers. They were obligated to do so by Washington State's Clean Air Act.[12]

DEADLY WORK

For nearly twenty years, Lawrence Rouse went to work religiously, believing his small efforts were making a difference. He dutifully signed up for the most dangerous jobs at Hanford's tank farm and the Plutonium Finishing Plant, where he was consistently exposed to chemicals and, on at least ten occasions, radiation as well. After two decades of this pernicious exposure, it finally caught up with him. Rouse now lives with a degenerative form of dementia. His last day at work was in 2012.[13]

"The disease that I have, toxic encephalopathy, I think that's how it's pronounced, from the time you're diagnosed you normally, it depends on every person, you normally have ten to twelve years and you're dead. You just end up, it eats your brain away," said Rouse.

Rouse's menacing disease has impacted not only the activities in his day-to-day life, but also the routines of those around him. After reading a poem his son had posted on social media about his father's dementia, Rouse became emotional, telling the local NBC affiliate in Pasco, Washington, "[My son] wrote this letter, this little poem and said that his dad is gone. He's not the same dad that he had growing up. It's hard for me to see that because that's not me."

His wife Melinda added, "I think the hardest part for me is knowing what he was and seeing what we've lost. Hard on the kids, hard on me."

According to Rouse, he and his coworkers would often not wear the proper protective gear. "Anytime you went into a [tank] farm to do any kind of work you'd smell something. Sometimes it would be a little one. Sometimes it would almost bring you to your knees . . . it would rain the chemical on you from the stack. That's why we wore the baseball caps."

This is a common theme that runs through the safety culture, or lack thereof, at Hanford: workers time and again attest to the fact that for decades, improper gear, lack of testing, management neglect, and outright malfeasance were manifest. The result was a dangerous, and deadly, work environment.[14]

NOBODY LISTENS

In March 2017, Lawrence Rouse went before a Washington State Senate committee with his wife Melinda by his side. She was there to serve as his interpreter and a firsthand witness to his suffering. They were to speak in favor of legislation that would ultimately give support to workers like Rouse who had been harmed by chemical and radiation exposure at Hanford.[15]

"He doesn't speak well," Melinda admitted to the panel. "I pretty much speak for him all the time now."

Melinda was furious that nobody was holding the DOE responsible, aside from a few persistent citizen groups. She passionately implored the state to do its job and hold the DOE accountable for the numerous safety violations at Hanford. She was fed up. For years, Melinda and her husband fought the agency to grant proper compensation to their family for Rouse's lost wages and the toll of ongoing medical treatment.

"Somebody has got to have the integrity to stop the self-governing Department of Energy," declared Melinda, speaking in support of Washington State's Department of Labor and Industries' initiative that would help workers who were sickened during their work at Hanford. By forcing the state to recognize that individual ailments were caused by conditions at the workplace, it would be far easier for employees, past and present, to receive compensation.[16]

Joining Melinda to speak on behalf of her husband was Abe Garza's wife, Bertolla Bugarin. Despite ample evidence that her husband had also fallen ill after exposure to chemical vapors, the state and DOE wrote it off as mere allergies and a bit of asthma. "It is the most toxic site in the United States," said an exasperated Bertolla. "I'm really angry no one is listening to us."

"To see a person who loves to learn and make his brain work get reduced to this, it's heartbreaking," Bertolla said of her husband. "It's totally heartbreaking to see a person's brain get wasted like that."[17]

Not only had nobody been listening to Melinda and Bertolla, some actively dismissed their cries for help. First up was attorney Natalee Fillinger, speaking on behalf of the Washington Self-Insurers Association, a trade group representing insurers who would be potentially liable for the workers' claims.

It will be "extraordinarily expensive," Fillinger insisted. "Before you make sweeping law changes, go find the actual internal reports that have been thoroughly reviewed and investigated issues."[18] Fillinger was arguing that greedy workers like Garza and Rouse would take advantage of these changes in worker compensation rules. Bob Battles, of the Association of Washington Business, concurred, complaining that it would set a "bad precedent," forcing employers to make hefty payouts to sick workers even if they didn't acquire their afflictions on the job.

Despite hefty pushback from industry, a similar bill was signed into law by governor Jay Inslee in March of 2018. While the initial legislation had failed in the Washington State Senate, this nearly identical bill later passed after a very serious accident at Hanford.[19] It was a bill that was long overdue.

RADIOACTIVE TUNNELS

In March 2017, as described previously, an underground tunnel storing radioactive waste at the Hanford nuclear facility collapsed, leaving a gaping four-hundred-square-foot hole in the earth. The tunnel, made of dirt and wood, had finally caved in. No workers were reported injured, but hundreds were forced to take cover. Like much of Hanford's aging infrastructure, the tunnel was an accident waiting to happen. But Hanford management predictably downplayed the event.[20]

The DOE also said there were no signs of a radioactive release and opted to fill the hole with fifty truckloads of dirt and a plastic cover. Behind this short-term fix a big question remained: would this stop future collapses that could have far more dangerous impacts? According to Doug Shoop, manager of the Department of Energy Richland Operations Office, the answer was no. "There is potential for more collapse," said Shoop.[21]

Accidents like these prompted the Local 598 (an active pipefitters union) and groups like Hanford Challenge to back another push for the bill. It took the tunnel's collapse, but they finally succeeded in passing it.

A FIGHT FOR WORKER'S COMPENSATION

In the five years leading up to the bill's passage, numerous worker compensation claims had been denied. Additionally, the Hanford workers' insurance program was set up in favor of the DOE, and numerous loopholes had been crafted into the policies that allowed the DOE to deny claims for trivial reasons. The new law not only closed those gaps, it also expanded labor rights, allowing any worker to file a claim at any point during their lifetimes.

"Washington State has recognized the often terrible price Hanford workers on the front lines of nuclear production and cleanup have to pay for their service to the nation," said Tom Carpenter, who testified in favor of the law. "This law removes the unfair barriers that prevent workers from qualifying for worker compensation, despite working at the most contaminated and hazardous site in the nation."

But while the state of Washington might have finally recognized the Hanford site's toll on the health of its workers, Washington, DC, and the DOE continued to ignore, if not outright dismiss, the workers' grievances. In an unprecedented move, in December 2018, President Trump's Justice Department sued the state of Washington, claiming the new law was discriminatory against DOE contractors and the federal government. Filing in a US District Court near Hanford, the Justice Department attempted to invalidate the new law and curb its enforcement.[22]

"DOE will bear the majority of the costs from this heightened liability, including for ailments not demonstrated to have resulted from employment at Hanford," alleged the lawsuit. The Department of Justice's legal maneuver was a blatant attempt to dismiss numerous instances when Hanford workers were injured or poisoned on the job. In the same vein as Trump's circus-like legal tactics, the Justice Department's suit was a cruel "fuck you" to workers like Abe Garza and Lawrence Rouse, their families, and the thousands of others who put their lives on the line while cleaning up Hanford's nuclear mess, all while their employers raked in huge profits at taxpayer expense.[23]

In August 2020 after two years of legal struggle, the Ninth Circuit upheld the state law, unanimously ruling that Washington state's legislation was in no way a violation of federal statute. The three-judge panel shot down the Trump administration's attempt to kill the law, arguing that, in 1937, Congress granted authority to individual states to decide whether or not to provide compensation when contractors were injured on the job while working on federal lands.[24]

"Washington State has recognized the often terrible price Hanford workers on the front lines of nuclear production and cleanup have to pay for their service to the nation," said Tom Carpenter. The Trump administration wasn't the only ones turning their back on workers. In September 2021, Biden's DOJ announced they would appeal the Ninth Circuit's ruling to the Supreme Court.[25]

THE PALOMARES DISASTER

The remediation of nuclear waste has long been a classified endeavor. Therefore, accidents, exposure to radiation, and worker injuries on the job rarely, if ever, make the newspapers where they would receive public scrutiny. This is, of course, intentional. The less oversight, the easier it is to mislead and to cover up mistakes. Take the case of the military's Palomares disaster.

On January 17, 1966, a collision occurred during a routine refueling operation of a B-52 bomber over Spain's Mediterranean coast.[26] The Associated Press reported first on the incident, writing that a KC-135 tanker with jet fuel had collided in mid-air with a B-52.[27]

"At least five of the eleven crewman aboard the two planes died in the crashes," wrote the AP. "They collided miles above the earth. School children walking to their classes heard the rending of metal, then watched as smoke clouds erupted from the big planes as they spiraled down, scattered burning wreckage over a wide area."

The startling reporting left out one important fact: when the KC-135 struck the B-52, four hydrogen bombs became dislodged and fell toward the unsuspecting countryside of Palomares. Had the nukes been armed, the result would have been unspeakably deadly. Nonetheless, each bomb was laced with plutonium, most likely Hanford-made. While the bombs them-

selves were not activated, other explosives on the aircraft detonated in the crash, causing the plutonium housed in the B-52's
warheads to scatter across Spanish homes and farmland below.

Had the AP news report of the accident included the tidbit
about radioactive particles raining down on innocent Span-
iards, there would have been an international uproar and a col-
lective call for an abandonment of nuclear arms. But the initial
communiqué from the Air Force was intentionally vague, if
not overtly misleading:

> A B-52 bomber from the 68th Bomb Wing at Seymour
> Johnson Air Force Base, North Carolina, and a KC-135
> tanker from the 910th air refueling squadron at Bergstrom
> Air Force Base, Texas, crashed today southwest of Cart-
> agena, Spain, during scheduled air operations. There are
> reports of some survivors from the crews of the aircraft. An
> Air Force accident investigation team has been dispatched
> to the scene. Additional details will be available as the in-
> vestigation progresses.[28]

Later, the military reluctantly admitted the bombs had
cracked, and estimated that only a "small amount of basically
harmless radiation" had been released. The United States was
not about to reveal the gravity of their mistake. It was not
uncommon throughout the Cold War for US aircraft to fly
during all hours of the day, in all types of weather, with live,
activated nuclear bombs attached to their bellies. In a way, it
was a lucky break that the Palomares disaster was not a nuclear detonation.[29] Yet plutonium is a tricky little element. A big
dose will kill you on the spot, but in most cases, plutonium bi-
oaccumulates, causing a host of problems down the road, like
various forms of cancer. The more you are exposed, the more
likely it is that plutonium will kill you later in life.

Such was the case for many of the Air Force personnel
assigned to secretly clean up the Palomares collision. Many

of the men who gathered soil and worked to remediate as best they could this wide swath of Spanish land had no special training or expertise to deal with such an event. As the *New York Times* reported:

> "[The] response crew [was] made up of low-ranking airmen with no special training—cooks, grocery clerks, even musicians from an Air Force band—[who were rushed] to the scene. Wearing nothing more protective than cotton coveralls and sometimes a paper dust mask, they cut down contaminated crops, scooped up contaminated soil, and packed the material in 5,300 steel barrels that were shipped back to the United States to be buried in a secure nuclear waste storage site in South Carolina."[30]

Victor Skaar, a chief master sergeant, was one of the men who would suffer from the covert work he performed as a young airman in Spain in 1966. Nearly two decades later, while receiving a routine military physical in 1982, Skaar learned something alarming: his white blood cell count was totally out of whack. His body was fighting an invader. Skaar, at that very moment, speculated about what the culprit could be. Plutonium was invading his cells—plutonium he had breathed in while cleaning up Spanish soil in the 1960s.

"First they told me there were no records, which I knew was a lie because I helped make them," he told the *New York Times* in 2019. "Then they told me I had been exposed, but the levels were so low that it didn't matter."[31]

Thousands of miles from Washington State, Skaar was living with the same physical and emotional trauma that so many Hanford workers were simultaneously experiencing. He was one more collateral sacrifice of the United States' nuclear obsession. Now, in his eighties, Skaar was fighting the very government he had once dutifully served. He was hoping for some recognition that the tasks the military assigned him when he was a young man were slowly killing him and some of his fellow servicemen.

Skaar's fight was not unlike that of Vietnam vets requesting compensation from the federal government for their exposure to Agent Orange. His story was just another part of a much longer story about US troops being treated as disposable, whether they were dying in the battlefield or suffering quietly at home. In February 2020, the Air Force doubled down, stating that the troops who had shoveled and removed plutonium debris in Palomares had not been exposed to any detectable amount of radiation. The government's proof was scanty. Skaar's lawyers had recently filed a lawsuit, which became a first of its kind, against the Department of Veterans Affairs for failing to acknowledge that he and his fellow soldiers suffered radioactive exposure while on the job for the US government.

Skaar mailed letters to each of the men who served with him during the Palomares event to inform them that his suit had been accepted as a class action. The letters were often returned, a note attached when applicable: they were gone. Most were dead, and Skaar suspected that many had died from cancer, a result of the work they did while in the Air Force.[32] With help from Yale Law School students, a federal appeals court heard Skaar's case in September 2020. Their main complaint was that the Air Force's method of collecting samples of potential radioactive exposure during the Palomares cleanup had not been scientifically sound. The Air Force contended that the urine samples they took in 1966 were enough to see whether or not the men were poisoned. Skaar, who was involved in the collection of these samples, knew they were not accurate.

"There was no time," said Skaar. "We had to find all the bombs and do the cleanup—that took priority."

An internal report by the Air Force—a report they have ignored—backs up Skaar's claim that the testing was done haphazardly. This lapse in protocol became the backbone of the class action lawsuit.[33]

"The VA has denied those veterans who are now elderly and facing a variety of health concerns benefits and has refused to recognize the conditions of their service for over fifty years," Yale student Lily Halpern told the US Court of Appeals for Veterans Claims during the hearing, which was held remotely. "So while this case is about unsound science, it is also about remedying a grave injustice."[34]

The Department of Veterans Affairs countered that "adverse acute health effects were neither expected nor observed, and long-term risks for increased incidence of cancer to the bone, liver and lungs (the target organs for plutonium) were low." They continued that "the Air Force Medical Service reconstructed the possible radiation doses for Veterans who participated in cleanup of the Palomares accident in 2013, using the highest measured doses obtained from biological monitoring at the time of the accident."

It was nonsense, and on December 17, 2020, Skaar and his fellow servicemen were victorious. The court accepted their argument that the government's methodology for measuring radiation exposure "ignored 98 percent of the radiation measurements taken from veterans after the incident." The class action suit is now moving forward.

"Thanks to the Court's decision and the continuing advocacy of Mr. Skaar and other class members, the VA must now justify its practice of arbitrarily dismissing the exceedingly high levels of radiation these veterans encountered and continue to suffer from…[and] fulfill its duty under law to assist these veterans and ensure their claims are evaluated using methods that are both scientifically and legally sound," said John Rowan, Air Force veteran and national president of Vietnam Veterans of America.[35]

TORTURE BY PLUTONIUM

The pernicious business of Hanford connects many people. The toxic remnants from plutonium manufacturing sickened hundreds of workers like Abe Garza and Lawrence Rouse, men, who like Victor Skaar, signed up for what they believed was their patriotic duty. The very government they put their trust in failed to reciprocate.

It's not as if the US government hasn't been aware of plutonium's dangers for decades. In fact, for years, the government studied its effects on humans. In an infamous set of tests between 1945 and 1947, the military exposed eighteen people to plutonium—not too unlike the grotesque Nazi experiments during the height of the Holocaust.[36] Test subjects weren't simply exposed but were intentionally injected with the atomic element by doctors working for the Manhattan Project as part of a covert scientific experiment. The government knew the outcome wouldn't be good. The subjects also had no idea what was really going on, nor what the military was injecting into their bodies.

Ebb Cade was one such victim. On March 24, 1945, Cade was involved in a motor vehicle accident while employed as a cement worker at a Manhattan Project construction site in Tennessee. Cade, who was Black, was a victim of a government that deemed his body as expendable as his enslaved ancestors. The accident left him with severe fractures of his right patella, right radius, ulna, and left femur. He was in excruciating pain, yet doctors at the Oak Ridge Hospital, which was located on the nuclear reservation in Oak Ridge, Tennessee, did not treat his broken bones. Instead, they injected him with 4.7 micrograms of plutonium, nearly five times the perceived safe limit at the time. The idea, doctors noted, was to let the radiation run through his body. Cade, whom they named HP-12 (Human Product-12), would not have his bones set for twenty full days after the plutonium infected his blood. He was fifty-three years old. Dr. Hymer Friedell, who oversaw the grotesque experiment, noted that Cade was a "well developed . . . well nourished . . . colored male." In other words, he was a perfect candidate for the government's racist torture program.[37]

The idea, Dr. Friedell said, was not to kill Cade outright, but to see what the injection did to his body over time. The doctors would measure his kidney functions and draw blood samples to help paint a better picture of what exposure to nuclear radiation does to a human body. There was no consent involved in this horrific procedure. Cade was completely unaware that he was being used as a test subject. While he lay helpless in his hospital bed, waiting in agony for surgery on his broken bones, fifteen of his teeth were yanked from his mouth. Cade was never given a reason as to why they pulled out his healthy teeth, which were sent off for testing. Doctors noted his gums were in a state of early decay, but that was just a poor excuse. They drilled deep into his bones to perform biopsies in an attempt to discover what damage the plutonium was doing to his marrow.[38]

It's too difficult to imagine what Cade must have been feeling as his doctors lied to him about why they put off surgery for weeks on end, refusing to tend to his shattered bones. Sensing that something was terribly wrong, Cade got up one night and left the hospital. He vanished. The sadistic doctors were upset, as they had planned to continue monitoring him as the years went on, jotting down what sort of havoc their plutonium injection was having on his aging body. Cade moved to Greensboro, North Carolina, where he suffered a heart attack and died on April 13, 1953, at the age of sixty-three, nine years after the fateful car accident in Oak Ridge. When historians talk about the secretive nature of the Manhattan Project, and the scientific ingenuity of splitting an atom to create a nuclear warhead, victims like Ebb Cade, a descendant of slaves in Georgia, are rarely mentioned.[39]

Ebb Cade was the first human to be injected with plutonium by the US government. His case was reminiscent of the Tuskegee syphilis experiments, in which poor Black men with latent syphilis were monitored for nearly forty years along a placebo group to see how the disease progressed, even though by 1947, penicillin was used as a standard and effective treatment for the awful disease. But no penicillin was administered. The men were only given mineral spirits and supplements. Most died of the disease in mental anguish. Others went blind. None of the men knew the full extent of these experiments performed on them. The plutonium experiments, while less well known, were just as racist and unethical.

It wasn't just Cade who was injected. Seventeen additional individuals were submitted to this excruciating treatment. Albert Stevens, known as CAL-1, survived the highest dose of plutonium given to anyone in the study. Stevens, a white painter from Healdsburg, California, was diagnosed with terminal stomach cancer. On May 14, 1945, he was given "many times the so-called lethal textbook dose" of plutonium. But Stevens did not have cancer. He had a common stomach ulcer, and like Cade, he had no idea that he was being injected with something that would likely kill him. Somehow, Stevens survived his nuclear torture and died of heart disease in 1966.[40]

The third human subject was Elmer Allen, a Black railroad worker working in California. At the time, it was thought that Allen had bone cancer. Known bureaucratically as CAL-3, Allen was injected with plutonium in 1947 and required amputation of his left leg soon after. While Allen did have cancer, he lived until 1999. After an autopsy, a pathologist confirmed that Allen did not have a terminal form of bone cancer, but rather chondrosarcoma, which develops in cartilage calls and usually does not metastasize for many years. In other words, similar to Stevens, Allen was not about to die anytime soon. There are other subjects, many of whom are still unknown. Two doctors, Joseph G. Hamilton and Robert S. Stone, were largely responsible for carrying out these poisonous, deeply unethical human experiments.

Elmer Allen's daughter, Elmerine Whitfield Bell, told an advisory committee in Washington, DC, in March 1995:

> I continue to be appalled by the apparent attempts at cover-ups, the inferences that the nature of the times, the 1940s, allowed scientists to conduct experiments without getting a patient's consent or without mentioning risks. We contend that my father was not an informed participant in the plutonium experiment. He was asked to sign his name several times while a patient at the University of California hospital in San Francisco. Why was he not asked to sign his name permitting scientists to inject him with plutonium? Why was his wife, who was college trained, not consulted in this matter?[41]

And it was not just plutonium that these sadistic doctors injected into unwitting human test subjects. Polonium, americium, and radium were also tested on human beings. In other words, the US government has long known the various impacts radiation has on the human body.[42] They've taken readings of radioactive exposure during numerous tests. They've poked and prodded animals and human victims of nuclear exposure. They've tested urine. They've performed autopsies. They've murdered countless humans with nuclear bombs. So, why would they not go out of their way to protect those who clean up their atomic messes? That's a question many want answered.

BLOWING IN THE WIND

Hanford is a vast, subdued landscape. Thousands of gallons of toxic chemicals bubble in ancient tanks, and crumbling buildings emanate radiation. It is one of the most dangerous work environments in the world.

In December 2017, the demolition of an old plutonium finishing plant was abruptly stopped. Several times over the course of a month, monitors recorded an active, pervasive spread of radioactive particles. Dust from the job site was airborne. In that soot, plutonium particles had latched on for the ride, landing on thirty-six vehicles, numerous pieces of clothing, and various work equipment. In all, 257 workers were feared to have been exposed. They might have unknowingly breathed in these nano-particles and carried plutonium home on their clothing. Seven homes were assayed, but no radiation was detected.[43] Even so, it was a startling incident, but not unfamiliar for Hanford.

CH2M Hill Plateau Remediation Co., which was in charge of this particular demolition job, attempted to write it off as a singular unfortunate event, not part of a larger, systematic problem. President of CH2M Hill Plateau Remediation Company, Ty Blackford, issued a curt statement to calm unsettled nerves.

"Mistakes were made at several levels that created a situation that is unacceptable for worker safety, protection of the environment, and service to our customer," said Blackford.

Blackford's press release was a half-witted attempt to cover for his company's mistakes. Workers were indeed poisoned. One, who tested positive for inhaling plutonium, told KING-5 News, "I'm pissed. I'm scared, like we all are, that sooner or later it's going to bite me and I'm going to end up with cancer," said the worker, who feared retaliation and requested to stay anonymous.[44]

Despite the known contamination, the crew resumed work. "We are appalled that they restarted work, without having fixed the problem," said Tom Carpenter of Hanford Challenge. "They put more people in harm's way. . . . Now they are paying the price."[45]

He was right. One worker who had already tested positive was later exposed as well, a double whammy. "I am not happy at all. I am anxious. This is not something I want to deal with," the worker said. "There is a general feeling throughout the plant that nobody trusts what they are being told. They [management] are not listening to the technicians and workers in the field."[46]

It wasn't just human beings who were being exposed to plutonium. Once the material is airborne, there is no telling where it will go, or what it will ultimately do, wherever it lands.

"If you get an airborne spread of contamination you risk contaminating rivers, agricultural products, and lands (and people), absolutely. So we want to make sure we're trying to rein in all that in as much as we can," said Alex Smith of the Washington state EPA.[47]

While CH2M Hill acted as if they had the situation under control, the reality on the ground was much different. "It was complete chaos. It was a mess," the exposed worker said. "We got in our cars and went home to our families. We hugged our wives, our children, our grandchildren and did our daily routines, so we don't know what we took anywhere."[48]

It wasn't the first time that year that something had gone awry at the plutonium finishing plant where this mishap occurred. In June 2017, 350 workers at the plant were told to find safety when a monitor nearby detected high levels of radioactive airborne particles. Thirty Hanford contractors later tested positive for inhaling "radioactive substances."[49]

It was just another day on the job at Hanford, but did it have to be? The work is certainly dangerous to begin with, given the nature of the materials these workers are tasked with cleaning up. But are there better protocols and safety measures that could mitigate the potential for accidents like these? Are there ways to ensure workers in highly radioactive buildings are prepared for such incidents? And why, knowing full well the dangers associated with inhaling or even touching radioactive materials laced with plutonium, would there not be the strictest rules and oversight of this work?

LACK OF ACCOUNTABILITY

It wasn't just the government that failed to protect workers at Hanford. CH2M Hill, in the process of adding shock protection to respirators worn by workers, somehow ensured the retrofitted masks would leak. Between 2012 and 2016, an estimated 560 workers were likely exposed to toxic vapors because the protective gear they were issued by their respective companies was defective. As of March 2020, the DOE has not conducted a comprehensive review of the issue, a further example of poor oversight that has put hundreds at risk. And without proper medical citation, these individuals, if exposed, could struggle mightily to track down their due compensation.[50]

Companies hired by the DOE, like CH2M Hill, will continue to assure the public that they are taking every necessary precaution. Yet time and again there are events at Hanford that put workers at great risk. Even when the companies know employees were impacted by an accident on the job, they downplay or outright ignore workers' ailments, as in the cases of Abe Garza and Lawrence Rouse. It's a persistent disregard for the welfare of Hanford contractors. It's important to understand the culture that makes this pattern commonplace at Hanford. A deadly disconnect stretches between management and those risking their lives in Hanford's trenches. The motivation for speeding along on these dangerous jobs had to do with one thing, and one thing only: the quest for profit.

Media investigation and public scrutiny of such events causes problems for the DOE and its contractors. The more the public knows about what is happening at Hanford, the more pressure those in charge receive to increase transparency and report incidents when they occur.

TOXIC SMOKE SIGNALS

Take the case of a small but fierce fire that broke out at the Perma-Fix Northwest plant in May 2019, located just outside Hanford's official boundaries. In a kiln firing with nuke waste, radioactive gunk was pulled from an oven baking at 2,100 degrees Fahrenheit. The toxic material was so hot it turned into glass. The workers, not really knowing how long to let it cool, placed the chunk of steaming glass on a wooden pallet, causing the entire thing to go up in flames. A frantic group of workers rushed to put out the toxic flames with chemical retardants. Luckily, it didn't spread and was finally put out by Richland's fire department.

In 2019, two such fires occurred at the highly radioactive Perma-Fix Northwest facility. Neither, however, were reported to state regulators. The incident is important for three reasons. First, without regulators called in to investigate, the public has little chance of knowing exactly what's going on at Hanford in one of its most important and dangerous undertakings: turning plutonium-laden sludge into glass. Second, the fires are proof the whole endeavor is risky business and potentially catastrophic. Third, since Perma-Fix is officially not on Hanford property, it is not required to hire union labor and can more easily scoot around public accountability.

In a groundbreaking investigation, Hanford Challenge found that accidents and mistakes like the ones which caused the Perma-Fix fires happened all the time, calling into question whether the Atlanta-based Perma-Fix had any business handling radioactive waste trucked over from Hanford.[51]

After scouring thousands of government documents obtained through Washington state's Public Disclosure Act, Hanford Challenge found that Perma-Fix had paid $550,000 in state and federal fines from 2009 to 2019. This raised an immediate question: should Perma-Fix and their nonunion workforce be allowed to handle Hanford's waste at all? There's little oversight of the Perma-Fix's work, and that's not likely to change if they continue to operate offsite. The report also noted that Perma-Fix was operating on a hazardous waste permit that expired in 2009.[52] Moreover, radioactive exposure occurred on multiple occasions over the years, including one incident in which three workers "were seriously overexposed to radiation, with one of them suffering an exposure over 10,000 times higher than the dose received by the highest exposed worker at the Hanford Site during the same time period."

"This is work that Hanford workers have done well in the past and should be doing now. Hanford has the built-in capacity to handle this waste and to handle it in a safer, more transparent and more accountable manner," wrote the report's author, Robert Alvarez, a former Clinton administration official with the DOE, who worked as a consultant for Hanford Challenge's investigation.

Alvarez contended that accountability was paramount because of the enormous amount of plutonium the company had handled—enough to make two nuclear bombs. Why was that so risky? More than thirty-two thousand people live within five miles of the plant, with the majority under the age of eighteen.[53] But of course, the more waste Perma-Fix handles, the more money they pocket. And nonunion labor is cheaper for the DOE, though it doesn't produce better results.

The Perma-Fix problem is a microcosm of a much larger issue facing virtually every aspect of the Hanford cleanup: both the companies that profit and the DOE that oversees the work have little incentive to invite scrutiny. When and if they do, the public is likely to be made aware of an insanely complex and mismanaged venture that thrives on never really being completed. In other words, a toxic Hanford is a profitable Hanford. That's the way the DOE's contractors see it, at least. But there's one big problem: the DOE isn't paying the bills, taxpayers are. This brings us to the topic of the unions and their role at Hanford. One would assume that in a grueling work environment so wrought with occupational health risks, unions would not only be vibrant, but also collectively minded, and always acting in the best interest of the members they represent. It's true that Hanford's unionized workforce has been able to negotiate decent wages and benefits over the years. Yet there is a persistent theme in discussions I've had with Hanford union workers: that union leadership often sides with management and contractors over rank-and-file members. Additionally, compared to other unions that represent workers at other DOE-controlled sites around the United States, Hanford's have consistently been far more timid in their negotiating tactics.

Take the case of atomic laborers in Oak Ridge, Tennessee. In June 1987, 4,100 workers from seventeen different unions walked off the job at the Y-12 plant after failing to come to a contract agreement with their employer Martin Marietta Corp.[54] The dispute lasted 107 long days.[55] A couple of months later in September 1987, three thousand workers at the Air Force's nuclear Tonopah Testing Range in Nevada stopped work over a similar conflict. This big strike included ten unions and lasted a total of ten weeks.[56] Hanford's unified workforce could have acted in solidarity with the other unions in their industry and staged similar walkouts. But in 1987, Hanford's unions did not strike, and labor officials did not openly support worker efforts at Tonopah or Oak Ridge.

Over the years, various tales of corruption and mismanagement have plagued Hanford's labor leaders. One of the more egregious allegations was levied at longtime union leader Jim Watts, who served as the regional president of the Oil, Chemical and Atomic Workers Local 1-369, the largest union within the Hanford Atomic Metal Trades Council (HAMTC). Watts, who never led a single strike comparable to those waged at other US nuclear facilities in 1987, was accused by members and others of utilizing materials from the Hanford site to construct his family's private home in the tri-city area of Washington. Whether or not there's any truth to the mafia-esque allegation, it's clear that Watts, who died in 2018 at the age of eighty-two, was not entirely the beloved labor leader he was often made out to be.[57] Watts was viewed by many as in the pocket of contractors, not on the side of the unions he represented. His failure to back other nuclear labor struggles in the late 1980s supports this sentiment.

Aside from the historical distrust of union leadership, there's another, larger conundrum facing Hanford and its unions: no unified voice represents these workers. Two large organizations operate independently of one another: HAMTEC, which negotiates for fifteen Hanford unions and is made up of 2,700 workers, and the AFL-CIO's Central Washington Building & Construction Trades Council (CW B&CTC), made up of sixteen unions and thousands of workers (some of which do not work at Hanford).[58] To complicate matters further, depending on the specific contract or job being done at Hanford, workers may be represented by either HAMTEC or CW B&CTC.

No doubt, a fractured labor movement is exactly what big, profit-driven contractors like Bechtel desire. If Hanford workers aren't on the same page, they are much less likely to strike or act in solidarity. Some union members I spoke to, who prefer to remain anonymous, would like to see a merging of these two large umbrella organizations. "It's time for a real change around here," one longtime member of Union 598 of the AFL-CIO told me. "A major reshuffling of Hanford's [union] structure will take a lot of political will and a hell of a lot of organizing."

Hanford B Reactor, © Mark Ruwedel 1994

CHAPTER FIVE

TO KILL A WHISTLEBLOWER

THE CASE OF ED BRICKER

I always was sticking my neck out. I thought I was doing it for my country, getting this rogue agency reined in.

—Ed Bricker

It's never been easy to be a whistleblower at Hanford, and certainly not in the late 1980s, when the area was still operating inside a foggy cloud of government secrecy.

As a third-generation local and the son of a Hanford worker, Ed Bricker knew full well what sort of task he was undertaking when he was offered a job as a nuclear materials processor at his hometown site. Bricker, a well-built man with a bit of a bulldog grimace, believed that the work, much like his life in the community of Richland, was one of patriotic duty. A devout Mormon and father of five, Bricker never imagined living anywhere else. Richland and Hanford both were home.

Bricker remembers racing out to Hanford in September 1963 in the back of his father's 1959 Buick for the groundbreaking ceremony of the N Reactor. President Kennedy flew in on a helicopter for the celebration, just two months before that fateful day in Dallas.

"I shook JFK's hand. I was about nine. It happened so quickly," Bricker recalled.[1]

In the late 1970s, Ed Bricker and his high school sweetheart, Cindy, took jobs at Hanford upon graduation. It was the only game in town, and they were happy to have work as well as the money to support their young family. But all was not well at Hanford, and Bricker saw the blatant and egregious mismanagement firsthand. It was rampant corner-cutting that proved fatal.

Early on in Bricker's tenure at Hanford, his childhood friend died in a crane accident after Bricker, following orders, did not connect a safety alarm that would have prevented his friend's death. The sad event changed the course of Bricker's life.[2]

Initially, Bricker was hired to work at Hanford's waste storage facilities, but quit to attend a local college. He was rehired after finishing his program, this time with more responsibility and a new job at the Z Plant, a code name for the Plutonium Finishing Plant. Z Plant was shut down in the 1970s but resurrected in 1983 when President Reagan began to ramp up US weapons development. "This place was designed for production first and safety second," said Bricker. "Now it's cleanup first and safety second."[3]

Z was a mess, and Bricker quickly earned a reputation for speaking his mind and confronting management about the avoidable mishaps he saw day in and day out. The plant was meant to produce plutonium "buttons" for bomb cores, but it wasn't fit to operate. "I could see the problems clearly," said Bricker. "It was horrifying. Z Plant should never have started up when it did." Bricker's safety diligence soon got him elected steward for the Oil, Chemical and Atomic Workers union. That's when the trouble began. His complaints, many of them made directly to Jim Albaugh, the head of Rockwell's Safety and Quality Assurance, piled up by the day. They included a report about a control room that had been left unattended, an instance where plutonium was handled in a room with unsealed windows, a note to his higher-ups about fires that had gone unreported, and even a case of plutonium being piped to the wrong location. These complaints were all ignored by his employer Rockwell, a contractor that operated under the guidance of the Department of Energy.[4]

Bricker didn't last long at Z and requested a transfer. His rub with management wasn't getting any easier. The issues he raised were continually suppressed. Workers began to turn against him. He was labeled a "crybaby" by one dismissive boss. Workers called him a "cocksucker" and a "whiner."[5] In 1984, Bricker finally left his post at Z and moved over to Hanford's Tank Farms. The new job didn't stop Bricker from pointing out various safety violations downplayed or outright ignored by Rockwell and the DOE. He continued even though fellow workers, many of whom were once allies, were now teaming up with management to paint him as the villain. "I was honestly concerned that these facilities were being mismanaged," said Bricker. "I always was sticking my neck out. I thought I was doing it for my country, getting this rogue agency reined in."[6]

He could have made a much bigger stink, but Bricker refrained from taking his concerns to the press. This didn't mean he was afraid to up the ante. By 1986, Bricker was so fed up he decided to contact a congressional investigator to dig into why his complaints were being swept under the rug. Until this point, all of Bricker's concerns had been raised internally, following an archaic protocol laid out in Hanford's employee manual. The managers above Bricker, including those in charge at the DOE, didn't follow the same tack. In March 1986, Bricker left a voice message for DOE Hanford manager Mike Lawrence. According to Hanford guidelines, the message should have been confidential. But Lawrence immediately rang up Rockwell's president to tell him about the pot of trouble their employee Bricker was stirring.[7]

That same month, Bricker and his team were put in charge of cleaning up a radioactive spill, a result of a piping mistake. While these sorts of accidents weren't novelties, this particular misrouting occurred along a road that Washington governor Booth Gardner was planning to travel during a meet-and-greet trip out to the Hanford site. Bricker and his team had been instructed to remove all signage about radiation dangers and cut the ropes that blocked the roadway. It was a dangerous order, as any toxic dirt turned up by Gardner's or his escort's van could spread radioactive particles for miles.[8] Bricker was stunned. He believed that allowing the road to be used was a substantial threat and told the congressional investigator as much. The incident would later make the news after an internal investigation deemed the removal of the signage an "improper decision," resulting in the suspension of three managers.[9]

"While the levels of contamination involved were low and the decision was made believing that safety would not be compromised, it was a clear violation of our procedures," said Paul Lorenzini, director of Rockwell at the time.[10]

In 1987, the *Seattle Times* reached out to Bricker for an interview. Later, ABC News picked up the story as well. "It was pretty apparent after I spoke out the first time that I would never be forgiven for what I had done; for taking things out from under the Hanford cloak," recalled Bricker.[11] Of course, his contractor Rockwell, and later the company's successor Westinghouse, saw him as a useless troublemaker. Management was not on his side, but Bricker stayed the course, believing he was slowly making a difference. If the public knew about the problems at Hanford, the DOE would have no choice but to fix them.

Questions about Bricker's mental/psychological fitness began to flare up. He was sent to an array of psychologists in an effort to label him as unfit. In two separate meetings, Bricker was asked, "How do you feel about your fellow workers, your employer, and do certain things tick you off?" They would ask questions like, "How do you feel about your mother? Do you kick the dog?" "I was terribly embarrassed," Bricker remembers. "It's humiliating, degrading."[12] The plot to get rid of him picked up speed after Bricker conducted an interview with the *Seattle Times*. Bricker told the reporter he was convinced his employer already knew he'd talked to the press, even before any story was even published. Internal memos detailed exactly what transpired.[13]

HANFORD'S MERCENARIES

In January of 1987, Rockwell general manager Clegg Crawford met with three others to discuss the future of Z, which they were trying to get back up and running after it had sat idle for three long months. Rockwell was set to lose its contract after the company was outbid in a war with Westinghouse, which meant Crawford would likely be out of a job. They had six months to figure something out. Crawford hoped that restarting Z could extend Rockwell's work at Hanford beyond their deadline. Shortly after the meeting, memos reveal, Crawford was approached by at assistant plant manager, John Fulton, who said a worker named William Cook had informed him who was passing along insider information to the press. Cook had been contacted by a *Seattle Times* reporter about a Hanford story at the direction of Bricker, who believed he was passing along a valuable, like-minded source. Cook immediately pegged Bricker as the one who'd been leaking to the press over the previous months.

Crawford, steaming, immediately assembled a group of colleagues to discuss the best way to oust Bricker. By now they were all convinced that Bricker leaked internal documents, and, without evidence, blamed him directly for Z's closure after various safety issues at the plant were made public.[14]

During Bricker's tumultuous ordeal, he reached out to Tom Carpenter, then working for the Government Accountability Project. "I would drive out to visit him at his home and we would notice a black van parked near his house. It was everywhere we went," remembered Carpenter. "We were certain the damn thing was following us, which caused Ed to become pretty paranoid about the situation."

Carpenter was intent on finding out who was behind the mysterious black van that was tailing them, so he filed a subpoena to get a list of all vehicles purchased by Rockwell. He couldn't believe what those records uncovered: a 1987 purchase order for an unmarked van—to this day he keeps the document tacked above his desk as a sort of souvenir of his early years fighting for whistleblowers. It reads:

> 1987 RHO [Rockwell] SECURITY PROJECTS MASTER PLAN
>
> 17. Pa 230 TACTICAL COMMAND/INVESTIGATION VANS
>
> Purchase an unmarked van which is equipped with surveillance equipment, emergency lighting, radio communications, and is completely self contained. The criminal investigation group requires a mobile unit equipped to handle sensitive investigations and to conduct surveillance as necessary to support customer directed activities

"It was evidence we weren't *crazy*," confirmed Carpenter.

Later, the Department of Labor released a report investigating Bricker's complaints and divulging Rockwell's scheme to ruin his career. The report revealed that Rockwell was covertly targeting Bricker in a dirty counteroperation scheme called "Special Item-Mole." John Spear, the DOL's special investigator on the Bricker case, spent over a year gathering information, eventually producing four binders worth of discovery.[15]

The operation to target Bricker was run by Wit Walker, a veteran air force counterintelligence operative under the direction of Hanford Chief of Security, General Bill Brooksher. Walker and Brooksher had real power at Hanford. Walker was the chief of Hanford's security, a miniature private mercenary outfit with a police force of three hundred officers who had access to machine guns, helicopters, and other counterintelligence equipment. Their mission was to defend Hanford from spies, criminals, and Russian terrorists—anyone they deemed a threat to Hanford's secrecy. Bricker, a mid-level whistleblower, was the biggest threat to business as usual at Hanford, a business Walker and Brooksher were paid big money to defend.[16]

In a testy deposition, Tom Carpenter confronted a surprised Brooksher about the unmarked van that had stalked them and likely other Hanford troublemakers. "[Brooksher] repeatedly denied they had a van, and that's when I showed him the purchase order with his signature on it," says Carpenter. "Brooksher was totally pissed, screaming at me 'Where did you get that!?!' before he stormed out of the room!"

By catching Brooksher, Carpenter exposed the lengths to which Rockwell was willing to go in order to silence those who spoke out about Hanford's dangerous working conditions. There was one golden nugget in John Spear's investigation: the mole in Rockwell's "Special-Item Mole" operation was likely Bricker's good friend Jack Manis.

THE MOLE

Jack Manis was a man of habit. A nuclear processor like Bricker, Manis often visited the Bricker family in the evenings and was also tracked to their home by Rockwell's counterintelligence operation. While both Bricker and Manis were Mormons, Walker had strayed from his faith and had money and marital problems. Like Bricker, Manis was harassed by his superiors. Hanford at the time was still an operating nuclear site. All workers had to pass a psychological evaluation and background checks, but some, like Bricker and Manis, faced more stringent questioning.

Manis was grilled about his petty debts, which Rockwell argued made him vulnerable to recruitment by a foreign adversary like the nettlesome Soviets. They also accused Manis of cheating on his wife, a claim he vehemently rejected. Rockwell's security team responded to his repeated denials by tossing photos on the table in front of him as proof he'd been surveilled, and proof he'd been sleeping around on his wife. It was like a scene from a Hollywood B-movie, but it was earth-shattering. The photos could easily ruin Manis and destroy his marriage. But there was a way out. What did he know about Ed Bricker, they asked? How well did he know him? What did they talk about all those evenings Manis spent at the Bricker home? If Manis helped them nail the *son-of-a-bitch* Bricker, they promised, his tribulations would dissipate. It was taxpayer-funded blackmail—do what they demand or pay the price.

Reluctantly, Manis signed on to become their mole. His job was simple: spy on his pal, an assignment he carried out judiciously. He took pictures and stole Bricker's mail and shared details about their conversations and Bricker's work concerns. These efforts went on for weeks. Manis was a decent informant, but Rockwell wanted more. The problem was, unlike Manis, Bricker was a devout family man. He didn't booze and gamble. He paid his bills on time. He stayed home at night with his family and went to church services on Sundays. Bricker led a wholesome, seemingly infallible Mormon life.

Rockwell's goons weren't having it. They were getting pushy. While Manis had been feeding them information, none of it was very useful, and certainly none of it was enough to send Bricker packing. They needed much more, and ordered Manis to wear a wire and entrap his longtime friend. It was time to raise the stakes. Manis, however, was getting nervous. Snooping on his buddy to bury his own faults was becoming too much to handle. He'd gone along with Rockwell's scheme for long enough; a wiretap was a line too far. He finally broke down and told Bricker what he'd been up to.

"That's when Ed told Jack to call me for legal advice," recalled Carpenter, who'd never heard of anything quite like what Manis was confessing. "I couldn't believe what he was telling me, but with all that was going on, it made perfect sense."

Spear's investigation proved that the "Special-Item Mole" was conjured up in an attempt to "terminate" Bricker in a timely fashion. His report detailed the many ways Bricker's rights had been violated by Rockwell, Westinghouse, and the Department of Energy. Spear found that the mole operation "had the effect of stirring management and employee sentiment against Bricker as evidenced by his being sent to a psychologist against his will, unfavorable performance appraisals, and general workplace hostility."

"I was a good, safe employee that followed procedures," Bricker stated after the report was released. "They didn't want anybody that followed procedures."[17]

Manis, the mole, was only one piece of Bricker's puzzling and distressing saga. They wanted Bricker, and no tactic was too extreme in the quest to take him down. "They went at Ed with everything they had," recalls Carpenter. "They even tried to kill the poor guy."

ATTEMPTED MURDER

One perilous day while working at Hanford's Z Plant, Bricker, outfitted in a hazmat suit with an oxygen tank strapped to
his back, was tasked with hiking alone into a high-radiation
processing canyon for a cleanup reconnaissance. The area was
so chock-full of dangerous radioactive particles that workers
jokingly referred to it as the "one sniff, you're stiff" zone.[18]

"While he was down in there, his oxygen regulator came
loose," Carpenter explained to me. "He had to try and hold his
breath and get out as fast as possible. It was intentional, they
tried to kill him, no doubt about it."

Carpenter believes that the air regulator, which had been
fastened by one of Bricker's coworkers the night before, was
attached loosely in an attempt to sabotage him, forcing Bricker to inhale enough radiation that he'd eventually die. When
Bricker realized his air canister was failing, he reached for his
backup, but it was taped shut. Almost suffocating, Bricker
raced out of the canyon as fast as he could, inhaling as little
air as possible as he trudged up the side of the steep canyon.
When he was finally safe, he fell over, exhausted and out of
breath. Carpenter believes Bricker was nearly murdered that
day in a brutal retaliation for simply trying to make Hanford
a safer work environment. No criminal investigation followed,
and no charges were ever filed. Why would Bricker's fellow
union members turn a blind eye to this nearly deadly episode?
That's a question that is still in search of answers. Perhaps a
few of them were involved in the sabotage, or perhaps they
believed Bricker had it coming. We will likely never know.

The exposure, along with other Hanford-related incidents,
took a ravenous toll on Bricker's health. Today, areas on his
skin are covered with melanoma, and he has an ongoing
battle with chronic pulmonary disease, a lung disorder that
includes emphysema and chronic bronchitis—ailments he

blames on toxic vapor inhalation and that treacherous day in the polluted canyon.

When asked why he kept at it, despite his employer's alleged murder attempt, Bricker replied, "I may be one person, but I didn't like the way they were treating me, the public, or taxpayers' money. To me, it was clear they didn't know what they were doing or how to fix the problems, and they weren't interested in what the workers had to say."[19]

In January 1986, Bricker learned about the Whistleblower Protection Act, which he believed may have given him cover for reporting on the unsafe practices of his employer and the DOE. After work, Bricker and his wife Carol stayed up late, typing up reports that they handed over to Tom Carpenter and congressional investigators. Thanks in large part to Bricker's efforts, pressure was mounting. The DOE was being forced to come clean. The site was laden with safety mishaps: issues that could not only kill workers but also impact the general public. In February of 1986, Michael Lawrence, the DOE's director at Hanford, announced they had nothing to hide and released nineteen thousand pages of declassified material. Much of Hanford's toxic history was first revealed in those documents, from past accidents to the intentional release of radioactive pollutants during the Green Run event in 1949.[20]

The Department of Labor investigation and the work of Tom Carpenter eventually helped to exonerate Bricker. In 1990, the Department of Labor backed Bricker's claim that Rockwell, Westinghouse, and the DOE had sought to get rid of him because he was attempting to bring Hanford safety issues to light. Four years later, Bricker settled for two hundred thousand dollars.[21]

"I lost a lot of good friends as a result of being a whistleblower," says Ed Bricker, who has no regrets. "I was trying to protect people, in my own way."[22]

CHAPTER SIX

TOXIC AVENGERS

TOP ENGINEERS AND SCIENTISTS BLOW THE WHISTLE ON HANFORD SAFETY

> Bechtel is the best at playing the game of getting the most taxpayer money to address technical issues that are their responsibility.... It's the only business where not doing it well leads to more profits.
>
> —Walter Tamosaitis

In 2011, outrage was brewing at Hanford. Some prominent employees working on the project were blowing the whistle over what they believed to be dismissals of internal scientific assessments. They were also concerned about alleged abuses of managerial power that they had called to the attention of the Obama administration, to no avail. The whistleblowers asserted that the DOE lacked the critical expertise to oversee the project, pointing to institutional failures within the DOE and Hanford contractor Bechtel. They also alleged that Bechtel rushed through shoddy design plans to pocket quick cash. The consequences, they argued, not only jeopardized public safety and put the project at risk of failure; they were also likely to cost taxpayers even more money, should fatally flawed construction ultimately require a complete overhaul. At the tail end of sum-

mer 2011, Donald Alexander, a high-level DOE physical chemist working at Hanford, told me he was about to head off on a
weekend camping trip with his son in northern Idaho. While his
spirits were high at the thought of his upcoming retreat, Alexander's assessment of Hanford's situation was somber.

"We need alternatives to the current plan right now," admitted Alexander, who is now retired but stays involved in
Hanford issues. "We need a different design and more options
on the table. This appears to be a hard thing for [DOE and
Bechtel] management to accept. They have spent years of time
and money on a bad design, and it will delay the project even
more. . . . One of the main problems at Hanford is that DOE
is understaffed and overtasked. As such, we cannot conduct in-
depth reviews of each of the individual systems in the facilities.
Therefore there is a high likelihood that several systems will be
found to be inoperable or not perform to expectations."

It was damning stuff. Donald Alexander's whistleblowing,
which I first covered in *Seattle Weekly*, was one of the largest shakeups Hanford and the DOE experienced in the last
decade, largely because Alexander was, and remains, well re-
spected among his peers. What made him such a powerful
whistleblower, unlike most who came before him, was that he
was nearly impossible to silence. Alexander knows his nuclear
disasters well; he was part of one of the DOE's first scientific
delegations to Russia's Mayak nuclear facility in 1990.

Alexander was speaking out at a tumultuous time. The same
year he spoke to me, the Defense Nuclear Facilities Safety
Board (DNFSB), an independent organization tasked by the
executive branch to oversee public health and safety issues at
the DOE's nuclear facilities, reviewed thirty thousand documents and interviewed forty-five staffers. Their report was
devastating but unsurprising to those familiar with Hanford's
efforts to silence critics and whistleblowers.

The DNFSB report noted that those who went against the grain and raised concerns about safety issues associated with construction design "were discouraged, if not opposed or rejected without review." In fact, according to the DNFSB, one of these scientists, Dr. Walter Tamosaitis, was removed from his position as a result of speaking up about design problems.

Today, it's not just the DNFSB that is concerned with the safety and management culture at Hanford. The Government Accountability Office (GAO) has released numerous reports detailing the extent to which Hanford contractors have underestimated costs and timelines.

In 2004, GAO dropped a report critical of the DOE and Bechtel's cleanup plans, warning of faulty design and construction of the Tank Waste Treatment and Immobilization Plant (WTP), a structure that is still a critical part of the cleanup effort. The report affirmed that the WTP building was not designed to withstand a strong earthquake, but only after prodding from the DNFSB did the DOE force Bechtel to go back to the drawing board to ensure the plant could withstand a quake. As a result, Bechtel's design and cost estimates to finish construction skyrocketed from $4.3 billion to more than $10 billion overnight. And in 2006, GAO released another paper critical of Bechtel's timeline and cost estimates, which change almost yearly, saying they have "continuing concerns about the current strategy for going forward on the project."

Various flawed design plans have flown under the radar because the DOE did not have enough staff to thoroughly review every design piece put forth by Bechtel, Alexander told me. It's a problem that persists to this day. As a result, expensive mistakes like these will no doubt occur again. The lack of key DOE staff to oversee Bechtel's work still plagues the WTP project.

The concerns of the GAO, the DNFSB, and Alexander all pointed to a flawed relationship between the DOE and Bechtel, which is both the design and construction authority on WTP. Once operable, the plant is to turn the millions of gallons of radioactive sediment currently in Hanford's waste tanks into glass rods by combining the toxic gunk with glass-forming material. The rods will then be shipped to an offsite location to be stored indefinitely.

The DOE is tasked with overseeing the project and signing off on their recommended procedures, but the agency is incapable of proper oversight. "In the past forty-five years, about four hundred thousand people . . . have been irradiated [because of the Mayak disaster]," reflected Alexander. "It's quite possible that a similar accident could happen here. That's why it is so important that we get the Hanford cleanup facilities up and running properly, as soon as possible."

EXPEDIENCY FIRST, SAFETY SECOND

Rick McNulty, who in 2011 held the position of organizational property management officer, said running out of money was but one of many risks facing the future of the Hanford cleanup. On August 4, 2011, McNulty—also a lawyer and president of Local 788 of the American Federation of Government Employees, largely made up of Hanford scientists and engineers—requested a dual stop-work order of Bechtel and the DOE to force them to immediately halt welding tops on the WTP's so-called "non-Newtonian vessels."[1] These five large containers hold "pulse jet mixers" designed to mix radioactive waste within the vessels when the plant is finally operable. Alexander first explained that if these materials cannot stay consistently mixed, WTP would never be able to turn the radioactive waste into glass rods.

McNulty was also concerned that Bechtel and DOE management consistently ignored sound science, moving forward with a project that failed small-scale testing on numerous occasions. The tests showed that solids ended up accumulating into small piles, causing the mixers to malfunction. The substances that built up during the mixing process, these studies noted, were far more dense and cohesive than originally thought. Consequently, the mixers would likely fail. If these small-scale studies proved correct, and the pulse jet mixers start mixing waste, it could cause a radioactive accident.

Perhaps even more frighteningly, as Alexander pointed out, is that these same tests show that erosion will likely occur in the so-called "black cells"—the areas around the vessels that house the pulse jet mixers. These areas would become off-limits to maintenance crews once the vessels begin to operate, like a radioactive coffin surrounded by cement.

"[A] significant risk [is] that the vessel bottoms could be eroded through," a distressed Alexander explained. "If the [pulse jet mixers] erode the vessel floor, then the [radioactive] contents of the vessel will drain into the black cell that they are entombed in. Because there is no access for men or equipment into black cells, there is no way of providing maintenance within them. The black cell itself would likely have to be abandoned."

Like Alexander, McNulty was worried that there would be no turning back once the vessels became operable because the radioactivity within them would be too high for workers to enter— meaning that the black cells' mechanisms, from the vessels to the piping, would have to last the lifetime of the machine. Any malfunction of any part would end the vessel operation altogether, creating a potentially deadly nuclear accident.

"We're talking about dealing with nuclear waste here, so we have to make sure everything is functioning properly," warned McNulty. "This whole thing will be shot if these well heads are sealed with a faulty design inside. We need this thing to work; it's not worth rushing."

McNulty's complaint and subsequent request to halt construction came as a result of the aforementioned small-scale studies conducted by Alexander. In an internal "differing opinion" report circulated among DOE management and contractor staff, which challenged Bechtel's notion that the pulse jet mixers would work, Alexander wrote in June 2011:

> The Contractor Reports [which are submitted to DOE for review] are neither conservative nor do they provide a realistic portrayal of vessel physics and therefore there is no justification for continued design, procurement, and installation. Contractor Decision Papers are not technically sound and therefore do not Support a Decision to Weld Heads ... The Design is not Licensable and management should STOP WORK.

Alexander's tests of the pulse jet mixer design plans showed that the model was faulty, yet his pleas to stop construction went unheeded by his DOE project director, Dale Knutson. In early August 2011, the DOE announced that it was moving forward with welding the tops on the vessels, much to Alexander's dismay.

"We took Dr. Alexander's report into consideration and determined there was no imminent risk to safety if the heads were welded on [the non-Newtonian vessels]," DOE spokesperson Carrie Meyer told me. "In the end we looked at the bottom line of the project, and it was a business decision to move forward."

In a leaked internal email I obtained dated August 4, 2011, Alexander addressed his concerns directly to the DOE's chief of nuclear safety, Richard Lagdon, writing:

> Unfortunately the Decision to Weld the Non-Newtonian Vessels was made a day too soon. Based on the testing yesterday evening and the recent testing results it is clear that the Decision to Weld will require rework and place unacceptable liability upon the government. . . .I was the only

scientist present to observe these tests. I guess the project
doesn't really care about the test results. Testing over the
last two weeks demonstrates that we are now at the point
where a very expensive contingency option will have to be
exercised. This involves either the implementation of design
and fabrication of a new vessel or significant modification
of the existing vessel. Either option will be extremely cost-
ly. . . . This could have been avoided if the DOE technical
staff recommendations and those of the DNFSB (among
numerous others) had been fairly considered.

A month later, on September 1, 2011, Knutson and Bechtel
WTP project director Russo released a joint statement asserting they would sidestep further small-scale testing and instead
conduct large-scale analysis in the future, once the units were
sealed with the pulse jet mixers inside. "Testing is performed
to validate the safety and quality of design and construction,"
Russo said. "We are confident, based on the results of our
small-scale testing, that the mixing design of the vessels meets
the safety design basis."

"It's a classic case of management overriding technical staff,"
asserted McNulty, who spoke from years of experience working at Hanford. "The DOE is in a state of absolute denial about
this whole thing. They need to rein [Russo] in. They can't allow
him to continue to misrepresent all the internal studies that
show [the pulse jet mixers] are simply not going to work."

In the fall of 2010, the pulse jet mixers were welded inside the non-Newtonian vessels, but the tops were not sealed
shut. Despite opposition from Alexander and other scientists,
this portion of the project was pushed forward by Bechtel and
DOE management. "I raised issues within DOE, but Bechtel
was convinced these pulse jet mixers would work," Alexander
claimed. "The result was that Bechtel was able to get DOE management to sign off on welding the mixers within the vessels."

Once the weld heads encapsulate what studies show to be defective pulse jet mixers, years of research and development will be wasted and billions more will have to be spent to fix what could have been prevented.

While Russo refused to be interviewed on the matter, Bechtel spokesperson Suzanne Heaston passed along to me the following statement via email:

> Assuming the vessel mixing systems work as designed, welding the heads on now will save taxpayers significant cost and avoid delays in treatment of the waste in the tank farm ... If further testing associated with the mitigation actions determines that they will not perform adequately and operational controls are not adequate, design changes could be required. The timing of the welding of the heads on the vessels is a management decision to proceed. ... The potential costs of potential rework are less than the known costs of delay.

In other words, even though no small-scale tests have ever shown that the pulse jet mixers will work properly, Bechtel, with the DOE's blessing, planned to still move forward with welding the heads to the tops of the vessels.

"WALT IS KILLING US"

This illogic totally mystified Walter Tamosaitis, a former systems engineer who was employed for more than forty years by Bechtel subcontractor URS. "So Bechtel charges ahead, welds the heads on [the non-Newtonian vessels], and then waits for the answers that will tell how the tanks need to be changed," Tamosaitis told me in response to Bechtel's statement. "What then? Cut the heads off the tanks? Start over building new tanks? Wow. That sounds like a low-cost approach."

In an additional email sent August 2, 2011, Alexander described how Bechtel management disregarded his early report that their design for the pulse jet mixers was flawed:

> In the spring I raised a series of concerns with respect to the performance of the non-Newtonian vessels. Because I raised the issue, Frank Russo directed me to write my issues in a paper over the Easter weekend and deliver the paper on Monday April 5, 2010. . . . As a consequence the [Bechtel] manager labeled my issues as the 'non-Newtonian curve-ball.' Since when are DOE staff supposed to take direction from Contractor management?. . .Mr. Russo also directed Dr. Walter Tamosaitis to gather as many top flight PhDs as possible together to discredit my paper. I requested that my paper receive appropriate peer review but that request was denied. Walt had trouble even assembling a team. Walt knew that my issues were technically correct and he never submitted a counter paper.

Shortly after he refused to counter Alexander's internal paper warning about the problems with the pulse jet mixer design, Tamosaitis blew his own whistle, exposing what he saw as safety failures at WTP and citing concerns that the pulse jet mixer design issues would prohibit the plant from operating correctly. As a result, Tamosaitis was removed from the project.

"The drive to stay on schedule is putting the whole [WTP] project at risk," Tamosaitis told me. "'Not on my watch' is a standard mantra among [DOE and contract] management who like to intimidate naysayers like me. These guys would rather deal with major issues down the road than fix them up front. . . .Cost and schedule performance trump sound science time and again."

On March 31, 2010, Tamosaitis emailed Bechtel managers Michael K. Robinson and Russo regarding concerns about pulse jet mixer failures that were first raised by the DOE's Alexander, to which Russo replied, "Please keep this under control. The science is over." In an internal email string dated April 14, 2010, Robinson wrote to Russo that he would "just have to keep [Tamosaitis] in line."

"As soon as Russo came on board, the chain of command was altered," Tamosaitis pointed out. "Before Russo, I had to report directly to Bill Gay, a URS employee (a Hanford subcontractor), but Russo removed Gay from the command chain and [made me communicate] directly to Mike Robinson [of Bechtel]. I think Russo believed it was easier to drive ahead with his cost and schedule push if he didn't have two URS managers directly under him."

In an email dated March 31, 2010, Russo updated President Obama appointee Inés Triay on the situation. Triay served as assistant secretary for environmental management and oversaw the DOE's Hanford work until July 2011, at which time she stepped down.

"It was like herding cats," Russo said to Triay about a meeting he'd had with senior contract scientists and engineers regarding his quest to stay on schedule. "Scientists . . . were in lock step harmony when we told them the science is ending. They all hated it . . . I will send anyone on my team home if they demonstrate an unwillingness or inability to fulfill my direction."

"Walt is killing us," Russo later emailed Bill Gay of URS on July 1, 2010, who, though removed from the chain of command, still had to sign off on Tamosaitis' removal. "Get him in your corporate office today."

"He will be gone tomorrow," Gay replied.

"This action [Tamosaitis' removal from the Hanford project] was initiated by Dale Knutson probably not knowing the sensitivity," Gay emailed to another employee in response to the decision to get rid of Tamosaitis.

In a sworn statement sent to the Department of Labor, Knutson denied that he was in any way involved in the decision to demote Tamosaitis.

Tamosaitis was punished, and while he was still employed by URS until 2013, he was confined to a windowless basement office in Richland, where no management spoke to him in over a year. He was cast away. His daily work routine was not that of a normal URS scientist, and he was not even sure what official title he had. It was clear retaliation. URS shipped him around the country to work on various company projects as a sort of in-house consultant.

In 2011, Tamosaitis sued Bechtel in Washington State, as well as URS and the DOE at the federal level over his ousting at Hanford. "It is my opinion that [Dale] Knutson and Frank Russo are in lockstep," he asserted. "Due to the constant managerial turnover [on the WTP project], these guys won't likely be there in a few years, so they'd rather have these problems happen on someone else's clock, even though it is always more expensive to fix something later then to do it right the first time."

The vessels are one day to be the first stop for Hanford's tank waste once it enters the site's pretreatment facility. Already, over thirteen years behind schedule and billions of dollars over its initial budget, the vessels still aren't finished.[2]

If these $100 million vessels have to be rebuilt, the costs will skyrocket. As a result, the entire project could fall apart, as Hanford Challenge and others note. That means taxpayers will again have to foot the bill for WTP's redesign and construction, postponing its operation indefinitely.

"Clearly, the management system or 'safety culture' is broken," Don Alexander wrote in an August 2, 2011, email to Rick McNulty. "I have been under tremendous stress for more

than a year. It seems to me that this is beyond a purely technical issue and is a whistleblower issue."

WHISTLEBLOWER AVALANCHE

A flurry of whistleblowers began to speak out about Hanford
safety issues in 2010 and 2011. Along with the DOE's Alexander and URS's Tamosaitis was Donna Busche, who was
also employed by contractor URS as manager of environmental and nuclear safety at Hanford's Waste Treatment Plant.
In November 2011, Busche filed a discrimination complaint
under the federal whistleblower protection statutes with the
US Department of Labor, alleging retaliation against her for
reporting problems at the WTP.

Climbing the corporate ladder in the male-dominated engineering world was no easy feat. But Busche, as numerous
coworkers told me, is tough, politically savvy, and scientifically
skilled. After attending graduate school at Texas A&M University and before arriving at Hanford, Busche was the chief
nuclear engineer and manager of nuclear safety at the DOE's
Waste Isolation Pilot Plant in Carlsbad, New Mexico.

Busche's job at Hanford was to ensure the site's contractors
produced adequate documentation to support the contractor's
compliance with federal environmental and nuclear safety
laws. In other words, virtually no aspect of construction could
take place at the WTP until Busche said it was safe to do
so. "I'm where the nuclear safety buck stops," Busche would
proudly say.

If Busche said "stop," the work had to stop. But saying "stop"
to the wrong guys, Busche claimed, got her in a heap of trouble with Hanford higher-ups.

Among other grievances, Busche said she was sexually harassed by URS manager Bill Gay.[3] In Busche's official complaint,

she explained that Gay made inappropriate and sexist comments to her in a meeting, "including comments that women react emotionally while men use logical thinking." Gay also allegedly told Busche that, as an attractive woman, she should use her "feminine wiles" to better communicate with her male cohorts. Gay also apparently said that if Busche were single, "he would pursue a romantic relationship with her." Busche notified Human Resources shortly after Gay made these remarks, and, as result, he later apologized.

Even more damaging were Busche's claims that beginning in 2010 Bechtel shirked safety compliance, signing off on shoddy work to meet deadlines that would earn the contractor large financial incentives. For example, Busche backed Donald Alexander's claim that radioactive-waste stirrers were faulty and had numerous design problems, such as erosion and potential leaking. Despite her concerns, Bechtel pushed through testing saying they were sound.

The company's timing was impeccable. It was late June 2010, and if their plans were finalized by the end of the month, Bechtel would receive a $5 million bonus for reaching cost and schedule goals. Busche said that during this time she was viewed as a roadblock to meeting these financial incentives. As a result, her concerns were suppressed and Bechtel managers allegedly sought ways to retaliate against her. Management at Bechtel and the DOE, however, had no idea whom they were dealing with. In October 2010, Busche took her concerns to the Defense Nuclear Facilities Safety Board. After her comments were made during a public hearing with DNFSB on October 7, Busche claimed she was "openly admonished by former DOE assistant secretary Inés Triay for her testimony."

In her Department of Labor complaint, Busche alleged that after her testimony, Triay told her "If [your] intent was to piss people off [with your testimony, you] did a very good job."

When Busche showed up for a second day of hearings, she claimed she was approached by Frank Russo—who ran the WTP project for Bechtel—as well as by Bill Gay and Leo Sain, a senior URS vice president. They all urged her to recant her earlier testimony when she met with the DNFSB. She replied that she would not.

Even worse, when Busche returned to work after the hearings, she alleged WTP management kept her isolated and out of meetings that she was both authorized to and required to attend. She also said that since Bechtel "controls the work and supervision of persons assigned to [her]," that the company has "actively sabotaged her work since [Bechtel] employees go around her, defy her efforts to supervise them. . .all without consequence."[4]

Busche's story, when coupled with that of the DOE's Dr. Alexander, provides ample evidence that management at both Bechtel and the DOE at best ignored, and at worst actively retaliated against, experts with inconvenient opinions. And because it's nuclear waste that's being dealt with, their alleged negligence could prove deadly.

"If you're an executive, your job is to bring in quarterly earnings. But it's different for me," Busche told author Tom Mueller for Mueller's book *Crisis of Conscience*. "I hold a professional engineering license, which legally obligates me to investigate certain things. By signing some documents, like environmental dangerous waste permits, I'm personally certifying that the procedure is safe, under penalty of jail. I'm not going to jail just because some idiot manager is in a hurry!"[5]

Busche, with help from the Department of Labor and Hanford Challenge's Tom Carpenter, hired a lawyer and filed a lawsuit against URS and Bechtel, a suit her employer was not too pleased with. But her colleagues wrote a report to DOE complaining that Busche was the problem at WTP. In 2014,

Busche was canned. It was two years later when the DOE reached a settlement with the US Department of Justice, Bechtel Corp., and AECOM (formally URS) for a whopping $125 million. The civil lawsuit alleged taxpayer funds were mismanaged and that both companies performed shoddy work. The lawsuit also claimed that government funds were illegally used to lobby members of Congress. Brought on by whistleblowers Gary Brunson, Donna Busche, and Walter Tamosaitis, the settlement was one of the largest in DOE history.[6]

A CASH GAME

In May 2011, evidence emerged in a lawsuit filed in a Washington state court by Dr. Tamosaitis, implicating high-level DOE employees in the silencing of Tamosaitis, who was removed from his management position at the WTP after he raised concerns about the plant's faulty design.[7] During a deposition, Frank Russo, who ran Bechtel's Hanford operation at the time, verified the names of DOE officials with whom he had discussed Tamosaitis: Dale Knutson, federal project director for the DOE at Hanford, DOE deputy secretary Daniel Poneman, and former US assistant secretary for environmental management Inés Triay. Poneman and Triay were Obama appointees.

In the deposition, Tamosaitis' lawyer, Jack Sheridan, asked Russo whether he had, via email, told his boss, Bechtel president David Walker, that Triay, Poneman, and Knutson all "understood the reason for Walt's departure" and that "DOE can't be seen as involved." Russo confirmed this, admitting to telling Walker that he had briefed Triay and Poneman on the issue.

In early November 2011, Tamosaitis filed a second lawsuit against Bechtel and the DOE in federal court.[8] Among other things, Tamosaitis' suit alleged that Bechtel management and DOE brass were concerned that the issues Tamosaitis was raising could put an additional $50 million of WTP funding in jeopardy. It was all about the money.

The DOE retaliated and filed a motion to delay certain evidentiary aspects of Tamosaitis' case from being allowed in future court proceedings.

Soon after, in early December 2011, Tamosaitis testified in front of the US Senate's Homeland Security and Governmental Affairs Subcommittee. At the hearing, he explained how he was removed from his job and forced to work in an offsite windowless basement office as a warning of sorts to others who were contemplating speaking out.

Tamosaitis set off a minor earthquake at Hanford. Following his lead, two veteran Hanford scientists spoke to me about their experiences with the saga, exposing blatant corruption and mismanagement at Hanford's WTP. With these endeavors, they claimed, DOE management was not only complicit but also took direct actions to hide glaring technical problems from the public—problems that could lead to a catastrophic nuclear accident.

A CRIPPLED OPERATION

In 2011, David Bruce, a longtime Hanford nuclear chemical process engineer, was seventy-eight, and his enthusiasm to do his job right was as genuine as ever. Many of his coworkers over the years saw Bruce, who worked for various Hanford contractors for nearly fifty years, as a mentor of sorts—a man whose words were worth heeding.

"The pursuit to stay on schedule has crippled the entire operation," Bruce told me of the WTP. "This sucker is not going to run as currently designed, plain and simple, and a heck of a lot of people around here know it but are too afraid to speak up."

In December of 2011, Bruce decided he'd had enough. He was aware of glaring technical flaws, such as problems in the mixing design that could lead to lethal leaks at the WTP and prevent it from ever running properly. These problems had not yet been addressed, and in a meeting with top management, including Russo, Bruce stood up and made his points.

"After that meeting, [Frank] Russo came up to me and asked to meet with me later to discuss the issues that I raised," Bruce explained. He was a bit surprised; it was the first time anyone that high up in Bechtel management had seemed concerned with the issues he was raising. While he thought the meeting went well and felt that Russo heard him out, he still had very serious doubts about whether necessary changes would ever be made.

Russo and Bechtel would not comment directly on the claim that management overrode technical staff, but the company insisted that "[Bechtel's] responsibility to the American taxpayer is to ensure that balance in designing and building a plant that will safely and effectively operate to protect people and the environment from the hazards of and risks from the radioactive waste."

Yet on January 13, 2012, the DOE's Office of Health, Safety and Security (HSS), which is tasked with overseeing work carried out at the DOE's nuclear sites, released what some called the most scathing review of Hanford ever to come out of the independent oversight committee. The document was direct in its criticism of the culture that permeated Hanford's work environment, finding that "only 30 percent of all survey respondents feel that they can openly challenge decisions made by management." The report went on to state, "There is a strong perception that you will be labeled or red-flagged, and some individuals indicated that they were transferred to another area by their supervision after having raised concerns."

Russo responded to the HSS report by telling his employees in a letter, "I want to re-emphasize how important it is for everyone to have a questioning attitude, to stop and ask questions if something doesn't seem right, and if there is a concern, to raise it so it can be addressed."

Getting Russo to acknowledge even this much was an arduous slog. In late September 2009, frustration with their supervisors' failure to address ineffective designs had grown so high that Bruce and URS senior advisory engineer Murray Thorson, both devout Christians, retreated to their work cafeteria to pray together. Their request to their Lord was simple: they asked, if their perceptions were correct, to expose what they saw as waste and corruption within the DOE and contractor management.

During the previous six months, the two had worked diligently to come up with a design to eliminate precipitation in the ion-exchange system at the WTP. Buildup of precipitation in the feed to the ion-exchange columns, integral parts of the process of turning nuclear waste into glass, would cause the columns to plug or fail to function, jeopardizing the operability of the entire WTP facility.

Bruce and Thorson had been reaching out to management with their concerns since 2007. After being repeatedly ignored, they met with the DOE to outline the serious technical flaws in Bechtel's proposed design. Only then did Bechtel agree to do something about it.

An ad hoc group was formed, with Bruce and Thorson on one team and another set of engineers from Bechtel and URS on another. The two pursued a fix for the buildup of precipitation, which became known as the Equipment Option, while the other group developed an alternative Operating Solution. The Equipment Option was projected to take five fewer years to process Hanford's nuclear waste into glass. At an operating cost of roughly $1 billion per year, that meant a $5 billion savings for taxpayers. The Operating Solution, on the other hand, would temporarily fix the issue, but provide less reliability and less flexibility, plus it would increase the amount of time needed to process nuclear waste. More important to Bechtel, however: The Operating Solution would cost less in construction dollars to implement.

Bechtel took both options to the DOE, stating their recommendation of the Operating Solution option. DOE, however, ended up opting for Thorson and Bruce's design.

Tamosaitis, then serving as URS management advisor for the precipitation study teams, said, "Murray [Thorson] and Dave [Bruce] had the undisputed answer to the problem. Everyone knew it, but despite this fact, Bechtel management did not want to accrue the costs of the fix. So they picked the cheaper, less adequate solution.

"Bechtel knew darn well DOE would [not pick the Operating Solution], and would go with the Equipment Option," Tamosaitis continued. "But they pursued this approach anyway, so that DOE would ultimately cover the cost"—because, according to their contract, if the DOE picked a more expensive solution to a problem, they, rather than Bechtel, had to cover the costs by adding funds to Bechtel's [baseline] budget.

"Bechtel is the best at playing the game of getting the most taxpayer money to address technical issues that are their responsibility," said Tamosaitis. "They wait for DOE to give them more money. This maximizes their profits at taxpayer expense. If they don't get the money, they just move on. It's the only business where not doing it well leads to more profits—all of which is taxpayer money."

Bechtel spokesperson Suzanne Heaston defended her company via email, stating, "The Operations option fully met all technical requirements and had a lower installed cost."

"Bechtel was not very excited about our approach," said Bruce with a chuckle before turning serious. "Murray Thorson is a brilliant engineer, one of the best I've ever worked with, and the fact that Bechtel didn't even really want to hear what we had to say on the issue was very disheartening, to say the least."

Thorson's accomplishments at the WTP are well-documented. From 2002 to 2008, he led a highly successful effort that resulted in changing the type of resin used in the WTPs ion-exchange columns. This resin acts as a sponge to separate radioactive cesium from the waste, helping to decontaminate Hanford's radioactive material before it is processed into glass. Bechtel was not supportive of Thorson's efforts, however, because more than $11 million worth of research and testing was required to develop and qualify the resin, despite its potential long-term savings of billions of dollars. Another resin already existed, and despite all its problems and associated high costs, Bechtel contended it was acceptable, and told Thorson to stop his development effort.

All indications were that the original resin was not going to work—it gummed up the system, potentially causing it to fail. Even so, URS and Bechtel management disagreed with staff recommendations and claimed the resin was fine as it was. The DOE thought otherwise, and the agency's federal director at the time, John Eschenberg, authorized the group Thorson was working in to move ahead with the new resin development, agreeing to cover the research costs, which were added to Bechtel's WTP budget. After several years of research and testing, Thorson's efforts paid off, and his resin was demonstrated to be a tremendous success.

The new resin was substantially less expensive than the original resin. When all is said and done, Thorson's resin will have saved taxpayers at least $3 billion.

THE DAMAGE DONE

Shortly after the DOE chose Thorson and Bruce's Equipment Option, Thorson wanted out. He did not feel his work was being adequately appreciated at the WTP, though he'd saved the project billions of dollars. When an opening arose at Hanford's Tank Farm, which handles the underground storage containers that hold the toxic site's remaining nuclear waste, Thorson went after it, even though it carried a lesser title.

"I want to be clear: Bechtel did not force me to leave my job at WTP," said Thorson. "But the environment they created there, where good work isn't recognized, was one that I could no longer [work in]. I wanted WTP to operate properly, and believed my new job would continue in these efforts."

Thorson's next job was to work on an oversight group called CLIN 3.2, responsible for looking at long-term operability issues at the WTP. Though technically still a URS employee, Thorson would be working for a company called Washington River Protection Solutions (WRPS), which led CLIN 3.2's evaluations. WRPS is a joint company accountable under their contract to URS.

CLIN 3.2 stood for Contract Line Item Number 3.2, which was included in Hanford's Tank Farm contract between the DOE and URS, the company put in charge of Tank Farm operations. The Tank Farm contract is separate from the WTP contract. Bechtel was not involved in the Tank Farm contract, but URS acts as its lead contractor, responsible for safely retrieving, treating, storing, and disposing of Hanford's Tank Farm waste, which is still sitting in those 177 underground concrete tanks that are grouped into eighteen "farms." As of May 2020, the Tank Farm contract was worth $13 billion.[9]

Waste from the farms will one day move to the WTP through piping and different treatment facilities. The hope is that this final phase of this process will turn this processed waste into glass. So the Tank Farm and the WTP are to work in conjunction to ensure optimum success. In the Tank Farm contract, CLIN 3.2 called for the establishment of biannual independent evaluations to ensure the WTP would run properly.

"This isn't your typical project design," admitted Thorson, referring to areas in the WTP called black cells that hold piping and equipment.

One of the primary tasks assigned to the CLIN 3.2 evaluation group was to ensure everything inside these black cells would function as designed. Two sources, who worked as managers and engineers at Hanford and are familiar with the contract, say that CLIN 3.2 was a "top objective" of the Tank Farm contract, which would help ensure that Bechtel was kept honest since they would have a stake in both the Tank Farm and the WTP contracts.

The first CLIN 3.2 report was issued in September 2010 and found numerous risks, including problems with reliability, operability, maintainability and throughput, hydrogen-vent control, precipitation of solids that could plug equipment, control-system documentation, and contamination control.

After the report was issued, Bechtel said they would not answer design questions or support any reviews, asserted Thorson. "Since DOE did not require them to do so—which Bechtel argued was not required by their contract—it really knocked the wind out of us." Though the reviews would benefit the WTP's potential success, Bechtel claimed they had no money to do reviews unless the DOE handed over more funds. Essentially, CLIN 3.2 was an elite technical review board without any real teeth.

The DOE refused to comment on Thorson's claim that they did not require Bechtel to address the issues raised in CLIN 3.2's first report. But, says Thorson, "It was clear that Bechtel was not pleased with the long-term operability issues we had raised [regarding the WTP]. DOE was simply not supportive of [CLIN] 3.2's original scope."

WRPS soon reduced CLIN 3.2 from a twelve-person operation to half that. Even with the significant downsize, Thorson and others continued to work to put together an annual report—the "Annual Waste Treatment and Immobilization Plant (WTP) Operational Support Report (For Fiscal Year 2011)." Once again, the evaluation found serious vulnerabilities with the WTP that would likely require design changes and testing to remedy. The results of the report were briefed to the DOE.

At that point, however, the report's classification was revised, then reissued as "business sensitive" and for "official use only," rather than being released publicly as intended. "The stated reason from the DOE at the meeting was to keep it out of the hands of potential critical reviewers such as the [DNFSB]," said Thorson.

"Why wouldn't they want it in the hands of [DNFSB]?" asked Tamosaitis. "Because it would bring a big spotlight to the whole WTP operation."

Asked about the delay in releasing the September report, DOE spokesperson Carrie Meyer did not directly address the allegation, stating "The report will be checked for factual accuracy, and released in the spring."

"[Bechtel and DOE] do not want to look at long-term operability of WTP," Thorson added. "They'd rather build the thing and let the problems be fixed later. But you can't do that in the black cells. This is not a normal construction job, it's a first-of-a-kind with a lot of unforeseen issues if it doesn't work right."

In 2012, I obtained a copy of the September report. It is the same as the version still classified as "official use only," a DOE source confirmed. The report's authors identify numerous vulnerabilities, including the potential for hydrogen buildup due to faulty venting that could lead to a shutdown of the WTP—or worse, a nuclear explosion. Despite such potential calamities, at the end of 2011, the DOE verbally requested in a meeting that all CLIN 3.2 evaluations of the WTP in the form of annual reports be stopped indefinitely. Thorson said he and others were also instructed by management to halt work on CLIN 3.2. Additionally, a draft alteration to WRPS's contract with the DOE has been circulated outlining this change in CLIN 3.2's work scope.

No immediate justification was given by the DOE, but Meyer told me the DOE was to implement a "one-system integrated approach" that does not eliminate the CLIN 3.2 analysis, but rather combines work and safety reviews of the Tank Farm with those taking place at the WTP.

"Despite what they say, they aren't going to allow us to do any more long-term operability analysis at all," Thorson responded. "Since Bechtel doesn't believe a factual accuracy check is in their contract, there is no mechanism to ever release the report or get the issues addressed—apart from DOE direction."

One reason the DOE may be supporting Bechtel's decision to largely ignore CLIN 3.2's work could have to do with a March 2011 paper titled the "2020 Vision." I obtained an internal copy of the "2020 Vision" plan, which was primarily put together by WRPS, DOE, and Bechtel personnel who, as the documents state, were "tasked with identifying the optimum approach to startup, commissioning, and turnover of WTP facilities for operations."

The plan, marked "Business Sensitive and Proprietary," reads in part "An important feature of our proposed approach is acceleration of the transition" of activities "from the WTP line item to operating expense." The goal, the 2020 Vision noted, is to ensure that the WTP cost is capped at $12.263 billion. With this, the "2020 Vision" lays out a plan for Bechtel to stay within their proposed budget. They didn't, of course, and by 2020 the $12.263 billion jumped to Bechtel's estimate of $16.8 billion. However, even that number is underestimated: the GAO says WTP could cost taxpayers $41 billion when all is said and done.[10]

What this means is that the WTP shifted some of their research work to the Tank Farms, as I was informed by a URS employee who wished to stay anonymous. The URS Tank Farm contract was not nearly as strapped for cash as Bechtel's WTP contract. By moving some work to the Tank Farm contract, Bechtel and the DOE were able to publicly contend that WTP costs were lower than they actually were.

That the WTP budget was apparently not growing provided cover for the project, protecting against interrogation from outside watchdog groups and organizations like the Government Accountability Office and DNFSB, claimed Tamosaitis. But all that cash can't be hidden in the mattress forever.

"[Bechtel] management here turns over every three years, and guys like me stay around to see the damage they've caused," claimed an engineer who has worked for Bechtel for well over a decade and wishes to remain anonymous for fear of being fired for speaking out.

"The Bechtel mantra is 'Build Something, Be Paid, Be Gone,'" added Tamosaitis.

The Bechtel engineer said this is a clear sign that they don't have the project under control, and the DOE's Alexander admitted his agency does not have enough technical staff to oversee the WTP project.

With the CLIN 3.2 oversight group's objective essentially dismantled, Murray Thorson was once again frustrated. As was David Bruce. "If Bechtel won't listen to the issues I am raising, I'm going to make a big, big stink," he promised, saying that if he isn't given a fair hearing, he'll identify many more design flaws. "[Management's] shenanigans have gone on for far too long."

HOLLOW JUSTICE

What a long, strange trip it was for engineer Walter Tamosaitis. Well, perhaps not so much strange as it was heart-wrenching. He was fired in 2013 after spending over forty years on the job. Yet every once in a while, those who are maligned end up being vindicated. That's exactly what happened in August 2015 for Tamosaitis, who'd been entangled in five years of strained litigation against his former employer URS (now owned by AECOM).

On August 12, 2015, Tamosaitis agreed to a $4.1 million settlement of his federal whistleblower retaliation lawsuit against Hanford contractor URS.[11] While AECOM refused to acknowledge any wrongdoing, they clearly didn't want to drag on a case that could have made the contractor look even worse than it already did.

"We are very pleased that Walter can get on with his life after five years of litigation, and that he has been vindicated," said Jack Sheridan, the Seattle attorney who represented Tamosaitis, "This settlement sends a message to whistleblowers everywhere that integrity and truth are worth fighting for, and that you can win if you don't give up."

What URS didn't expect was that Tamosaitis would refuse to go down without a fight. He was open about a greedy management culture at Hanford run amok. He was candid in explaining that the Hanford cleanup was a cash cow for URS and its parent contractor Bechtel, the same company accused of bilking taxpayers over its botched Iraq reconstruction projects. As such, he was honest and vocal about how the whole operation put profits above the safety of its employees and the public.

In 2011, Tamosaitis filed a federal whistleblower complaint under the Energy Reorganization Act (ERA).[12] By 2013, Tamosaitis was let go for "lack of work." Initially his case was dismissed by Federal District Court Judge Lonny Suko, who found that there was insufficient evidence to support his retaliation claim and that he didn't have the right to a jury trial under ERA. In 2014, the Ninth Circuit Court of Appeals overruled Judge Suko, stating there was "plenty of evidence that Bechtel encouraged URS E&C to remove Tamosaitis from the WTP site because of his whistleblowing, that URS E&C knew that Tamosaitis's whistleblowing motivated Bechtel, and that URS E&C carried out the removal."[13]

The Ninth Circuit also found that Tamosaitis indeed had a right to a jury trial. In July 2014, Los Angeles–based AECOM announced it would acquire URS for $6 billion and has since been pushing for a resolution.[14] While no parties admitted liability, with a $4.1 million settlement, it's clear who was victorious. Of course, the bigger question is if this case has set a precedent, and if it will help ensure that future Hanford employees aren't afraid to step forward and voice concerns about public health and environmental safety.

That's the hope, insists Tom Carpenter of Hanford Challenge.

"This is great news for Walt and great news for the public. Walt is a hero who staked his career to raise nuclear safety issues that could have resulted in a catastrophe down the road," Carpenter said after the settlement announcement. "His issues were investigated and validated, and those safety issues are being scrutinized and corrected. This settlement brings justice to Walt and is a necessary step in the quest to address a broken safety culture at Hanford that has historically punished employees for bringing forward concerns."

A PAINFUL EXIT

A late afternoon phone call in May 2020 found Walter Tamosaitis in a reflective mood. It could have been due to the two months he'd been quarantining with his wife at their family home in Richland, where they were hoping to stave off the coronavirus. Or it could have been that despite being vindicated in court, things still have not ended up the way he envisioned. The years of legal battles and the shunning by coworkers, some of whom he considered friends, took their toll. He felt as if his life's purpose has been stolen, never to be returned. People often believe that a large settlement like the one Tamosaitis received will heal all wounds. That's not always the case.

"It was never about the money. If they hadn't fired me, I would now have fifty years of service under my belt. I put work first in my life," Tamosaitis, now in his early seventies, somberly told me. "Outside of my family, work was my drive. I enjoyed my job and thought I was contributing to it. It's all left me so empty."

Engineering was all he'd ever known. In 1970, straight out of college, Tamosaitis began working for a series of companies controlled by DuPont, a career he never wanted to leave. Tamosaitis may have been one of Hanford's most impactful whistleblowers, exposing how contractors put profit above science and safety, but he still believed the work was vitally important.

"While I was in my yard the other day, a neighbor asked me how I was enjoying retirement. He couldn't believe my answer, that I absolutely hate it and wish I was still going in every day. My wife sees it in me...that I am not happy."

Tamosaitis was open about the emotional struggles he's dealt with over the past ten years since first speaking to me for pieces I was doing on his case for *Seattle Weekly*. Back then, he was still employed, fighting the good fight. Now, with the fight over, he was not sure the tribulations he endured would do anything to change the spoiled culture at Hanford.

"I am now seven years retired, and I really miss the energy of the work, the accomplishments, the challenges, the crisis of the moment. I was really good at my job," he told me. Tamo-saitis admitted to being diagnosed with post-traumatic stress disorder (PTSD), and our conversation, I fear, brought back some of the suffering he'd been working to overcome.

Even so, he said he'd speak out and do it all over again. "Still," he explained, "nobody has any idea what they took away from me, and no amount of money can cure or remedy the pain they've caused."

A portion of the reporting in this chapter first appeared in Seattle Weekly *and has been adapted and updated here for context and clarity.*

CHAPTER SEVEN

HANFORD'S INDIGENOUS STRUGGLE FOR ENVIRONMENTAL JUSTICE

THE LEGACY OF RUSSELL JIM

He was the catalyst in my belief that Indian tribes should be treated as full, equal participants in the process.

— James Asselstine

There are not a lot of heroes out here. Few in recent memory have risen to the daunting challenge, immersing themselves in Hanford's scientific complexities and its historic and cultural implications. If there are any champions of the cause, Russell Jim (Kii'ahł) was certainly one of them. The "Quiet Warrior," Jim was a lifelong advocate for the Yakama Nation. The "conscience of the cleanup," Jim was considered by many to be the spiritual leader of the Hanford resistance. Jim served as the head of the Confederated Tribes and Bands of the Yakama Indian Nation's Environmental Restoration and Waste Management Program (ERWM), a position he essentially created. In 2018, Jim passed away after battling heart trouble and pneumonia after a long bout of cancer, which he believed was a direct result of the time he spent in and around Hanford's radioactive haze.[1]

"I think he's been a major player in the Hanford cleanup and he's been one of the sharpest critics of the process and a very constructive one," said John Bassett, president of Heritage University, when Jim was awarded an honorary doctorate in 2017.

Illustration by Becky Grant.

By all accounts, Jim had an unwavering moral compass and was the rare advocate who possessed the ability to peer through the layers of Hanford's bureaucratic stratum. He was able to envision its future while never losing sight of the past and the gainful lives that the region provided his people over many centuries. The Yakama Nation, in defiance of their forced relocation, refused compensation from the federal government. They have never stopped fighting back against the settler colonialism that has destroyed their Native lands.

"The Hanford area was our wintering ground, the Palm Springs of the area. And the winters were milder here, and so, therefore, we moved here and dispersed to all other parts of the country when the spring came. And our usual custom places involve Canada, Western Montana, northern Arizona, northern California, and the Pacific coast," Jim said in an interview with the Atomic Heritage Museum in 2003.[2] He continued:

> So consequently in the Treaty of 1855, we included such language as accepted by the United States of America, in a contract called a treaty. And as a consequence, we thought that we would forever have the right to utilize the natural foods and medicines and to hunt and fish and all use of our custom places. We lived in harmony with the area, with the river, with all of the environment. All the natural foods and medicines were quite abundant here. And as the snows receded, we followed back up clear into the Alpine areas, into the fall season. And then storing our food that we had gathered all spring and summer, we picked it up on the way back here to Hanford.

BEACONS OF DESTRUCTION

When the Yakama weren't wintering, they were often downriver at Celilo Falls, known to them as Wy-am, which acted as the Columbia River's great trading post. Today, as you travel along the Columbia, the mammoth river below has an almost lake-like stillness. It appears to be barely moving, if at all. Dams have discouraged and interrupted this giant river's natural flow, slowing it down, widening it, restricting its enormous power. Engineers would call the dams' creation an ingenious act of energy cultivation. The dams stand as a testament to the white man's prowess. But environmentalists and Indigenous tribes don't see the Columbia River dams, of which there are fourteen, as feats of human ingenuity. They rightfully view them for what they are: monuments of colonialism and beacons of destruction. They are, no doubt, efficient—efficient at killing off native salmon and the humans who have lived off their sustenance for millennia. And while the wild salmon that once nourished the great tribes of the Pacific Northwest barely hang on, the spiritual rhythm of the river faintly beats, hoping to one day be released from its imprisonment.

Wy-am, like the giant chinook salmon and the tribes that once gathered there, has been forced to adapt or face extinction. Until the 1950s, this stretch of waters, which flows down from the Canadian Rockies, was home to sacred fishing grounds, where skilled tribes used industrious nets to catch salmon as they swam upstream en route to their mating grounds. For thousands of years, wild salmon, after fattening themselves in the ocean, swam up Wy-am's narrow channels between its large pillar-like rocks, leaping out of the water and over tumbling waterfalls, working their way upstream to the pools for breeding and hatching. If they could make it. Tribal fishers utilized wooden platforms and dip-nets for their catch, which they would submerge below the water in turbulent areas, hiding between the forty-foot-high rocks. As the salmon swooshed against the currents, they would be caught in nets and yanked to the shore.[3] It's a sustainable method of fishing that is now all but extinct in this region, since Wy-am was mercilessly flooded after the completion of the Dalles Dam in 1958, twelve miles away. No longer could tribes fish using their traditional fishing methods; the falls were gone. The rocky chutes where they'd drop their dripnets had vanished. Their way of life—what little actually remained by the 1950s—was eliminated.

ROLL OVER COLUMBIA

As a settler, it's hard to imagine what Wy-am meant to these Indigenous nations. It's also difficult to ponder what lies beneath the Columbia today, below its controlled current. The amount of water that rushed over Wy-am during spring melt is estimated to have been ten times greater than the amount of water that spills over the picturesque Niagara Falls today.[4] Wy-am was a sanctuary to the half-dozen Columbia tribes and thousands more that congregated here to celebrate the salmon, their shared spiritual heritage, and the love and respect they had for one another and the land.

Archeological records indicate the area's first human inhabitants date back at least eleven thousand years. And the first recordings by Meriwether Lewis and William Clark estimated that by 1805, upwards of ten thousand people lived along the Columbia River.[5] Wy-am acted as a nexus of a great Native trading network that stretched from the Alaskan interior to the coasts of Southern California, where buffalo meats, hides, salmon, obsidian, pipestone, and much more were exchanged among tribes.

The Yakama were originally made up of five tribes from the mid-Columbia Basin that spoke the same Sahaptin dialect.[6] After losing the Yakama War of 1855, the tribes were forced into a single, defining tribe known as the Yakama, and expelled from their lands and onto the present-day reservation located in south central Washington state. Today, the Confederated Tribes and Bands of the Yakama Nation is a federally recognized tribe that is made up of Wallawalla, Wanapam, Wenatchi, Klikitat, Palus, Wishram, and Yakama peoples.

As a teenager, Russell Jim would trek with his family to the ancient fishing sites of Wy-am. The place etched itself into his spiritual psyche.[7] "It was quite an experience," remembered Jim, "I was very young. . . . Gee, I was happy." When Jim was in his twenties, Wy-am was flooded by the electric machinations of the Dalles Dam, which no doubt left Jim with a firsthand account of what the white man and their vicious government were capable of in the name of "progress." Wy-am served as a better education than the organized schooling Jim received in his youth.[8]

"When I came home from the Chemawa Indian Boarding School," recounted Jim, "I described the horror stories to my aunt, and she went to my father and said, 'You can send the rest of your children back to that school if you want to. This one is not going.' And she said, 'If he has to go to school, you find a place close by here where I can watch him. If you do not, I'll take him to the hills and you'll never find us.'"[9]

Even the folk music hero Woody Guthrie, long viewed as an anticapitalist champion of the working class, played an organizational role in destroying the Columbia River and the people who called it home. After Guthrie left New York City in 1940, he landed in Los Angeles and soon headed north to Portland, Oregon, where he became a hired gun for the US Department of Interior. In a one-month span, Guthrie penned twenty-six songs while on the Interior's payroll, including his well-known, overtly patriotic "Roll On, Columbia, Roll On," which acted as a rallying cry for the construction of electricity-producing dams on the river. While Guthrie may still be viewed as a socialist champion to some, his music acted as the soundtrack of colonialism for many others.

"Guthrie's was a voice of the displaced and dispossessed, yet this down-to-earth propaganda music helped to dispossess and displace people that had for millennia lived on and from the river he sang about," writes Cornell professor and musicologist David Yearsley.[10] "Perhaps the broadest irony is that Guthrie's bardic gift—flowing if not with the power of the Columbia, then at least with unsurpassed fluency—yields 'natural' music that praises the destruction of nature."

Yes, the dams created jobs. They created electricity. They laid the ground for the white, liberal Pacific Northwest lifestyle of today. And as the Columbia's waters were tamed, the region's great ancient forests, with trees ranging from 250 to 1,000 years old, were also ravaged in the name of US expansionism. Today, only around 10 percent of these old-growth trees remain in Washington and Oregon, a grotesque patchwork of clear-cuts that are visible from nearly every hilltop.[11] In less than one hundred years, 87 percent of the old-growth forest was razed. The Columbia River dams and the government-sponsored exploitation logging came at a great cost to the Indigenous peoples of the area. Cinder block by cinder block, as the dams were constructed, the way of life that Russell Jim and his ancestors enjoyed for thousands of years was quickly demolished. They were removed from their ancestral lands. Their fisheries were gone. They were victimized, demonized, and relegated as second-class citizens in this new cruel world, dominated by capitalist greed and the white man's Christian entitlement. Natives, in short, were expendable. Today, the very dams that Woody Guthrie once championed remain as fanciful colonialist landmarks, not unlike South Dakota's Mount Rushmore, where the chiseled faces of white men are carved into the Lakota's sacred Tunkaslia Sakpe Paha.[12]

"The false religious doctrine of Christian discovery was used by the United States to perpetrate crimes of genocide and forced displacement against Native Peoples," says Yakama Nation chairman JoDe Goudy.[13] He continued:

> The Columbia River dams were built on this false legal foundation and decimated the Yakama Nation's fisheries, traditional foods and cultural sites. We are calling on that action (removal of the dams) to happen, because when you go back, and you understand the truth, with regard to what has materialized—this lake behind us all—once one of the greatest, one of the mightiest big rivers in the world. Our way of life, of the Natives, is fading. What we can collectively do to sustain our way of life from now to as far as we can see into the future, because if we do not, then we will cease to be.

Once your eyes are open to the pain and sorrow these dams have inflicted and continue to inflict, not only to the mighty wild salmon that spawned in its waters but also to the Natives who cared for the river for eons, there is no looking away. The reality is just too brutally honest and emotionally fraught. The dams, by whatever means necessary, must go.

FINDING HIS VOICE

While Jim's early connection to the Columbia River began during his teenage voyages to the sacred grounds of Wy-am with his kin, it was the government's militarist efforts upstream that galvanized him to action. With his long, gray braids and metal-rimmed glasses, Jim's eloquent and passionate defense of the Hanford area for his people and the environment was unmatched.

The government saw Hanford as an "isolated wasteland" where the people were "expendable . . . therefore the Manhattan Project was justified here," said Jim in an interview with the

Atomic Heritage Foundation. "White men look at that place, and they see a wasteland," Jim said in 1983. "We look and see chokecherries, rabbits and foods that come out of the ground; but who in their right mind, knowing the contamination they have put there, would go and gather that food now?"[14] The Yakama people have also been negatively impacted by Hanford's nuclear production.

"[We] are suffering the consequences, health-wise," Jim continued.

> [Hanford's land] means our health being affected also as a result of the environment being affected. The health of the Yakama people depends on the health of the environment through today and it will be through tomorrow. There is a concerted effort now by the Yakama Nation to influence the cleanup of the site. We know that it will never be returned to pristine status in the next five hundred years, but at least there should be an effort to set the stage for cleanup . . . There is a lot of activity out here but hardly any cleanup.

Early on, Jim noticed that rheumatoid arthritis was rampant among Yakama elders and even many younger adults. He was quick to realize there may be a link between these ailments and the radioactive releases from Hanford. "During my work here on the Hanford Reservation, I was called by a doctor out of Tennessee and asked if I was the guy that was making this statement. I said, 'Yes.' And he said, 'Well, I want you to know that,' he studied a mining operation, every type of mining operation for years, and he found that uranium causes a malady very similar to rheumatoid arthritis," Jim recounted in an interview with Brian Bull of Wisdom of the Elders.[15] "But even before that, by 1976 and '77, I suspect that many of our problems came out of Hanford because of the releases, although they denied there was any major releases out of Hanford."

Of course, there were many releases, most of which were not publicly known at the time. This was proven in 1986 when the DOE was forced to publish thousands of pages of internal documents, detailing the quantity of radioactive particles that Hanford facilities had knowingly released during their operative years. Perhaps even more than the formally trained scientists themselves, Jim knew that it would take generations of hard work, tenacity, and a willingness to deal with nearly insurmountable bureaucratic hurdles to remediate these lands.

"You younger generations have to realize what you are going to be faced with and perhaps your children and grandchildren also," Jim told a small crowd at the University of Washington during a public forum on Hanford in May 2013.[16] "Over the past fifty years, some 440 billion gallons of contaminated liquids were directly disposed to the ground. Enough to create a poisonous lake the size of Manhattan, 120 feet deep. . . . We have a magnificent problem, and some of you may wonder why is the Yakama Nation involved. As most of you may know, we have a treaty with the United States of America. A *contract*. We feel it's supposed to last until the end of time."

Jim became a full-time advocate when he realized what was really going on at Hanford in 1977. At the time that Jim was immersing himself in all the inner workings and complexities at the site, government officials were starting to consider Hanford as a formal dumping ground for the nation's growing cache of radioactive and chemical waste. They had a lot to get rid of, and still do. The United States has five times more spent nuclear fuel than Russia, the world's second leading producer. The Hanford land, the government argued forty years ago, was already so destroyed that dumping truckloads of more nuclear byproducts wouldn't make matters all that much worse. A young Russell Jim saw things much differently.

First, Jim understood the tribes of the area were not stake-holders like the farmers, fisheries, and folks who lived down-stream from Hanford. They were, in fact, sovereign nations, independent governments that had legal rights that many stakeholders do not. This gave Jim power to have his voice not only heard but acted upon.[17]

GROWING ANTI-NUKE SENTIMENT

While Russell Jim's activism on behalf of the Yakama was sprouting at Hanford, anti-nuclear sentiment was simultaneous-ly growing throughout the world. By the late 1970s, many people were growing wary of nuclear proliferation. The anti-nuke move-ment, particularly overseas, was rapidly building. In Wyhl, Ger-many, activists put the brakes on a nuclear power plant that was set to be constructed. This success inspired a robust anti-nuke movement that expanded across Europe.[18] In France, anti-nuke opposition was also taking shape and spreading to the Pacif-ic, where, in 1972, early Greenpeace activists, including David McTaggart, sailed a boat into the heart of France's dangerous nuclear testing zone. There, McTaggart was physically assaulted by the French military, his boat ransacked. But he didn't give up. By 1974, McTaggart's campaign was victorious, and France put an end to their atomic weapons testing program. In Spain, activ-ists were equally successful, helping to quash numerous plans for nuclear development in the country. The anti-nuclear movement didn't find its footing in the United States during this period, as the Vietnam War remained the focal point among many activ-ists. But later accidents like Russia's 1986 Chernobyl meltdown as well as Hanford's toxic legacy (which began drawing national attention during the 1980s, largely thanks to the work of people like Jim) would alter the United States' trust in nuclear technol-ogies, especially among the youth.

Despite growing awareness, the potential for a deadly nuclear accident at Hanford was something still largely unknown
aside from a few river advocates and Native tribes. For those
keeping tabs on Hanford throughout the 1980s, like the Yakama, the situation was ominous. By 1985, four decades after
Hanford began producing plutonium, not a single independent
study looked at the cumulative damage the site had unleashed
on nearby communities or Native tribes. DOE officials blew
off calls for such an inquiry and contended that it would be
unworthy of the department's time. They argued that radioactivity was all but nonexistent outside of Hanford's boundaries. Citizen activists noted an uptick in certain cancers in their
communities and believed a longitudinal study on the human
population was the only way to get a handle on Hanford's
long-term impacts.[19] "I don't know what else as citizens we
can do but count bodies," said artist and former Hanford-area
resident Joan N. Moortry. In the mid-1980s, Moortry helped
found the Hanford Education Action League, an early Hanford watchdog group that was unconvinced by the DOE's
assurances that Hanford's atomic demons were continually
monitored and safely contained.

Terry R. Strong, who served as head of the Radiation Control
Section of the Washington Department of Social and Health
Services in 1985, strongly disagreed with the DOE's lack of
monitoring and openly criticized the state of Washington for
allocating a meager $87,000 a year to keep an eye on Han-
ford's environmental impact. The threat was so grave, Strong
believed, that the state should have been spending at least
$2.5 million. Others, including British physician Dr. Alice M.
Stewart, who helped author a study of Hanford workers during
the early 1980s, argued the government was also far too lenient
with its radiation safety levels. The study found a connection
between low radiation doses and cancer deaths—particularly

multiple myeloma—among workers. Hanford employees, the study reported, experienced at least a 5 percent higher risk of developing cancer than the general population. "If they stick to present safety levels," warned Dr. Stewart, "they will have more trouble than they think they are going to have."[20]

Radioactive wastes, however, weren't the only poisons befouling the site; hazardous chemicals were also a byproduct of Hanford's weapon operations. "We have mainly acids and caustics, some solvents, trichloroethylene, PCBs, pentachlorophenol, sulfuric acid, chlorine, fluorine, mercury, chromates," said Carl G. Welty in 1985, who worked as a toxicologist for the DOE's environmental protection division. "You name a problem, and we probably have it."

A CHALLENGING ADVERSARY

Russell Jim knew there was a major problem at Hanford and the government was planning to make it worse. By the late 1970s, Hanford and Yucca Mountain were the two prime contenders to become depots for spent nuclear fuel. While the Western Shoshone stood their ground and tried to fight the use of Yucca as a repository, they ultimately lost. Jim, representing Yakama Nation, took the lead on keeping the stuff out of Hanford. The waste was to sit in man-made tombs for the next ten thousand years. Flabbergasted at the thought of such an idiotic undertaking, Jim took his fight to the United States Senate. Testifying before a Senate subcommittee on nuclear regulation in 1980, Jim made an impassioned plea to the senators about his peoples' connection to the land, hoping they'd consider viewing the Hanford issue from his point of view: "There is something you need to understand that is unique between my people and yours. Yakama Indian people do not get most of their food supply from the local A&P or

Safeway store," said Jim. In fact, he later wrote in a newspaper article, the Yakama still use more than seventy different types of plants as food. "Our religion and culture are deeply interwoven with the gathering of our foods the Creator provided us. Our blood has melted into that particular part of the Earth where our people are buried."[21]

Jim not only intimately understood the science behind the nuclear mess at Hanford, he also was well-versed in the laws and the rights of his people. The time he spent in Washington speaking at various hearings and meeting personally with numerous Senators and staffers was beginning to pay off. When the Nuclear Waste Policy Act of 1982 was passed, it included specific language that recognized Indian sovereignty. It was powerful language. As a result of Jim's efforts, tribes like the Yakama, along with states, could veto their lands from becoming nuclear waste depositories. And it would take a majority of both houses of Congress to overturn such vetoes.

"He can be a most challenging adversary when he wants to be," said J. Bennett Easterling, director of policy for DOE's civilian radioactive program during the mid-1980s, shortly after the passage of the 1982 act. "Russell has mastered his subject. He knows the law and knows what it guarantees. . . . He can tell me the department is 'dead wrong' on an issue and not make it a personal insult to me."

Jim had a graceful and emotive way of expressing the traditions and concerns of his people. In a speech, along with a set of written comments, Jim shared these oft-misunderstood views with the Subcommittee on Nuclear Regulation in 1987 when Hanford was being chosen as a dumping ground.

> We have learned in the past year of over forty years of both accidental and intentional releases of radioactivity to the earth, the atmosphere, and the waters that are sacred to the Yakama. This is an agency that for nearly three decades

used the Columbia River for once-through cooling of its
reactors. . . . This is the agency that for thirty years put
liquid, high-level wastes in single-shell tanks just below the
surface of the ground, and assured us that the practice was
safe, only to have many of those tanks leak their deadly
contents . . .

Jim was right. He was right about the risks and right about the
DOE's numerous failures. How could these people be trusted
to do it correctly? And more importantly, how could it even
be done right in the first place? It couldn't, and Jim knew it.
You can't bury nuclear waste near groundwater supplies; there's
simply no way to keep it from seeping out as the earth shakes,
contorts, erodes, and shifts over the course of tens of thousands of years. If water were to ever enter the nuclear-laden
cavity, it would likely boil over, causing radioactive lava to spill,
or worse, produce a quasi-volcanic eruption. At the very least,
Jim argued, the stuff would one day leak, as it had been out
of the existing underground tanks for decades. The Columbia
River would be impacted. Fish would be impacted. Humans
would be impacted, and Jim's people, no doubt, would suffer
the worst of it.

"I wanted to know what was coming through our reservation
on Highway 97, leaving Hanford, what was coming through
Hanford . . . and I could not get an answer," said Jim during
his 2013 talk at the University of Washington.[22] "We were the
only tribe to testify before the Senate subcommittee in January
of 1980. And from that point the only tribe to try to contribute
to the parent legislation that became the Nuclear Waste Policy
Act of 1982 . . . we immediately filed for effective status and
received it by April 1983. . . . We eventually showed that Hanford, technically, was not the place to put this material."

Jim's activism during this time forced the federal government to drop their insidious idea of using Hanford as a nu-

clear dumping zone. He had won. His people had won, and
so had the environment that had sustained them for generations. While others had joined the cause, without Jim's tenacious work, Native voices would have been ignored, as many
senators admitted they believed the states would speak up in
Natives' interest. Jim, of course, straightened them out, making it clear they were more than capable of speaking for themselves. "Russell had a significant effect on my thinking," said
James Asselstine, who was appointed by Ronald Reagan to the
Nuclear Regulatory Commissioners. "He was the catalyst in
my belief that Indian tribes should be treated as full, equal
participants in the process."

A BATTLE WORTH FIGHTING

This big victory was only the beginning of Jim's long career as
an advocate for the Yakama Nation. His foray with the federal
government in the late 1970s and 1980s was not his last. The
land, in Jim's eyes, was worth fighting for. The 1855 treaty had
ceded over ten million acres from the Yakama tribes to the
federal government. While they signed over the lands, they
never expected the seizure to last.

"We could not pick up and move as the transients that work
here," said Russell Jim in 1996.[23] "The Yakama culture and religion [are] directly tied to this land. We can't pick up our culture
out of the ground and move it somewhere else. . . . We managed the land successfully for countless generations," added Jim.
"And the newcomers managed to defile it in a few short years."

Jim was being polite. The newcomers didn't just defile this
land, they nuked it and poisoned his people and the landscape
they depended upon. "Abnormally high incidence[s] of thyroid
tumors and cancers have been observed in populations living
downwind from Hanford," reported Dr. Helen Caldicott, a sci-

entist and anti-nuclear activist. "Strontium-90, Cesium-137, and Plutonium-239 have been [atmospherically] released in large quantities, as was, between 1952 and 1967, Ruthenium-106. People in adjacent neighborhoods were kept uninformed about these releases—before, during, and after—and none were warned that they were at risk for subsequent development of cancer."[24]

Jim knew the toll on the Yakama was great, not only to cultural heritage, but to their health. No big decision was made at Hanford without input from Jim, and while it didn't always go his way, he never backed down. He was prescient and brave. He was able to articulate the lunacy of the Hanford project and the government's continued ignorance and outright deception. His quest for information and knowledge about what was actually taking place at Hanford forced an immeasurable amount of transparency, which remains all too important if the DOE and its contractors are to ever be held accountable. Up until his death in April 2018 at the age of eighty-two, Jim was working hard to fight the federal government's effort to declassify Hanford's nuclear waste, which would allow the radioactive leftovers to be more freely transported and dumped, with obviously grave implications.

Out on the cold North Dakota plains, as Indigenous activists, environmentalists, and others gathered at Standing Rock in opposition to the Dakota Access Pipeline, the spirit of Russell Jim was there, his spirit helping to carry on the opposition, despite the rubber bullets and freezing temperatures. His heart, too, would be bleeding with Line 3 water protectors who are battling Enbridge's tar sands pipeline in northern Minnesota, which violates the US treaty rights of the Ojibwe, Anishinaabe, and other tribes.[25] It's Jim's resistance, his connection to these sacred Indigenous lands, and his perseverance, that now runs through the call for a Red New Deal—the Indigenous climate plan that calls for change from below and a replacement of the system that has created the very problems facing our Earth today.[26]

"He's just irreplaceable," said Hanford's tribal program manager Jill Conrad. "There's just not going to be anyone with his knowledge and experience. He was working on Hanford issues longer than many of the senior managers at Hanford—he will be missed."

As a result of Jim's legacy, the Yakama Nation will have a seat at the table, and while Jim's voice will no longer be heard, his echoes will continue to reverberate, guiding the future involvement of the Yakama with the site. Along with Jim's tribe, the Nez Perce and the Confederated Tribes of the Umatilla Reservation are active in the Hanford cleanup, largely thanks to the groundbreaking activism of Russell Jim.[27]

THE YAKAMA'S FIGHT CONTINUES

"The long history of our ancestral lands started prior to Hanford's establishment. There needs to be a reminder that Yakama Nation was here before Hanford, before Washington became a state, before the Treaty of 1855 at Walla Walla, and before Lewis and Clark," explains Jim's successor and longtime colleague Alfrieda Peters, who now serves as education and outreach specialist for the Yakama Nation Environmental Restoration and Waste Management Department (ERWM). "Now there is an overlapping and combined history between Yakama Nation and Hanford. The public must realize that Hanford is within Yakama Nation ceded-area lands, and we still have ceded-area rights. The Columbia River, the lands, and the salmon tie us to Hanford."[28]

The Indigenous movement that Jim shepherded during his decades of work at Hanford continues, and Peters, who labored alongside her friend on behalf of the Yakama Nation for much of that time, believes the road ahead will be more tumultuous than before. Even so, Peters gracefully envisions a land where Hanford was not a nuclear dump, and a white, colonial government kept its word and upheld its treaties.

"[W]e would be there, actively living our way of life. Fishing, collecting our traditional foods and medicines, going to sacred areas," adds Peters, who is eloquent, soft-spoken, and as fierce of an advocate as her mentor Russell Jim. "I believe our families would still be walking the lands and our elders would be telling stories of the land. I can imagine them saying, 'You know the moccasins of your great-great-grandparents walked here.' The prayer songs of our people would drift whatever direction the air carried them over the lands, water, and wildlife. The songs are not just for tribal people. The Yakamas would ask for blessings of all life—not just human life. A cultural reverence."[29]

It's this perspective that gives Peters the tenacity to keep the struggle going, despite the obstacles—be they bureaucratic or scientific. Like Jim, Peters considers this land sacred, connecting her people to this place and to the river despite the wounds that have been inflicted upon it.

"I find myself returning over and over to my birthplace: Celilo. Even though Celilo Falls is underwater, I feel the pull and reminisce. I remember the sound and mist from the water. The activity of the fishermen. Families filleting fish. I remember my grandmother's dried salmon in the smoke sheds—the aroma was very inviting. I knew there would be many enjoyable meals," reflects Peters. "Now I go down to the water and revitalize myself, wash myself with the water from the river. It is my own spiritual feeling—home."[30]

Following the death of Russell Jim, his name, out of deference for his next journey, was not spoken for an entire year.[31] "I acknowledge and honor his acute insight on the consequences of the Hanford Nuclear Site in our backyard and his testimony that ensured the Yakama Nation and other tribes have an active voice and input in the cleanup," maintains Peters. "When we speak about Yakama Nation and Hanford, it is the message of Atwai[32] Dr. Jim, now an ancestral elder, that goes forward."[33] While these lands will never return to their historic beauty, and while the Columbia River won't be free-flowing and dam-free in our lifetimes, it is comforting to envision the future Jim sought. It may take a thousand years, but if the conditions of his people, the land, this air and water, are to ever improve, it will largely be because of the dogged efforts of the Quiet Warrior, Russell Jim, and the Indigenous voices he has empowered to carry on his struggle.

CHAPTER EIGHT

DESTROYING THE PLANET TO SAVE THE PLANET

THE FALLACIES OF NUCLEAR TECHNOLOGY

By artificially accelerating the expansion of civilian programs, subsidies to nuclear technology. . .exacerbate the
already challenging problems of weapons proliferation. . .

—Union of Concerned Scientists

The consensus is not good. In fact, it's downright awful. There's little debate in the scientific community about the ravaging impacts climate catastrophe has in store for our little blue planet. No longer are we debating who is responsible, or what kinds of emissions are contributing to these drastic alterations. Humans and our fossil fuel addiction are to blame. On August 9, 2021, the UN's Intergovernmental Panel on Climate Change (IPCC) re-leased its most comprehensive report since 2013, stating that it is "unequivocal that human influence has warmed the atmosphere, ocean and land." No matter what we do, the report bluntly pre-dicted, the planet will continue to warm for the next thirty years, and that's even if we were to stop all global emissions tomorrow. It's a dire warning and one we should swiftly heed.[1]

No region of the planet will escape the approaching climate devastation. Much of it has already begun to arrive. Heat waves will intensify. Droughts will plague enormous swaths of land. Rivers and lakes will vanish. Forest fires will burn with increased fury, polluting our air and poisoning our lungs. Hurricanes will overwhelm us. Summer heat waves will become unbearable and deadly. Oceans will heat up and acidify. Glaciers will continue to melt. Sea levels will rise. Scores of animal and plant life will be killed in what paleontologists call the sixth great extinction. The world's most impoverished communities, from Malawi to Honduras to Papua New Guinea, will suffer the most. Millions will lose their homes, whole cities will become unlivable. Water wars will break out. Crops will die. People will starve. Any way you look at it, the forecast is grim and apocalyptic. If global greenhouse emissions are not drastically cut immediately, the IPCC warns, the situation will only worsen.[2]

The IPCC broadly and succinctly lays out the reality we face. The Earth has not been this hot in over 125,000 years, CO_2 levels in the atmosphere haven't been this high in nearly two million years, and even if we moderately curb emissions, the planet is still likely to heat up 2.1 to 3.5 °C. The rosiest of scenarios the IPCC paints is not rosy at all.[3] It's nightmarish. The changes the Earth is facing are irreversible. This means that fossil fuels must stop being incinerated at once. If we do not end our use of these polluting energy sources, future generations will arrive to a planet that is virtually uninhabitable. In a rational society, greenhouse gases would not be reduced, they would be phased out and ultimately banned like we did with DDT back in 1972. This moratorium must be permanent and untethered from the marketplace.

Our language around global warming must change right along with our energy policy. We also need to stop talking about global warming as being a "problem" that can be fixed. It's no more a "problem" than cancer is a "problem." The Earth is a living cell and we need to treat it as such, as British scientist James Lovelock hypothesizes.[4] This cell is diseased and the species it hosts are in peril. Humans are causing the sickness, yet we still have the power to heal it or at least bandage its wounds. Unfortunately, the remedy some are prescribing, including the elderly Lovelock (he's 102 as of this writing), is to treat the ills of climate catastrophe with a heavy dose of nuclear technology. Bill Gates is even getting in on the fun, starting his own nuclear power company called Natrium, which is Latin for sodium. The first plan for Gates is to build a small and "safe" sodium-cooled reactor in Wyoming. But, critics note, Gates's atomic dreams will be short-lived. Sodium-cooled nuclear plants have always failed in the past, largely because they are at higher risk of breakout fires, which means a higher risk of accidents. In other words, Gates is wasting his money on a dangerous idea when there are plenty of reliable renewable technologies ready to go.[5]

For decades, the Left has largely been in opposition to atomic energy and in agreement that nuclear weapons are dangerous, and that the future of our planet ought to be free of the risks they pose. Yet as climate change becomes ever more real, some on the Left are hoping and advocating for an atomic renaissance.

Columnist George Monbiot has praised nuclear power in the *Guardian*, believing it to be a vital component to weaning the world off climate-warming fuels. In a column titled, "Why Fukushima Made Me Stop Worrying and Love Nuclear Power," Monbiot writes, "Some Greens have wildly exaggerated the dangers of radioactive pollution. . . .Every energy technology carries a cost; so does the absence of energy technologies. Atomic energy has just been subjected to one of the harshest of possible tests, and the impact on people and the planet has been small. The crisis at Fukushima has converted me to the cause of nuclear power."[6]

Monbiot's position would be laughable if it weren't so tragic. As the Japanese and the Pacific Ocean faced the world's largest nuclear accident in a quarter century following the meltdown of Fukushima, one of the leading progressive voices in the UK went out of his way to defend the very technology that was responsible for it. In most cases, Monbiot has been careful to defend his positions with valid supporting evidence, even chastising others for not measuring up to his standards. But to defend his stance on nuclear power, Monbiot is satisfied with cherry-picking scientific facts from the infamous 1986 Chernobyl disaster.

"The Chernobyl meltdown was hideous and traumatic. The official death toll so far appears to be forty-three: twenty-eight workers in the initial few months and fifteen civilians by 2005," wrote Monbiot, who cited the World Health Organization and the United Nations Scientific Committee on the Effects of Atomic Radiation as his source.[7] However, even the World Health Organization concluded that approximately four thousand people would eventually die as a result of radiation exposure from Chernobyl, a statement Monbiot seemed content with dismissing.[8]

Even so, both the UN and WHO seem to have drastically underestimated the actual human cost of the Chernobyl meltdown. In 2009, the New York Academy of Sciences released the most significant English-language report on the deaths and environmental devastation caused by Chernobyl. After poring through thousands of reports and studies conducted in Eastern Europe and Russia, the academy concluded that nearly one million people have died as a result of radiation exposure from the nuclear disaster.[9]

Dr. Janette D. Sherman, who co-edited the volume, explained the discrepancy between the UN's assessment of Chernobyl and the Academy's. "[The UN] released a report," said Dr. Sherman, ". . . and they only included about 350 articles available in the English language, but [the New York Academy of Sciences] looked at well over five thousand articles . . . by people who were there and saw what was going on. We are talking about medical doctors, scientists, veterinarians, epidemiologists, who saw what was happening when people in their communities were getting sick and dying."

In the Academy's groundbreaking report they argue that the World Health Organization and the International Atomic Energy Agency, which reports to the UN, formed an agreement in 1959 which states one will not release a report without the agreement of the other. "This is like having Dracula guard the blood bank," attests Dr. Sherman, "because [the World Health Organization] is beholden to IAEA before they can release a report."

Additionally, the IAEA was set up to promote nuclear power, so any evidence that damages its credibility directly challenges its mission. In fact massive protests have taken place in Geneva in an effort to stop this agreement, which is still in place.

Of course, it's not only Chernobyl that exposed the dangers of nuclear power. In 1961, when an explosion at the Nuclear Reactor Testing Station in Idaho Falls killed three people, their bodies were found laced with radiation.[10] Michigan's Enrico Fermi Nuclear Generating Station, which sits on the banks of Lake Erie, experienced a partial meltdown in 1966, leaking radioactive material. Critics argue a major incident at the site was narrowly avoided, which could have destroyed the entire city of Detroit.[11] The 1979 Three Mile Island incident resulted in significant leaks; even the conservative US Nuclear Regulatory Commission admits that two million people were exposed to radiation as a result, and the fallout could have been far worse.[12] There was the 1986 accident at the Surry Nuclear Plant in Virginia that killed four workers. In 1989, a fire broke out at the Vandellòs nuclear power plant, damaging the cooling system, and the plant nearly experienced a full meltdown.[13] In 1992, Russia's Sosnovy Bor nuclear plant released radioactive iodine into the air, the extent of which is hard to gauge. Japan's Tokaimura accident in 1999 killed two workers, and the explosion caused a radiation leak.[14] A steam explosion and subsequent radiation leak at Japan's Mihama Nuclear Power Plant in 2004 injured seven workers and killed four more.[15] Then we have the 2011 Fukushima event, which some have deemed the worst nuclear power disaster ever.[16] A 2013 World Nuclear Industry Status Report states that Fukushima released radiation that was 5.6 and 8.1 times greater than that of Chernobyl. And while there have been few large health studies of the accident, some estimates put the ultimate death toll at ten thousand, largely from cancers caused by radioactive fallout.[17] This says nothing of the ruin it caused on the local environment and the animals that inhabit it. Monbiot argues that these small and large incidents (there are others) are just the cost of doing nuclear business. It's difficult to understand the twisted rationale that killing the planet will somehow save it. Regrettably, Monbiot is not the only one making this mushroom-cloud-sized-blunder.

In June 2021, Bhaskar Sunkara, founder of *Jacobin* and current president of *The Nation*, followed in Monbiot's radioactive footsteps and praised the potential of nuclear energy, writing in the *Guardian* that "nuclear is an idea whose time came and seemed to have passed, but may indeed have a future. For those of us looking for a solution to climate change, the least we can ask is that no plants like Indian Power close until we have a clean, dependable and scalable alternative already in place."[18]

Sunkara also argued that we can easily separate the science of nuclear power from the technology of atomic weapons. "Some of the paranoia is no doubt rooted in Cold War–era associations of peaceful nuclear power with dangerous nuclear weaponry. We can and should separate these two, just like we are able to separate nuclear bombs from nuclear medicine."

Sadly, Sunkara, like Monbiot, is echoing dangerous myths and perpetuating naive and simplistic anecdotes to support their cause. First, nuclear power and atomic bombs, like the tiny elements that create them, are intricately linked. The Army Nuclear Power Program, which began in 1954 and ran through 1976, was initially conceived to promote and develop mobile nuclear power technology for the United States military. The project churned out hundreds of nuclear power operators and facilitated the further development of nuclear capabilities and reactor designs.[19] Additionally, the US government's role in any future nuclear power development will also be a calculated one. More nuclear power plants means more facilities to enrich and reprocess uranium. More of these plants means more materials for nuclear weapons. In the United States, nuclear power is more expensive than wind and solar, and is only competitive if the market is leveled through taxpayer-backed subsidies, which in turn support nuclear arms proliferation.[20] In a 2011 report by the Union of Concerned Scientists titled "Nuclear Power: Still Not Viable Without Subsidies," the authors explained:

> Just as coal production generates carbon and other externalities that need to be integrated into pricing if economies are to make sound energy choices, the link between civilian nuclear power and nuclear weapons also cannot be ignored. As noted by Sharon Squassoni, director of the Proliferation Prevention Program at the Center for

Strategic and International Studies, the 'dual-use [civilian and military] nature of nuclear technology is unavoidable. For the five nuclear-weapons states, commercial nuclear power was a spinoff from weapons programs; for later proliferators, the civilian sector has served as a convenient avenue and cover for weapons programs.' By artificially accelerating the expansion of civilian programs, subsidies to nuclear technology and fuel-cycle services worldwide exacerbate the already challenging problems of weapons proliferation. To date, the negative externality of proliferation has not been reflected in the economics of civilian reactors.[21]

NUCLEAR PLANTS IN THE MIDSTS OF WAR

As Russia's invasion of Ukraine demonstrated, the threat of nuclear war is not solely dependent on the detonation of atomic weapons. Nuclear power plants, when located in contested regions or on active battlefields, also pose a grave risk. If hit by artillery or missile fire, an unforeseen tragedy could quickly unfold. One such frightful scenario nearly occurred as Russian forces shelled the Zaporizhzhia power plant in the southern Ukrainian city of Enerhodar in late February 2022. As blasts occurred around the facility, a fire erupted in a nearby building and was later extinguished. Reports claimed no radioactivity was released during the blaze, but given the nature of the conflict, no independent investigation was conducted to ensure its safety.[22]

Built between 1980 and 1986, Zaporizhzhia, Europe's largest nuclear power complex, houses six 950-megawatt reactors, and any battles in or around the plant could lead to a dangerous release of radioactivity. Prior to the shelling of Zaporizhzhia, Russia also captured Chernobyl and its one-thousand-square-mile contamination zone.

In all, fifteen nuclear facilities were located in the theater of war, where any mishap or intentional attack could have caused an atomic explosion and a subsequent fallout of radioactive particles.[23] Before the bombing started the plants already posed a threat. Ukraine's aging nuclear plants were designed in the Soviet Union, and in 2021, none met internationally recognized safety standards. The plants were sitting ducks, making for easy targets of military or terror attacks.

Nuclear power facilities require a constant flow of water and electricity to operate, so even a slight disruption could lead to an accident or cataclysmic meltdown. Even at the nearly empty and decaying Chernobyl, electricity is needed to keep its 20,000 spent fuel rods cool. Shockingly, the plant lost power in early March 2022 as Russia took over the plant and workers were forced to jump start its backup generators to keep the electricity flowing. As Russia's forces engulfed Ukraine's major cities, the situation at Chernobyl became dire and news was hard to come by.

IAEA released an alarming statement, reporting that "remote data transmission from safeguards monitoring systems installed at the Chernobyl NPP had been lost," and while workers have "access to food and water, and medicine to a limited extent," the "situation for the staff was worsening." By March 10, 2022, the IAEA announced all communication with Chernobyl had been lost.[24] [25]

"I'm deeply concerned about the difficult and stressful situation facing staff at the Chernobyl nuclear power plant and the potential risks this entails for nuclear safety," IAEA Director General Rafael Grossi said as Russia took control of Chernobyl. "I call on the forces in effective control of the site to urgently facilitate the safe rotation of personnel there."

After three long weeks, exhausted and overworked staff at Chernobyl were finally allowed to rotate out, replaced by local volunteers.[26] Nonetheless, grave dangers persisted. A day after Chernobyl's exhausted employees had left their posts, a fire broke out in a radioactive forest near Chernobyl, arousing worries that radiation in the smoke could travel to nearby towns and beyond. Worried Ukrainian officials claimed the flames were ignited by Russian artillery.[27]

The catastrophic risks of atomic weapons and nuclear war are well known, but a military conflict in the midst of fifteen nuclear power plants is equally troubling. And the only way to ensure the worst never happens in Ukraine, or any place nuclear plants are located, is to end the technology in all of its hazardous forms.

CARBON UN-NEUTRAL

While Monbiot and Sunkara ignore the concerning relationship between nuclear weapons and nuclear power, they get a lot more wrong as well. Most importantly, despite the common misconception, atomic energy is not, and has never been, a carbon-free fuel source. Advocates often cite industry-funded PR data claiming that nuke power will reduce CO_2 emissions by upwards of 50 percent. This is blatant misinformation.[28]

When each cycle of energy development is taken into account, nuclear falls well behind solar and wind with regard to CO_2 emissions. These life cycle analyses (LCA) find that nuclear power, when every stage is taken into account, actually has a larger carbon footprint than natural gas plants, and almost double that of wind energy and a significant amount more than solar. How is this even possible if nuclear energy itself does not produce CO_2 emissions? It's because there are carbon dioxide emissions at every stage of the nuclear fuel chain. From plant and reactor construction, uranium mining, milling, and fuel fabrication to the transport of waste, emissions aren't far behind. Physicist Keith Barnham points out that proponents of nuclear power flagrantly ignore this reality and brush aside the fact that uranium mining is extremely carbon intensive.[29] "Nuclear fuel preparation begins with the mining of uranium containing ores, followed by the crushing of the ore then extraction of the uranium from the powdered ore chemically. All three stages take a lot of energy, most of which comes from fossil fuels," writes Barnham. "The inescapable fact is that the lower the concentration of uranium in the ore, the higher the fossil fuel energy required to extract uranium."

Then there's also the reality that existing uranium mines are nearing the end of their life spans. Andrea Wallner of the Austrian Institute of Technology writes that:

> Newly constructed nuclear power plants are supposed to have an operational life time of 60 years and a lead time between planning and operation of a facility of 10 to 19 years. Nuclear power plants which are currently being planned, would reach their end of expected life time in the period of 2080—2090; power plants now starting to operate, would be shut-down at the end of 2070 . . . [Estimates assume that the] currently operated uranium mines would be exhausted between 2043 and 2055. If we assume this scenario to occur, it would not be possible to supply a nuclear power plant built now with uranium until the end of its lifetime.[30]

MINING SACRED LANDS

Uranium mining is an energy-demanding, brutal process and in the United States, it is also a neocolonial practice. Uranium is a phenomenal element that provides insights into the formation of our planet. This radioactive metal has a half-life of 4.5 billion years, meaning it sticks around for a long, long time, even by geological standards, and paints a picture of the earliest days on planet Earth. The largest uranium deposits in the United States are located on the Colorado plateau, home of the Diné (Navajo) people.[31] During the height of the country's nuclear weapons program, the government extracted 250,000 metric tons of usable uranium from one hundred million tons of uranium ore. The mines, which were full of radioactivity, were largely worked by Indigenous Diné. During the height of the country's uranium craze of the 1970s, there were twelve thousand miners employed in the United States and a disproportionate number, upwards of five thousand, were of Diné descent.[32]

Paid very little, at times less than minimum wage, these miners would enter deep uranium shafts and chip away at the walls, often 1,500 feet below the earth's crust. They filled their wheelbarrows with this uranium ore, all while choking on soot and dust particles. It was dark. There was no ventilation. It was tremendously difficult, perilous work.

"The bitter tasting dust was all pervasive, coating their teeth and causing chronic coughing. They ate in the mines and drank water that dripped from the walls. The water contained high quantities of radon—a radioactive gas emanating from the ore," writes epidemiologist Eric Feigl-Ding of the Federal of American Scientists. "Radon decays into heavy, more radiotoxic isotopes called 'radon daughters,' which include isotopes of polonium, bismuth, and lead. Radon daughters' alpha particle emissions are considered to be about twenty times more carcinogenic than x-rays. As they lodge in the respiratory system, especially the deep lung, radon daughters emit energetic ionizing radiation that can damage cells of sensitive internal tissues."

Radon exposure causes lung diseases, the dangers of which were well-known to scientists and the medical community decades prior to World War II. But the Diné and other miners were deemed expendable. Many developed lung cancers as a result; one estimate put the risk at thirty times greater for those who worked the mines as opposed to those who did not. The government later recognized their afflictions, and with the 1990 Radiation Exposure Compensation Act, paid out $100,000 per victim and issued a formal apology. But the damage was done.[33]

In addition to the impact on Diné health, their land, too, was ravaged. Upwards of three billion metric tons of waste was created as a result of uranium extraction on Diné lands, a dizzying amount that continues to poison Native communities throughout the Southwest to this day.[34] Any call for new nuclear power development, especially from advocates on the Left, mustn't ignore these past horrors or the potential that this ugly imperialistic past could repeat itself.

Today, the United States imports most of the uranium it uses in nuclear processes. Many reports note this same deleterious impact that uranium extraction has on those who mine it and the land that contains it. Uranium mines are notoriously poisonous operations, no matter how they are managed or regulated. Heap-leach mining, which uses sulphuric acid and cyanic salts in its processes, poisons water supplies.[35] Underground uranium mines produce uranium yellowcake, which often ends up in large, toxic dumps. Surface and open-pit mining, often deemed the best method, has plenty of risks aside from the blatant landscape alteration.[36] As with utilizing mountaintop removal to extract coal in Appalachia, open pit uranium mines increase erosion and have the potential to kill entire waterways during landslide events. Such an incident occurred in 1979 on Diné land, when a dam broke, flooding the Puerco River near Church Rock, New Mexico with ninety-four million gallons of radioactive waste.[37] CO2 emissions aside, uranium mining is a nasty, destructive enterprise, yet it's vital to nuclear power generation.

Then there's the issue of what to do with all the waste that atomic energy produces, which is essentially now the problem Hanford is grappling with. The radioactive leftovers have to go somewhere, but they can't just go anywhere. The Yucca Mountain Nuclear Waste Repository, which is currently closed, remains on the shortlist for atomic dump sites. But it's a dangerous gambit. Geological faults run through the proposed site, which would include a one-thousand-foot shaft, dug deep into the mountain. Yucca is also a sacred site to the Western Shoshone, who vigorously oppose the mine and have thus far been victorious.[3839]

Nuclear power proponents like Monbiot like to pretend future nuke plants won't produce as much waste as the rickety old ones, that the amounts are small and manageable. Yet the reality is that they will still produce waste, and nobody knows exactly how much.[40] Where will it all go? We know the poor and disadvantaged, and often Indigenous, will end up dealing with the consequences. Currently, the United States produces nearly more than two thousand metric tons of radioactive waste every year. No energy source that produces a radioactive waste that lasts millennia ought to part of the climate solution.[41]

OBSOLETE ENERGY

In addition to waste concerns, the risks of nuclear power production are substantial. While there are many negative impacts of wind and solar, especially in the mining of materials used in renewable batteries, they appear less significant compared to the potential hazards inherent in nuclear technology. Whether any renewable energy source is truly sustainable is a vitally important discussion. The dirty mining of rare earth minerals poses a real threat to Indigenous communities and the environment, whether it's the Pebble Mine near Alaska's Bristol Bay or in lithium mines in the mountains of Bolivia.[42 43] Yet one thing is for certain: if we are to envision a future that is free of nuclear weapons, we must also contemplate a world that is free of its technology, which means nuclear power must one day also become obsolete.

So how should we address our energy needs and also battle climate change? Can we eliminate the use of fossil fuels and not swap them out for nuclear power? While it's constantly debated, there are plenty of scientists who believe it's possible for the world to be carbon free without the use of nuclear power.[44] In an April 2021 report "The Sky is the Limit," UK-based nonprofit Carbon Tracker shows how wind and solar don't just have the potential to meet the world's growing energy demand, but to exceed our electricity needs one hundred times over.[45] Carbon Tracker concludes there is absolutely no need for any new nuclear power; in fact, we could decommission all existing plants. We just need to tap into the power of the sun. For example, every rooftop in the United States could house solar panels, the installation of which would create tens of thousands of green jobs, far more than nuclear plant construction ever would.

"The world does not need to exploit its entire renewable resource—just 1 percent is enough to replace all fossil fuel usage," says report co-author Harry Benham. "Each year we are fueling the climate crisis by burning three million years of fossilized sunshine in coal, oil and gas while we use just 0.01% of daily sunshine."

We have no choice. We must think outside the box if we are to protect our natural resources and put the brakes on our runaway climate. Nuclear power, despite what George Monbiot, Bhaskar Sunkara, and others maintain, is not, and will never be, a part of the world's carbon-free energy future. The risks of nuclear power generation are simply too great.

CHAPTER NINE

THE CHERNOBYL-IN-WAITING

The attitude and spirit and assumption that we will go ahead
with these nuclear advances and that things will take care
of themselves—it begs the question of "is this a wise path?"

—Paul Loeb

It was December 2020 and Donald Trump was obsessive-
ly lying that the election was stolen when his Department
of Energy quietly released a report on the alleged benefits of
reclassifying the nation's high-level radioactive waste.[1] Like
many other sleepy DOE reports, it didn't make a big news
splash, but the study's thirty-seven pages did raise the hack-
les of those keeping tabs on Hanford's complex and obscure
inner workings. They had good reason to be alarmed. In their
document, the DOE argued that upwards of 80 percent of the
hot bubbling waste sitting in Hanford's leaky tanks should be
reclassified as "low-level." Doing so, they argued, would make
the whole Hanford cleanup a hell of a lot easier. If the waste
was no longer deemed "high-level" then it could be dealt with
in a totally new way, one that would require a lot less money.

"Back-end costs would generally be lower on a unit basis
as the complexity of the disposal facility is reduced," ran the
DOE report. "For the Hanford West Area tank waste . . . cost
savings are based on the amount of Hanford tank waste meet-

ing Nuclear Regulatory Commission Class C limits in the grout form, the cost of treating and grouting the waste, then shipping it off-site for disposal. The grouting estimate is based on production of cast stone, a durable cementitious grout."[2]

This was not the first time the DOE had talked about turning Hanford's radioactive waste into a grout-like substance. The initial flawed iteration of the grout concept began in the early 1980s as the site was slowly discontinuing its operations. Then, unlike now, grouting waste was floated as a way to store waste because Hanford's tanks were already overflowing. But it wasn't just theory. The grout program lasted ten years, from 1983 to 1993, and cost taxpayers $200 million. That's an equivalent of $450 million in 2021, and it was a huge waste of money. Over the past thirty years nothing has changed when it comes to grout technology. No real improvements have been made. There have been no leaps in understanding. It remains a plan conjured up by professional contractors and their allies in Washington as a quick fix for the problems plaguing the Hanford cleanup, which become more apparent every year.

Yet nobody actually believes it will be a quick fix, and some argue it will only delay the process that is already underway. "[T]he original grout program failed for insurmountable technical challenges that remain insurmountable today," watchdog group Hanford Challenge said in response to the DOE's rehashing of its failed idea. "Without credible solutions to these challenges, it would be a mistake to waste more time and money chasing this mirage."[3]

When the DOE pulled the plug on the grout program in 1993, it was decided that grout would never work. Despite claims that radioactive grout was easy to produce, the reality was that it was nearly impossible. An internal DOE document in 1992 stated that the grouting process could not be demonstrated, despite ten years exploring the option. A Government

Accountability Office (formerly the General Accounting Office) report in 1993 explained:

> DOE is facing technical uncertainties with the grout process. When radioactive materials are grouted, heat is produced, and generally speaking, the amount of heat rises with the level of radioactivity. If the temperature rises above ninety degrees centigrade, the grout may effectively immobilize liquid wastes. . . . In laboratory demonstration projects conducted in the 1990s, DOE used gram-sized samples of low-level waste stimulant to determine the estimated temperature of waste that would be grouted. Test results revealed that the estimated temperature of the grout would likely exceed ninety degrees centigrade due to the heat generated from the solidification of grout and the decay of radioactive waste components in the grout.[4]

In other words, grouting Hanford's tank waste was a bad approach then and remains a horrible one today. Then there is the problem of what to do with the stuff once it's in grout form. In the 1990s, Hanford technicians estimated that a total of 240 vaults would be needed to house the bricks of toxic grout. Each vault would hold upwards of 1.4 million gallons of grout. Those vaults, noted the GAO report, would "contain about as much radioactivity as would be contained in eight canisters produced by the high-level waste vitrification plant."[5] So what's the big problem? For starters, the DOE was unable to show that these underground storage encasements would be safe for the environment or human health. So the DOE proposed another bad proposal, which brings us to 2021. The DOE today, like the DOE of the 1980s, is proposing that the tank waste in grout form should be considered "low-level" waste and as such could simply be placed in shallow graves.

This brings us to the next problem, the grout, which would be chock full of radioactive technetium-99 and iodine-129, elements that take a very long time to break down (230,000 and sixteen million years, respectively).[6] What the hell could possibly go wrong during that time frame? Erosion and earthquakes, for starters. Anything buried near the surface will be exposed to these alterations, with escalating risks of contaminating groundwater supplies.[7] Radioactive grout won't be safe for one hundred years, let alone a million.

"The concrete won't last very long, and these materials are far, far too dangerous to entrust to that form and sitting atop one of the largest freshwater aquifers in the state," says Tom Carpenter of Hanford Challenge.

Even Hanford's old grout program manager admitted that radioactive particles would eventually leak. As a result of this reality and the risks of grout, Yakama Nation—with elder Russel Jim leading the charge—along with the states of Oregon and Washington all opposed the plan, until it was eventually abandoned.

Yet now the grout solution is back. "Successfully immobilizing the worst of Hanford's waste is too important for hastily made decisions that do not adequately and publicly resolve past performance issues," writes Hanford Challenge in their critique. "In that spirit, we present a summary of 'Current Claims and Past Failures' with grout to ensure that these issues are fully researched and addressed before making a decision. Valuable resources for cleanup should not be diverted without first providing validated and technically defensible solutions to the issues that caused the grout program to fail in the past."[8]

While grout is a horrible idea, turning Hanford's waste into glass has not proved an easy task. The technical challenges of vitrification are significant—which is why the process should not be rushed. To this day, turning Hanford's radioactive liquids into glass remains the best option available, and the one that taxpayers have been betting on even if they didn't realize it. To fully abandon it now would only draw out the inevitable. Grout, as we've seen during the 1980s and early 1990s, will face insurmountable hurdles, and public opposition will mount as a result. Reclassifying radioactive waste is also not allowed in Washington, so any attempt at doing so will most certainly face legal challenges.[9]

Such is the state of play at the Hanford Nuclear Reservation, where the most important environmental cleanup in world history takes place with so few paying attention. The costs, both financial and environmental, are too great to leave the job to an understaffed DOE and contractors whose main objective is to keep the profits flowing in. While Trump proposed cutting $760 million in funding for the Hanford cleanup, President Biden also believed too much money was being spent at Hanford, and his 2022 budget moved to slash $105 million. But some argue that the answer isn't slashing funds, but rather keeping tighter tabs on the money. Ensuring that money is being spent productively is far more pertinent than the budget itself. In other words, it's about accountability.[10]

IT'S NO ACCIDENT

It's started leaking, or rather, it's leaking again. In April 2021, the DOE alerted the public that a tank at Hanford was seeping radioactive waste for the second time that year. Not to worry, they advised, we've got it all under control. By August 2021, their teams were on to another bleeding tank, one that had gotten so bad they had to come up with a plan to remove its contents so they didn't experience a major disaster.

"It's not easy to access the tanks or move this kind of waste, and it takes specialized tools and techniques that have been developed, tested, and proven successful to meet this challenge," said Department of Energy's Hanford tank farms program director, Ricky Bang.

These grave situations are not anomalies, nor are they events to be taken lightly. They occur frequently and often in secrecy, far away from cameras, journalists, or government watchdog groups. Indeed, by the time you are reading this, there will likely have been more accidents on the dry plains of Eastern Washington. Maybe the leaks or mishaps will be small, perhaps they will be large in size, but they will happen again, and we can be sure the response will be the same. Deadlines for mitigation will be pushed back. There'll be talk of figuring out other, novel solutions like turning the muck into grout. And the threat of a nuclear accident, one that could decimate the Columbia River and poison the land and people from Portland, Oregon to Portland, Maine, will become ever more real. If we are to learn anything from Hanford, it's that nuclear technology, in all its forms, is a clear and present danger to all living things.

"The attitude and spirit and assumption that we will go ahead with these nuclear advances and that things will take care of themselves—it begs the question of 'is this a wise path?'" Paul Loeb, author of *Nuclear Culture*, said in an interview in 1986 of nuclear technology and the future of Hanford. "There are people out there, in the grass roots, who think it isn't."[11]

If someone tells you they know exactly how this will all play out, they are selling you a load of shit as radioactive as the boiling goop eating away at Hanford's underground tanks. Nobody knows what is going to happen, and few know what's really going on out there, which may be why officials are slow to press the panic button. But perhaps panic is what we need. The more the panic grows, the more awareness will be spread about the inherent dangers that Hanford and nuclear technology pose. Progress at Hanford comes in bits and pieces. In February 2022, a system started up that removes radioactive cesium from Hanford's underground tanks. The $130 million project was years in the making and was a small step toward one day turning the tank waste into glass.[12]

There are certainly no easy solutions. If there were, the decades-long process in dealing with Hanford's waste would be further along. But as long as much of the project continues to be conducted in a secretive manner, the public, which is footing the exponentially increasing bill, will *not* have valuable input in how the cleanup proceeds. This, of course, is the last thing politicians, the DOE, and connected contractors like Bechtel want. They'd rather operate in secret, out of sight and out of mind, where congressional hearings focusing on Hanford are not commonplace and the public doesn't regularly question their intentions, or even have a venue to do so. The complexities of the project at Hanford are often used as an excuse as to why the public has little understanding of the work. But this is a cop-out, or worse, part of a grand cover-up by a government that is failing to oversee the massive, corrupt pay-to-play venture. Many well intentioned, brilliant people are employed at Hanford, but they are caught in a broken system. Hanford's labor unions, which make up thousands of workers, are often stuck in the middle and are forced to stick up for themselves. If a union deems a site unsafe, they can potentially halt work, as they have done before. In 2016, a coalition of unions led by the Hanford Atomic Metal Trades Council, which works at the tank farm, issued a stop work order over concerns of vapor exposure.[13] If the culture is to change, solidarity with Hanford's over two-dozen unions is paramount. But solidarity is not enough. Hanford's unions, which are currently represented by Hanford Atomic Metals Trade and Central Washington Building & Construction Council, must merge their unions, forming a singular, amplified voice for the Hanford workers they represent.

No impartial scientist or engineer would ever downplay the risks posed by Hanford or the fact that it is a Chernobyl-like disaster-in-waiting. And no trustworthy observer would fail to acknowledge that the current modus operandi at Hanford is appallingly corrupt, wholly inadequate, and potentially lethal. Bechtel must be removed as the lead contractor. The system must be completely overhauled. There has to be governmental and corporate accountability, more public oversight, and a reckoning with how dire the situation actually is. Like our fossil fuel addiction and the wrath of climate change, the legacy of the United States' nuclear mania is a gargantuan, radioactive mess. Pretending the threat of Hanford is minimal and that the mess isn't really that bad is dangerous and deceitful spin that puts us all at risk. Nonprofit organizations like Tom Carpenter's Hanford Challenge and Hood River, Oregon—based Columbia Riverkeeper, along with Alfrieda Peters of the Yakama Nation, among others, are struggling to bring Hanford out from behind the curtain on to the main stage. A grassroots movement is needed to thurst Hanford into the national spotlight.

Hanford's nuclear reckoning is here. It's up to us, the public—journalists, activists, union members, government officials, academics, scientists, engineers, teachers, students, parents, farmers, humans—to ensure the job gets done in an equitable and transparent fashion that is safe for workers and for the environment, with public input at every step of the way. Future generations depend on it, even if they don't know it yet.

ACKNOWLEDGMENTS

The tale of Hanford has been told in many ways, over many years, from many different vantage points. While these accounts often provided important historical detail and context, I've felt that most lacked a critical lens and were told from the top down. They more often than not failed to critique US colonialism and the nuclear imperialism spawned by this entrenched white supremacy and how it played out at Hanford. These histories typically brushed over the brutality of Hanford's land seizures, its capitalist underpinnings, and the radioactive destruction our atomic weapons caused to Natives, to the Japanese, and to the environment. My hope is that this book adds a bit to this dialogue and does so in an insurgent manner, filling in the gaping holes in these patriotic narratives, helping to round out the people's story of Hanford—because its drama, in many ways, is just beginning to unfold. The effects of nuclear waste last millennia, and the decisions we make now will have an impact on future generations that are so very far removed from today's reality.

First and foremost, I need to thank my great friend and colleague Jeffrey St. Clair for exciting me about Hanford, explaining why it was such an important topic to pursue all those years ago. Without his wisdom and tenacity, I wouldn't have written any of the words printed here. I owe Jeff immensely. Tom Carpenter at Hanford Challenge was also instrumental. Tom was always willing to pick up the phone or meet with me if I had questions, and his expertise and advice remain unmatched. Tom is a lion, and Hanford is lucky to have him, even in retirement.

There are also not a lot of publishers out there that would even consider putting out a book like this, Haymarket being one of the few, daring exceptions. Julie Fain, Haymarket's tenacious publisher, was not only patient, she was more than understanding when the COVID-19 pandemic nearly paralyzed the project. She's one of those people who works tirelessly and rarely receives the credit she deserves. Julie is truly amazing and Haymarket is a powerhouse because of her and so many others who quietly labor behind the scenes. Thanks to Anthony Arnove for his expert vision and Jamie Kerry for making the book look so sharp, and to the Lannan Foundation and Wallace Action Fund for the financial backing.

Lucy Schiller, one of my favorite writers and a dear friend, was the first to read this manuscript and give crucial observations. I am so lucky she shared her talents with me. If this book is readable in any way, it is thanks to her diligence. Ashley Smith also provided impeccable edits and criticisms. His ideas and insights helped me work through my own arguments, and without him, this book would be lacking considerably. Ella Mahony, thank you, too, for your great proofreading and crucial feedback. The amazing illustrations were done by Becky Grant, and the images were taken by Mark Ruwedel, both of whom are amazing, renowned artists, and I am so honored they indulged my requests to include their work. I am also very grateful to the librarians that helped out along the way, especially Rick Mikulski and Kimberly Wilson at Portland State University, which is home to the Hanford archives. Much of the research for this book was carried out under their guidance, and I am eternally grateful. Librarians are true heroes.

On the homefront, I am indebted to my partner, Chelsea Mosher, who has probably heard more about Hanford than any one person ought to be subjected to. Without her unwavering support, this book would have never made it across the finish line. Thanks to Dianne Mack and Christine and David Mosher for providing sleeping arrangements (and full fridges of food) on my various trips to Seattle and Portland to conduct Hanford research. Along the way, so many other friends helped out in big and small ways as well. Jimmie Hines, Tyler Johnston, Roz Hunter, Sarah Mosher, Brice Biscoff, Dean Wareham, Ralph Nader, Onnesha Roychoudhuri, Roman John Carlos, Tiffany Wardle, Eric Draitser, Sam Blasucci, John LaForge, Lee Hall, Renée Chartier, the late Alfred Tyler, Louis Proyect, and Margot Kidder. Nathaniel St. Clair and the entire *CounterPunch* team, thanks for all of the feedback and input.

Above all, thanks to the countless people I've spoken to about Hanford over the last ten years, the numerous Yakama and Umatilla tribal members, the environmental and anti-nuke comrades, the brave whistleblowers, and others, thanks for shaping my views and understanding of what Hanford was, is, and should be. Thank you for fighting the good fight. If Hanford is to one day be safe, if its lands are to ever be renewed and returned to their rightful, Indigenous owners, it will be as a result of the work they are all doing, day in and day out. My hope is that this book can contribute to this cause in a modest yet tangible way.

NOTES

WHY HANFORD?

1 Benton County Auditor. "November 3, 2020 Election Results," Accessed October 1, 2021, https://results.vote.wa.gov/results/20201103/benton/.

2 Annette Cary, "Fairness or Bigotry? Kennewick Lawmaker's Bill Would Restrict Transgender High School Athletes," *Tri-City Herald,* January 12, 2020.

3 Jim Trumbo, "Tri-Cities always coming out on top," *Tri-City Herald,* March 14, 2011.

4 Ben Johnson, Richard Romanelli, Bert Pierard, "Lost in the Telling: The DuPont Company The Forgotten Producers of Plutonium," B Reactor Museum Association, March 2017.

5 United States Department of Energy, "2019, Hanford Lifecycle Scope, Schedule and Cost Report," January 31, 2019.

6 Associated Press, "Remaining Hanford Cleanup Cost Estimated at $110 Billion," February 25, 2015, https://komonews.com/news/local/remaining-hanford-cleanup-cost-estimated-at-110-billion-11-21-2015.

7 Annette Cary, "Congress Approves $2.6 Billion Hanford Budget. It's Far More Than Trump Administration Proposal, *Tri-City Herald,* Dec 22, 2020.

8 Annette Cary, "Hanford Strategy for Worst Nuclear Waste Criticized. Plant estimates skyrocket to $41 billion," *Tri-City Herald,* May 13, 2020.

9 Office of Management, "DOE Approves Modified Contract and Baseline for Hanford Waste Treatment Plant," December 16, 2016.

10 Lois Parshley, "Cold War, Hot Mess," *Virginia Quarterly Review* Fall 2021, Volume 97, Number 3.

CHAPTER ONE

1 Steve Olson, *The Apocalypse Factory: Plutonium and the Making of the Atomic Age* (W. W. Norton & Company, 2020), 69-70.

2　National Research Council. *Managing the Columbia River: Instream Flows, Water Withdrawals, and Salmon Survival* (Washington, DC: National Academies Press, 2004), 27-41.

3　Annette Cary, "Hanford Cleanup Costs triple. And That's the 'Best Case Scenario' in a New Report." *Tri-City Herald*, February 1, 2019.

4　Olson, *The Apocalypse Factory*, 69-70.

5　National Research Council. *Managing the Columbia River*, 27-41.

6　US Department of Energy, *History of Hanford Site Defense Production (Brief)*, by M.S. Gerber (Richland, WA, 1999).

7　United States Government Accountability Office, "DOE Lacks Critical Information Needed to Assess Its Tank Management Strategy at Hanford," 2008.

8　Michele Stenehjem Gerber, *On the Home Front: The Cold War Legacy of the Hanford Nuclear Site* (Lincoln: University of Nebraska Press, 1992), 22-23.

9　Kate Brown, *Plutopia: Nuclear Families, Atomic Cities, and the Great Soviet and American Plutonium Disasters* (Oxford Press, 2013), 32-36.

10　Gerber, *On the Home Front*, 22-23.

11　Cameron Addis, "The Whitman Massacre: Religion & Manifest Destiny on the Columbia Plateau, 1809-1858," *Journal of the Early Republic* 25, no. 2 (Summer 2005): 221-258.

12　Addis, "The Whitman Massacre," 221-258.

13　Olson, *The Apocalypse Factory*, 64.

14　Gerber, *On the Home Front*, 23-24.

15　U.S. Department of Energy Office of Scientific and Technical Information, *Fifth Semiannual Report of the Commission to the Congress: Atomic Energy Development, 1947-1948*, by David E. Lilienthal, Robert F. Bacher, Sumner T. Pike, Lewis L. Strauss, 1949.

16　Albert Einstein to Franklin Delano Roosevelt, August 2, 1939, in *E-World, https://hypertextbook.com/eworld/einstein/*.

17　S. L. Sanger, *Working on the Bomb: An Oral History of WWII Hanford* (Portland: Portland State University, 1995), 161-163.

18　Tanya E. Lee, "H-Bomb Guinea Pigs! Natives Suffering Decades After New Mexico Tests," *Indian Country Today*, September 13, 2018.
　　William Leonard Laurence, "Drama of the Atomic Bomb Found Climax in July 16 Test," *New York Times*, September 26, 1945.

19　Ross Pomeroy, "What It's Like to Actually See an Atomic Explosion *RealClear Science*, April 17, 2016, https://www.realclearscience.com/blog/2016/04/what_its_like_to_actually_see_an_atomic_explosion.html.

20　Ferenc Morton Szasz, *The Day the Sun Rose Twice: The Story of the Trinity Site Nuclear Explosion, July 16, 1945* (Albuquerque: UNM Press, 1984), 131-145.

21 Szasz, *The Day the Sun Rose Twice*, 79-145.

22 Dennis J. Carroll, "Downwinders Welcome Study of Trinity Blast's Impacts," *Santa Fe New Mexican*, January 25, 2014.

23 The International Campaign to Abolish Nuclear Weapons, "The Human Cost of Nuclear Testing," accessed October 2, 2021, https://www.icanw.org/nuclear_tests.

24 Hsuan L. Hsu, "Nuclear Colonialism," Environmental and Society Portal, accessed October 2, 2021.https://www.environmentandsociety.org/exhibitions/risk-and-militarization/nuclear-colonialism.

25 Leslie Groves, *Now It Can Be Told: The Story of the Manhattan Project* (New York: Harper & Row, 1962) 142–145.

26 Heather Mallick, "Bang. You Are Dead." *Toronto Star*, accessed June 19, 2019.

27 Mark Selden, "A Forgotten Holocaust: US Bombing Strategy, the Destruction of Japanese Cities & the American Way of War from World War II to Iraq," *Asian-Pacific Journal* 5, no. 5 (May 2007): 1-29.

28 AFP, "Japan Remembers Hiroshima on 71st Anniversary of Atomic Bombing," August 7, 2016.

29 Alex Wellerstein, "A 'Purely Military' Target? Truman's Changing Language about Hiroshima," Restricted Data, A Nuclear Secrecy Blog, accessed August 26, 2019, http://blog.nuclearsecrecy.com/2018/01/19/purely-military-target/.

30 Harry S. Truman, "Statement by the President Announcing the Use of the A-Bomb at Hiroshima," National Archives, August 6, 1945, https://www.osti.gov/opennet/manhattan-project-history/Events/1945-present/public_reaction.htm.

31 Dan Listwa, "Hiroshima and Nagasaki: The Long Term Health Effects," Center for Nuclear Studies, Columbia University, August 9, 2012, accessed June 1, 2019, https://k1project.columbia.edu/news/hiroshima-and-nagasaki.

32 D. L. Preston, E. Ron, S. Tokuoka, S. Funamoto, N. Nishi, M. Soda, K. Mabuchi, and K. Kodama, "Solid Cancer Incidence in Atomic Bomb Survivors: 1958-1998," *Radiation Research* 168, no. 1 (2007): 1-64.

33 Gabriel Popkin, "Seventy Years Later, Atomic Bombs Still Influence Health Research," *Inside Science*, August 5, 2015, https://www.insidescience.org/news/seventy-years-later-atomic-bombs-still-influence-health-research.

34 Listwa, "Hiroshima and Nagasaki."

35 Lily Rothman and Haruka Sakaguchi, "After the Bomb: Survivors of the Atomic Blasts in Hiroshima and Nagasaki Share Their Stories," *Time*, https://time.com/after-the-bomb/.

36 Howard Zinn, "The Bombs of August," *Progressive*, August 2000.

37   Gerber, *On the Home Front*, 58-59.

38   Brown, *Plutopia: Nuclear Families, Atomic Cities, and the Great Soviet and American Plutonium Disasters*, 37-43.

39   Dave Lindorff, "US bombings on Hiroshima & Nagasaki Were Not to End WWII But to Frighten Soviet Union," RT, August 9, 2019, https://www.rt.com/op-ed/466173-nagasaki-nuclear-bomb-soviet/.

40   Gar Alperovitz, *Atomic Diplomacy: Hiroshima and Potsdam; the Use of the Atomic Bomb and the American Confrontation With Soviet Power*, Simon & Schuster, 1965.

41   Henry Stimson, "Memorandum by the Secretary of War (Stimson) to President Truman," September 11, 1945, https://history.state.gov/historicaldocuments/frus1945v02/d13.

42   Gerber, *On the Home Front*, 61-62.

43   "Hanford Tank Waste Management," Washington State Department of Ecology, accessed October 4, 2021, https://ecology.wa.gov/Waste-Toxics/Nuclear-waste/Hanford-cleanup/Tank-waste-management.

44   Gerber, *On the Home Front*, 61-65.

45   Sanger, *Working on the Bomb*, 182-183.

46   Willis L. Shirk, Jr., *A History of the Atomic Space Age and Its Implications for the Future* (Indianapolis: Dog Ear Publishing, 2018), 42.

47   Associated Press, "Radiation Flowed 200 Miles to Sea, Study Finds," *New York Times*, July 17, 1992.

48   Curie (Ci): one of three units used to measure the intensity of radioactivity in a sample of material. This value refers to the amount of ionizing radiation released when an element (such as uranium) spontaneously emits energy as a result of the radioactive decay (or disintegration) of an unstable atom. Radioactivity is also the term used to describe the rate at which radioactive material emits radiation, or how many atoms in the material decay (or disintegrate) in a given time period. As such, 1 Ci is equal to thirty-seven billion (3.7 x 1010) disintegrations per second, so 1 Ci also equals thirty-seven billion (3.7 x 1010) Bequerels (Bq). A curie is also a quantity of any radionuclide that decays at a rate of thirty-seven billion disintegrations per second (1 gram of radium, for example). The curie is named for Marie and Pierre Curie, who discovered radium in 1898. (US Regulatory Commission, 2019.)

49   Washington Department of Health, "The Release of Radioactive Materials from Hanford: 1944-1972," 2000. Web archive, accessed May 14, 2019, https://bit.ly/2ZoLM4G.

50   World Information Service on Energy, "New Documents Reveal Story Behind Green Run," *Nuclear Monitor* 381 (October 30, 1992).

51 Advisory Committee on Human Radiation Experiments, "What We Now Know," 1994. Web archive, accessed June 13, 2019, https://ehss.energy.gov/ohre/roadmap/achre/chap11_2.html.

52 Advisory Committee on Human Radiation Experiments, "What We Now Know."

53 Advisory Committee on Human Radiation Experiments, "What We Now Know."

54 C. M. Grossman, W. E. Morton, R. H. Nussbaum, "Hypothyrodisim and Spontaneous Abortions among Hanford, Washington, Downwinders," *Archives of Environmental Health* 51, no. 3 (May–June 1996): 174–75.

55 Keith Meyers, "In the Shadow of the Mushroom Cloud: Nuclear Testing, Radioactive Fallout, and Damage to US Agriculture, 1945-1970," *Journal of Economic History* 79, no. 1 (March 2019): 244–74.

56 Chrissy Sexton, "1950s Nuclear Tests Exposed Millions to Radiation," Earth.com, December 26, 2017, https://www.earth.com/news/nuclear-tests-exposed-radiation/.

57 Susan McClure, "Final Report: Hanford-Linked Risk Negligible," *Hutch News*, July 3, 2002, https://www.fredhutch.org/en/news/center-news/2002/07/Hanford-linked-risk-negligible.html.

58 Advisory Committee on Human Radiation Experiments, "What We Now Know."

59 US Department of Energy, "History of the Plutonium Production Facilities at the Hanford Site Historic District, 1943-1990," *Hanford Cultural and Historic Resources Program* 1, no. 14 (June 2002).

60 Gerber, *On the Home Front*, 85.

61 Richard L. Neuberger, "Plutonium and Problems," *Nation*, July 30, 1949.

62 Gerber, *On the Home Front*, 123-130.

63 McClure, "Final Report."

64 Hal Bernton, "Hanford Waste-Processing Plants Closer to Startup, but Questions Remain about Cleanup," *Seattle Times*, April 28, 2019.

65 United States Nuclear Regulatory Commission, "Hanford Site Disposal Facility for Waste Incidental to Reprocessing," November 29, 2016.

66 Shannon Cram, "Wild and Scenic Wasteland: Conservation Politics in the Nuclear Wilderness," *Environmental Humanities* 7, no.1 (2016): 89-105.

CHAPTER TWO

1 Dr. Y, "Where Does the Plutonium Come From?" Federation of American Scientists, September 30, 2013.

2   Lesley Kennedy, "Why Reagan's 'Star Wars' Defense Plan Remained Science Fiction," History, January 18, 2019, https://www.history.com/news/reagan-star-wars-sdi-missile-defense.

3   Nate Jones, Peter Scoblic, "The Week the World Almost Ended," Slate, April 13, 2017, https://slate.com/news-and-politics/2017/06/able-archer-almost-started-a-nuclear-war-with-russia-in-1983.html.

4   Michael Getler, "Administration's Nuclear War Policy Stance Still Murky," Washington Post, November 10, 1982.

5   Economist, "America Withdraws From Intermediate-Range Nuclear Forces Treaty," February 1, 2019.

6   US Department of Defense, "US Withdraws From Intermediate-Range Nuclear Forces Treaty" by C. Todd Lopez, August 2, 2019.

7   Holly Ellyatt, "Gorbachev says Trump's Nuclear Treaty Withdrawal 'Not the work of a great mind'," CNBC, October 22, 2018, https://www.cnbc.com/2018/10/22/gorbachev-says-trumps-nuclear-treaty-withdrawal-not-the-work-of-a-great-mind.html.

8   Mike O'Sullivan, "Does The AUKUS Deal Point to War in the South China Sea?", Forbes, September 24, 2021, https://www.forbes.com/sites/mikeosullivan/2021/09/24/does-the-aukus-deal-point-to-war-in-the-south-china-sea/?sh=661468e68f78.

9   Council on Foreign Relations, "Territorial Disputes, South China Sea," March 21, 2022, https://www.cfr.org/global-conflict-tracker/conflict/territorial-disputes-south-china-sea.

10   Gerber, On the Home Front, 201-202.

11   William Bequette, "Journal: DOE Losing Trust of Nuclear Workers," Tri-City Herald, January 1, 1989.

12   Keith Schneider, "US Admits Peril of 40s A-Bomb Plant." The New York Times, July 12, 1990.

13   Pacific Northwest National Laboratory, A Short History of Hanford Waste Generation, Storage and Release, Pacific Northwest National Laboratory, by R. E. Gephart, Richland, Washington: October 2003, 8.

14   Research Department, Research and Engineering Division, Atlantic Richfield Hanford Company, 241-T-106 Tank Leak Investigation: Richland, Washington, November 1973.

15   Lee Dye, "Thousands Periled by Nuclear Waste," Los Angeles Times, July 5, 1973.

16   Robert Gillette, "Radiation Spill at Hanford: The Anatomy of an Accident," Science 181, No. 4101 (August 24, 1973): 728-730.

17   US Atomic Energy Commission, Report of the Safety and Industrial Health Advisory Board. AEC-10266, Washington, DC: US AEC, April 2, 1948, 70.

18   M. B. Tripplett et al, "Risks from Past, Current, and Potential Hanford Single Shell Tank Leaks," US Department of Energy, May 2013.

19   Gephart, "A Short History of Hanford Waste Generation, Storage
     and Release, Pacific Northwest National Laboratory," 10.

20   Natalie Wolchover, "Why is Plutonium More Dangerous
     than Uranium," *Live Science*, March 17, 2011, https://www.
     livescience.com/33127-plutonium-more-dangerous-uranium.
     html#:~:text=Plutonium%2D239%2C%20the%20isotope%20
     found,than%20beta%20or%20gamma%20radiation.

21   Gillette, "Radiation Spill at Hanford: The Anatomy of an
     Accident," 730.

22   Gillette, "Radiation Spill at Hanford: The Anatomy of an
     Accident," 730.

23   Dye, "Thousands Periled by Nuclear Waste."

24   Dye, "Thousands Periled by Nuclear Waste."

25   US Department of Energy Idaho Operations Office, *Operable
     Unit 3-14 Tank Farm Soil and Groundwater Remedial Investigation/
     Baseline Risk Assessment*, April 2006.

26   Spencer Heinz, "Pride, Nuclear Economics Bolster Life in Tri-
     Cities," *Oregonian*, May 14, 1985.

27   Richard Read, "Arms Race Leaves Legacy of Radioactive Wastes,"
     Oregonian, May 13, 1985.

28   Read, "Arms Race Leaves Legacy of Radioactive Wastes."

29   Read, "Arms Race Leaves Legacy of Radioactive Wastes."

30   Susannah Frame, "Hanford Officials Ignored Own Expert's
     Advice on Tunnel Safety for Decades," KING5 News, May 19,
     2017, https://www.king5.com/article/news/local/hanford/hanford-
     officials-ignored-their-experts-advice-on-tunnel-safety-for-
     decades/441051241.

31   Chad Skol, "Hanford Tunnel Collapse Prompts Some to Ask:
     What's the Long-Term Solution for Nuclear Waste?" *Associated
     Press*, May 12, 2017, https://www.spokesman.com/stories/2017/
     may/12/tunnel-collapse-prompts-some-to-ask-where-is-the-l/.

32   Annette Cary, "Workers Who Discovered Break in Hanford
     Radioactive Waste Tunnel Praised," *Yakima Herald,* May 14, 2017.

33   Douglas Perry, "Hanford Nuclear Site's Inspection Shortcomings
     Revealed in Watchdog Report; Parts of Vast Facility Not Entered
     in 50 Years," Oregonlive.com, February 25, 2020, https://www.
     oregonlive.com/environment/2020/02/hanford-nuclear-sites-
     inspection-shortcomings-revealed-in-watchdog-report-parts-of-
     vast-facility-not-entered-in-50-years.html.

34   Gary Peterson, "WESF High-Risk Cleanup Delayed," Northwest
     Energy Associates, September 24, 2020.

35   Perry, "Hanford Nuclear Site's Inspection Shortcomings Revealed."

36   Pacific Northwest National Laboratory, *A Short History of Hanford
     Waste Generation, Storage and Release, Pacific Northwest National
     Laboratory,* 5-10.

37 Thomas Rabal, "The Nuclear Disaster of Kyshtym 1957 and the Politics of the Cold War," Environment & Society Portal, *Arcadia*, no. 20 (2012).

38 Rabal, "The Nuclear Disaster of Kyshtym 1957 and the Politics of the Cold War."

39 Rebecca Clay, "Cold War, Hot Nukes," *Environmental Health Perspectives* 109, no. 4 (April 2001): 162-169.

40 A. David Rossin, "US Policy on Spent Fuel Reprocessing: The Issues," *Frontline*, accessed October 23, 2021, https://www.pbs.org/wgbh/pages/frontline/shows/reaction/readings/rossin.html.

41 Clay, "Cold War, Hot Nukes."

42 Clay, "Cold War, Hot Nukes."

43 Clay, "Cold War, Hot Nukes."

44 Rabal, "The Nuclear Disaster of Kyshtym 1957 and the Politics of the Cold War."

45 Rabal, "The Nuclear Disaster of Kyshtym 1957 and the Politics of the Cold War."

46 Zhores Medvedev, "Two Decades of Dissidence," *New Scientist*, November 4, 1976, https://www.newscientist.com/article/dn10546-two-decades-of-dissidence/.

47 William E. Farrell, "Ex-Soviet Scientist, Now in Israel, Tells Of Nuclear Disaster," *New York Times*, December 9, 1976, https://www.nytimes.com/1976/12/09/archives/exsoviet-scientist-now-in-israel-tells-of-nuclear-disaster.htm.

48 Farrell, "Ex-Soviet Scientist, Now in Israel, Tells of Nuclear Disaster."

49 Richard Pollock, "Soviets Experience Nuclear Accident," *Critical Mass Journal*, January, 1978.

50 Kate Brown, *Plutopia: Nuclear Families, Atomic Cities, and the Great Soviet and American Plutonium Disasters*, (Oxford Press, 2013): 239-240.

51 Pollock, "Soviets Experience Nuclear Accident."

52 Brown, *Plutopia: Nuclear Families, Atomic Cities, and the Great Soviet and American Plutonium Disasters*, 239-240.

53 Kenneth T. Walsh. "Presidential Lies and Deceptions," *US News and World Report*, June 6, 2008.

54 Rabal, "The Nuclear Disaster of Kyshtym 1957 and the Politics of the Cold War."

55 Pollock, "Soviets Experience Nuclear Accident."

56 Oregon Department of Energy, "Frequently Asked Questions About Hanford," August 2007, 2-4.

57 Shannon Dinney, "Nuclear Board Warns of Hanford Tank Explosion Risk," *Associated Press*, April 2, 2013.

58 Jake Offenhartz, "Wildfire Smoke Returns To NYC Skies," Gothamist, July 27, 2021, https://gothamist.com/news/wildfire-smoke-returns-nyc-skies.

59   United States Geological Survey, "How Far Did the Ash from Mount St. Helens Travel?" Accessed February 22, 2020, https://www.usgs.gov/faqs/how-far-did-ash-mount-st-helens-travel?qt-news_science_products=0#qt-news_science_products.

CHAPTER THREE

1   Kyle Mizokami, "The Cost to Clean Up America's Cold War Nuclear Waste Jumps to $377 Billion," *Popular Mechanics*, February 5, 2019.

2   James F. Nagle, *History of Government Contracting*, second edition (CCH Publications, 1999), 16–54.

3   Janet A. McDonnell, "A History of Defense Contract Administration," Defense Contract Management Agency, March 5, 2020.

4   Christopher R. Yukins, "The US Federal Procurement System: An Introduction," *Procurement Law Journal*, 2017.

5   Dwight D. Eisenhower, "Farewell Address," January 17, 1961.

6   Doug Whiteman, "The Financial Facts You Never Learned About World War II," Moneywise, December 23, 2020, https://www.yahoo.com/now/18-financial-facts-never-learned-145528611.html.

7   Guillaume Vandenbroucke, "Which War Saw the Highest Defense Spending? Depends How It's Measured," Federal Reserve Bank of St. Louis, February 4, 2020.

8   Whiteman, "The Financial Facts You Never Learned About World War II."

9   Merlin Chowkwanyun, "Five Questions with Noam Chomsky," *CounterPunch*, July 31, 2004, https://www.counterpunch.org/2004/07/31/five-questions-with-noam-chomsky/.

10   Sarah Pruitt, "Uncovering the Secret Identity of Rosie the Riveter," History.com, January 23, 2018.

11   Doris Goodwin, "The Way We Won: America's Economic Breakthrough During World War II," *The American Prospect*, December 19, 2001.

12   Goodwin, "The Way We Won: America's Economic Breakthrough During World War II."

13   Andrew Glass, "FDR Seizes Control of Montgomery Ward, Dec. 27, 1944," Politico, December 26, 2016, https://www.politico.com/story/2016/12/this-day-in-politics-dec-27-1944-232931.

14   Martin Glaberman, "Why Do Workers Strike?" *Jacobin*, May 30, 2018, https://www.jacobinmag.com/2018/05/no-strike-pledge-world-war-militants.

15   Mark R. Wilson, *Destructive Creation American Business and the Winning of World War II*, (University of Pennsylvania Press, 2016) 287-288.

16 US Congress Special Committee on Atomic Energy, "Hearings Seventy-Nine Congress First Session" 1945 and 1946," 560.

17 US Department of Energy, "The Maud Report," The Manhattan Project, An Interactive History, accessed July 3, 2021, https://www.osti.gov/opennet/manhattan-project-history/Events/1939-1942/maud.htm.

18 American Heritage Foundation, "The S-1 Committee," April 27, 2017.

19 US Department of Energy, "Oakridge and Hanford Come Through," The Manhattan Project, An Interactive History, accessed July 3, 2021, https://www.osti.gov/opennet/manhattan-project-history/Events/1942-1945/come_through.htm.

20 Sally Denton, *The Profiteers: Bechtel and the Men Who Built the World*, (Simon & Schuster, 2016), 66-67, Kindle

21 Forest Preserves of Cook County, "Site A at Red Gate Woods & The World's First Nuclear Reactor," accessed July 4, 2021, https://fpdcc.com/site-a-the-worlds-first-nuclear-reactor/.

22 Stephen I. Schwartz, "The US Nuclear Weapons Cost Study Project," Brookings Institute, August 1, 1998. Costs adjusted to 1996 dollar amounts using a base year of 1944 (the year of highest Manhattan Project expenditures).

23 Stephen I. Schwartz, "The Cost of US Nuclear Weapons," Nuclear Threat Initiative, October 1, 2008.

24 Schwartz, "The Cost of US Nuclear Weapons."

25 Annette Cary, "Tri-Party Agreement: Hanford Cleanup Began 25 Years Ago," *Tri-City Herald*, August 10, 2014.

26 Maria Gallucci, "A Glass Nightmare: Cleaning Up the Cold War's Nuclear Legacy at Hanford," IEE Spectrum, April 28, 2020, https://spectrum.ieee.org/hanford-nuclear-site.

27 Tim Newcomb, "Giant US Nuke Waste 'Vit' Plant Wraps Initial Construction," *Engineering News-Record*, January 7, 2021, https://www.enr.com/articles/50969-giant-us-nuke-waste-vit-plant-wraps-initial-construction.

28 Cary, "Hanford Strategy for Worst Nuclear Waste Criticized. Plant Estimates Skyrocket to $41 Billion."

29 Debra K. Rubin, "Bechtel National Names New Project Director for $12B Hanford Vitrification Plant," *Engineering News-Record*, July 9, 2013, https://www.enr.com/articles/7889-bechtel-national-names-new-project-director-for-12b-hanford-vitrification-plant; "Bechtel Names Project Director for Construction and Startup of World's Most Complex Radioactive Waste Treatment Plant," *Informed Infrastructure*, December 11, 2017, https://www.bechtel.com/newsroom/releases/2017/12/reilly-waste-treatment-plant-project-director/; "Bechtel Picks New Treatment Plant Chief at Hanford," *Exchange Monitor*, September 24, 2018, https://www.

exchangemonitor.com/bechtel-picks-new-treatment-plant-chief-hanford-2/.

30 John Stang, "Feds''Plan B' for Hanford Waste Cleanup Draws State Officials' Ire," *Crosscut*, June 5, 2019, https://crosscut.com/2019/06/feds-plan-b-hanford-waste-cleanup-draws-state-officials-ire.

31 "Becthel, Hanford Waste Treatment Plant," Bechtel.com accessed June 6, 2020, https://www.bechtel.com/projects/hanford-waste-treatment-plant/; Seattle Times Staff, "$12B May Not Be Enough to Finish Hanford Vit Plant," *Seattle Times*, August 30, 2011.

32 David R. Baker, "Bechtel Shares Blame in Big Dig Tragedy," SFGATE, July 11, 2007, https://www.sfgate.com/business/article/Bechtel-shares-blame-in-Big-Dig-tragedy-Federal-2552994.php; Denise Lavoie, "Contractors to settle Boston Big Dig suit for $450M," *Associated Press*, January 23, 2018, https://www.thestar.com/business/2008/01/23/contractors_to_settle_boston_big_dig_suit_for_450m.html.

33 Special Inspector General for Iraq Reconstruction, "Quarterly Report and Semiannual Report to the United States Congress," July 30, 2007.

34 Hanford Challenge, "DOE Identifies 'Potentially Unrecoverable Quality Issue' at Hanford Waste Treatment Plant," Press Release, March 16, 2018.

35 Jeff McMahon, "Bechtel Incompetent to Complete Hanford Nuclear Waste Cleanup: DOE Memo," *Forbes*, August 29, 2012, https://www.forbes.com/sites/jeffmcmahon/2012/08/29/bechtel-incompetent-to-complete-hanford-nuclear-waste-cleanup-doe-memo/?sh=10b33cc94e73.

36 McMahon, "Bechtel Incompetent to Complete Hanford Nuclear Waste Cleanup: DOE Memo," *Forbes*.

37 Annette Cary, "Hanford Contractor's Rating Drops Because of Investigations," *Associated Press*, December 12, 2019, https://m.washingtontimes.com/news/2019/dec/14/hanford-contractors-rating-drops-because-of-invest/.

38 Open Secrets, Bechtel Group, accessed July 5, 2021, https://www.opensecrets.org/orgs/bechtel-group/summary?id=D000000237; TCAJOB Staff, "Newsome invites new Energy secretary to tour Hanford," *Tri-Cities Area Journal of Business*, April 2021, https://newhouse.house.gov/media-center/press-releases/newhouse-invites-energy-secretary-tour-hanford-criticizes-politicization.

39 Jay Inslee, Bob Ferguson, "State of Washington Comments on US Department of Energy's Proposed Interpretation of the Term 'High Level Radioactive Waste' in the Nuclear Waste Policy Act (83 FR 50909)," January 7, 2019.

40   Laura Watson, Bob Ferguson, Phil Ridgon, et al, "Request to Rescind High-Level Radioactive Waste Interpretive Rule," Legal Brief, February 26, 2021.

41   Denton, *The Profiteers: Bechtel and the Men Who Built the World*, 66.

42   Denton, *The Profiteers: Bechtel and the Men Who Built the World*, 155-156.

43   Brian Hertzog, "How do we #LeadWithInfrastructure? Brendan Bechtel interviews US Secretary of Transportation Pete Buttigieg," blog, Bechtel.com, May 10, 2021.

44   Denton, *The Profiteers: Bechtel and the Men Who Built the World*, 132.

45   David Stout, "Caspar W. Weinberger Dies at 88," *New York Times*, March 28, 2006.

46   Iva Zagar, "Bechtel Enterprises' Daniel Chao Named to Export-Import Bank Committee," Bechtel, March 20, 2002.

47   Madelyn Pennino, "Sheehan Advocates Action, Ex-NATO Leader Speaks at E-town," Lancaster Online, March 12, 2021, https://lancasteronline.com/news/sheehan-advocates-action/article_157b5f6c-857e-5332-b102-94b48b7bf3c4.html.

48   Jeffrey St. Clair, "Straight to Bechtel," *CounterPunch*, July 4, 2021, https://www.counterpunch.org/2021/07/04/straight-to-bechtel-when-donald-rumsfeld-laid-pipe/.

CHAPTER FOUR

1   Annette Cary, "57% of Hanford nuclear site workers surveyed by WA State Report Toxic Exposures," *Tri-City Herald*, July 7, 2021.

2   Sydney Brownstone, "Will Trump Make Hanford More Dangerous Than It Already Is?" *Portland Mercury*, May 16, 2017.

3   Susannah Frame, "Hanford Continues to Mislead Workers about Toxic Vapors," KING5 NEWS, June 8, 2016, https://www.king5.com/article/news/local/hanford-continues-to-mislead-workers-about-toxic-vapors/236432342.

4   Frame, "Hanford Continues to Mislead Workers about Toxic Vapors."

5   Frame, "Hanford Continues to Mislead Workers about Toxic Vapors."

6   Hanford Challenge, "Chemical Vapor Exposures," accessed January 3, 2021, https://www.hanfordchallenge.org/chemical-vapor-exposures.

7   *Spokesman-Review*, "Samples Uncover New Danger in Hanford Tanks," September 22, 2004.

8   Shannon Dininny, "New Hazardous Chemical Turns Up in Tanks," Associated Press, March 16, 2011, https://www.seattlepi.com/local/article/New-hazardous-chemical-turns-up-in-tanks-1154727.php.

9   Simon Cotton, "Dimethylmercury and Mercury Poisoning:The Karen Wetterhahn story," *Bristol School of Chemistry*, October 2003.

10   Cathy Newman, "Pick Your Poison—12 Toxic Tales," *National Geographic,* February 18, 2009, https://www.nationalgeographic.com/science/article/poison-toxic-tales.

11   Frame, "Hanford Continues to Mislead Workers About Toxic Vapors."

12   Frame, "Hanford Continues to Mislead Workers About Toxic Vapors."

13   NBC News, "Sick Former Hanford Worker Speaks Out About His Deadly Disease and Federal Compensation for Sick Workers," June 5, 2014, https://www.nbcrightnow.com/archives/sick-former-hanford-worker-speaks-out-about-his-deadly-disease-federal-compensation-for-sick-workers/article_1976cb02-55fb-51c3-9cf9-5f122060e895.html.

14   NBC News, "Sick Former Hanford Worker Speaks Out About His Deadly Disease and Federal Compensation for Sick Workers."

15   Annette Cary, "State Senators Hear Emotional Pleas for Hanford Worker Compensation Change," *Tri-City Herald,* March 22, 2017.

16   Cary, "State Senators Hear Emotional Pleas for Hanford Worker Compensation Change."

17   Brownstone, "Will Trump Make Hanford More Dangerous Than It Already Is?"

18   Cary, "State Senators Hear Emotional Pleas for Hanford Worker Compensation Change."

19   Annette Cary, "Help On the Way for Ill Hanford Workers," *Tri-City Herald,* March 7, 2018.

20   Andrew Blankstein and Corky Siemaszko, "Hanford Nuclear Site, Tunnel Collapse Causes Workers to 'Take Cover,'" NBC News, May 9, 2017, https://www.nbcnews.com/news/us-news/hanford-nuclear-site-tunnel-collapse-causes-workers-take-cover-n756896; KING-5 NEWS, "Tunnel Collapses at Hanford; No Radiation Released, Officials Say," May 9, 2017, https://www.kare11.com/article/news/local/tunnel-collapses-at-hanford-no-radiation-released-officials-say/438233976.

21   Annette Cary, "Radiation Monitoring Led to Hanford Tunnel Breach Discovery" *Tri-City Herald,* May 13, 2017.

22   Hal Bernton, "Justice Department Sues Washington State Over Law to Compensate Sick Hanford Workers," *Seattle Times,* December 11, 2018.

23   Bernton, "Justice Department Sues Washington State Over Law to Compensate Sick Hanford Workers."

24   Associated Press, "Federal Appeals Panel Says State Can Protect Hanford Workers," August 19, 2020.

25   Dave Phillips, "Legal Win Is Too Late for Many Who Got Cancer After Nuclear Clean-Up," *New York Times,* February 11, 2020.

26 Susannah Frame, "Attorney General, Advocates 'Appalled' by DOJ's 'Cruel Effort' to Scrap Hanford Workers' Comp Law," KING5 News, September 14, 2021, https://www.king5. com/article/news/investigations/doj-petition-supreme-court-washington-hanford-works-comp-law/281-2c45cefa-9efd-477b-adfd-1968a4e64e99.

27 Associated Press, "B-52 and Tanker Collide Over Spain, 2 Dead, 5 Missing," New York Times, January 18, 1966.

28 Tad Szulc, The Bombs of Palomares, (The Viking Press, 1967), 68.

29 Tad Szulc, "Bomb Hunt on Spanish Coast Shifts to New Areas," New York Times, February 16, 1966.

30 Phillips, "Legal Win Is Too Late for Many Who Got Cancer After Nuclear Clean-Up."

31 Phillips, "Legal Win Is Too Late for Many Who Got Cancer After Nuclear Clean-Up."

32 Phillips, "Legal Win Is Too Late for Many Who Got Cancer After Nuclear Clean-Up."

33 Veterans Legal Services Clinic, "Skaar v. Wilkie Palomares Class Action," Yale Law School, accessed January 13, 2021, https://law. yale.edu/studying-law-yale/clinical-and-experiential-learning/ our-clinics/veterans-legal-services-clinic/skaar-v-mcdonough-certified-class-action.

34 Graham Keeley , "Ex-US Soldiers Nearing Resolution of Claims From 1966 Palomares Accident," Voice of America, January 18, 2021, https://www.voanews.com/a/usa_ex-us-soldiers-nearing-resolution-claims-1966-palomares-accident/6200883.html.

35 John LaForge, "Court Orders Veterans Affairs Department to Replace Flawed Science in Plutonium Disaster Case," CounterPunch, January 1, 2020, https://www.counterpunch. org/2021/01/01/court-orders-veterans-affairs-department-to-replace-flawed-science-used-to-deny-benefits-to-vets-poisoned-in-1966-plutonium-disaster/.

36 Dale M. Brumfield, "Inject with Plutonium," Medium, January 30, 2020, https://medium.com/lessons-from-history/a-child-came-to-the-u-s-for-cancer-treatment-but-was-injected-with-plutonium-sent-home-to-die-c55b154511db.

37 Brumfield, "Inject with Plutonium."

38 Brumfield, "Inject with Plutonium."

39 DOE Openness: Human Radiation Experiments, "The Manhattan District Experiments," ACHRE Report, accessed February 12, 2021, https://ehss.energy.gov/ohre/roadmap/achre/ chap5_2.html.

40 Gregg Herken and James David, "Doctors of Death," The New York Times, January 13, 1994.

41   DOE Openness: Human Radiation Experiments, "The
     Manhattan District Experiments."
42   Herken and David, "Doctors of Death."
43   Hal Bernton, "Work Halted at Hanford After Radiation Is Found
     to Have Spread," *Seattle Times*, December 22, 2017.
44   Susannah Frame, "'It Was Complete Chaos,' Says Hanford
     Worker Who Inhaled Plutonium," *KING-5 NEWS*, February
     13, 2018, https://www.king5.com/article/news/local/hanford/
     hanford-worker-who-inhaled-plutonium-im-scared-this-is-
     criminal/281-517526634.
45   Bernton, "Work Halted at Hanford After Radiation Is Found to
     Have Spread."
46   Frame, "'It Was Complete Chaos,' Says Hanford Worker Who
     Inhaled Plutonium."
47   Frame, "'It Was complete Chaos,' Says Hanford worker Who
     Inhaled Plutonium."
48   Frame, "'It Was Complete Chaos,' Says Hanford Worker Who
     Inhaled Plutonium."
49   Nicholas K. Geranios, "Radiation Alarm Prompts Order for
     Workers to Seek Cover," *The Spokesman Review*, June 8, 2017.
50   The Seattle Times Editorial Board, "Fix the Systems That Failed
     Hanford Workers," *Seattle Times*, March 25, 2020, https://www.
     seattletimes.com/opinion/editorials/fix-the-systems-that-failed-
     hanford-workers/.
51   Robert Alvarez and Hanford Challenge, "Risky Business
     at Perma-Fix Northwest," Hanford Challenge, accessed
     February 2, 2021, https://static1.squarespace.com/
     static/568adf4125981deb769d96b2/t/5fbde47518e72e5fdb
     9a8298/1606280319740/FINAL+PermaFix+Report.pdf.
52   Alvarez and Hanford Challenge, "Risky Business at Perma-Fix
     Northwest."
53   Hanford Challenge Press Release, "New Report Charges Federal
     Government with Exporting Unacceptable Nuclear Risks to
     Communities Near Hanford Nuclear Site," November 25, 2020.
54   "Oak Ridge Strike Has No Immediate Effect On Weapons
     Systems, Official Says," Associated Press, June 22, 1987; Clay
     Chandler, "No Progress Seen in Martin Marietta Strike,"
     Washington Post, June 24, 1987.
55   Frank Munger, "Changing of the guard at Oak Ridge labor group,"
     Knox News, December 28, 2015, https://archive.knoxnews.com/
     news/local/changing-of-the-guard-at-oak-ridge-labor-group-
     273523a2-de1e-5345-e053-0100007faa75-363533521.html/.
56   United Press International, "10-Week Strike at Nuclear Test Site
     Ends," *Los Angeles Times*, November 23, 1987.

57   Kristin M. Kraemer, "Tenacious Hanford union leader fought for Tri-Cities and more," *Tri-City Herald*, April 26, 2018.

58   Tri-City Herald Staff, "Hanford union workers agree to contract extension with pay raise," *Tri-City Herald*, October 14, 2019.

CHAPTER FIVE

1   Thomas Klause, "Welcome to Nuketown USA: A Look at the Company Town of the Hanford Site," *Spokesman Review*, May 14, 2017, https://www.spokesman.com/stories/2017/may/14/welcome-to-nuketown-usa-a-look-at-the-company-town/.

2   Kate Brown, *Plutopia: Nuclear Families, Atomic Cities, and the Great Soviet and American Plutonium Disasters* (Oxford University Press, 2013), 287-296.

3   Klause, "Welcome to Nuketown USA: A Look at the Company Town of the Hanford Site."

4   Brown, *Plutopia: Nuclear Families, Atomic Cities, and the Great Soviet and American Plutonium Disasters*, 287-296.

5   Brown, *Plutopia: Nuclear Families, Atomic Cities, and the Great Soviet and American Plutonium Disasters*, 287-296.

6   Eric Nadler, "The Plot to Get Ed Bricker—Hanford Whistle-Blower Was Tracked, Harassed, Files Show," *Seattle Times*, July 30, 1990.

7   Nadler, "The Plot to Get Ed Bricker—Hanford Whistle-Blower Was Tracked, Harassed, Files Show."

8   Tom Mueller, *Crisis of Conscience: Whistleblowing in An Age of Fraud* (Penguin, Random House, 2019), 437-443.

9   Matthew L. Wald, "Four Say Atom Industry Ordered Counseling and Harassed Them," *New York Times*, August 6, 1989.

10   "Radioactive Warning Signs Removed for Governor's Visit," UPI, August 12, 1986.

11   Nadler, "The Plot to Get Ed Bricker—Hanford Whistle-Blower Was Tracked, Harassed, Files Show."

12   Wald, "Four Say Atom Industry Ordered Counseling and Harassed Them."

13   Nadler, "The Plot To Get Ed Bricker—Hanford Whistle-Blower Was Tracked, Harassed, Files Show."

14   Nadler, "The Plot To Get Ed Bricker—Hanford Whistle-Blower Was Tracked, Harassed, Files Show."

15   Nadler, "The Plot To Get Ed Bricker—Hanford Whistle-Blower Was Tracked, Harassed, Files Show."

16   Nadler, "The Plot To Get Ed Bricker—Hanford Whistle-Blower Was Tracked, Harassed, Files Show."

17   Nadler, "The Plot To Get Ed Bricker—Hanford Whistle-Blower Was Tracked, Harassed, Files Show."

18   Mueller, *Crisis of Conscience: Whistleblowing in An Age of Fraud*, 439.

19   Brown, *Plutopia: Nuclear Families, Atomic Cities, and the Great
      Soviet and American Plutonium Disasters,* 287-296.

20   Brown, *Plutopia: Nuclear Families, Atomic Cities, and the Great
      Soviet and American Plutonium Disasters,* 287-296.

21   Ephraim Payne and Ray Ring, "The Hanford Whistleblowers,"
      High Country News, February 10, 2014, https://www.hcn.org/
      issues/46.2/the-hanford-whistleblowers.

22   Klause, "Welcome to Nuketown USA: A Look at the Company
      Town of the Hanford Site."

CHAPTER SIX

1   Ralph Vartabedian, "Safety Doubts Raised at Hanford Cleanup,"
      Los Angeles Times, November 30, 2013.

2   John Stang, "Effort to Lock Hanford's Radioactive Waste in Glass
      Faces More Delays," *High Country News,* November 19, 2019,
      https://www.hcn.org/articles/energy-and-industry-effort-to-lock-
      hanfords-radioactive-waste-in-glass-faces-more-delays.

3   John Stang, "Flashback: Hanford's Lack of a Nuclear Safety
      Culture," *Crosscut,* September 2, 2015, https://crosscut.
      com/2015/09/flashback-hanfords-lack-of-a-nuclear-safety-culture.

4   Ralph Vartabedian, "Manager Says Safety Issues Are Ignored at
      Hanford Nuclear Site," *Los Angeles Times,* February 13, 2013.

5   Tom Mueller, *Crisis of Conscience: Whistleblowing in An Age of
      Fraud* (Penguin, Random House, 2019), 482-483.

6   United States Department of Justice Office of Public Affairs,
      "United States Settles Lawsuit Against Energy Department
      Contractors for Knowingly Mischarging Costs on Contract at
      Nuclear Waste Treatment Plant," November 23, 2016, https://
      www.justice.gov/opa/pr/united-states-settles-lawsuit-against-
      energy-department-contractors-knowingly-mischarging.

7   Joe Davidson, "After a Complaint, He Landed in a Basement,"
      Washington Post, December 8, 2011.

8   Davidson, "After a Complaint, He Landed in a Basement."

9   Annette Cary, "New $13 Billion Contract Awarded for Hanford
      Tank Farm Cleanup," *Tri-City Herald,* May 14, 2020.

10   Cary, "Hanford Strategy for Worst Nuclear Waste Criticized.
      Plant Estimates Skyrocket to $41 Billion."

11   Nicholas K. Geranios, "Hanford Whistleblower Settles for
      $4.1 Million," Associated Press, August 12, 2015, https://www.
      seattletimes.com/seattle-news/hanford-whistleblower-settles-for-
      4-1-million/.

12   Patrick Malone, "Nuclear Cleanup Project Haunted by Legacy of
      Design Failures and Whistleblower Retaliation," Center for Public
      Integrity, September 1, 2015, https://publicintegrity.org/national-

security/nuclear-cleanup-project-haunted-by-legacy-of-design-failures-and-whistleblower-retaliation/.

13   "Hanford Whistleblower Gets $4.1 Million Settlement," NBC
      News Right Now, August 12, 2015, https://www.nbcrightnow.
      com/archives/hanford-whistleblower-gets-4-1-million-settlement/
      article_08b8db60-3fde-5a10-80b9-66aeb8edc9e7.html.

14   Chris Kirkham, "Aecom Finalizes $6 Billion Acquisition of
      Engineering Design Rival URS," Los Angeles Times, October 17,
      2014.

CHAPTER SEVEN

1   Anna King, "Yakama Nation's Hanford Warrior Russell Jim Dies,"
      NW News Network, April 10, 2018, https://www.nwnewsnetwork.
      org/history-and-culture/2018-04-10/yakama-nations-hanford-
      warrior-russell-jim-dies.

2   Russell Jim Interview, Atomic Heritage Museum, accessed March
      3, 2021, https://www.manhattanprojectvoices.org/oral-histories/
      russell-jims-interview.

3   Gordon Hewes, Handbook of North American Indians: Plateau,
      edited by Deward Walker. Washington, D.C., 1998.

4   Celilo Falls, Columbia River Inter-Tribal Fish Commission,
      accessed February 23, 2021, https://www.critfc.org/salmon-
      culture/tribal-salmon-culture/celilo-falls/.

5   Katrine Barber, "Celilo Falls," Oregon Encyclopedia, accessed
      March 3, 2021, https://www.oregonencyclopedia.org/articles/
      celilo_falls/#.YXdDdBDMJBw.

6   H. Shea, "The Grissom Site," Central Washington University, May
      2012.

7   Phil Ferolito, "Russell Jim of Yakama Tribe Spent Decades
      Monitoring Hanford," Associated Press, June 8, 2017, https://
      apnews.com/article/2bf0978712ce454e9dc0d6e2bad2b2ed.

8   "Russell Jim Oral History," The Oregon History Project, October
      16, 1999.

9   Brian Bull, "Program 304—Elder Wisdom, Wisdom of the
      Elders," June 17, 2011, https://wisdomoftheelders.org/program-
      304-elder-wisdom/.

10   David Yearsley, "Dam Nation and Woody Guthrie," CounterPunch,
      June 5, 2020, https://www.counterpunch.org/2020/06/05/dam-
      nation-and-woody-guthrie/.

11   "The Pacific Northwest Old-Growth Forest—A Unique
      Ecosystem," Oregon Wild, accessed February 21, 2021, https://
      oregonwild.org/pacific-northwest-research-station-old-growth-
      unique-ecosystem.

12   Amy McKeever, "The Heartbreaking, Controversial History of
      Mount Rushmore," National Geographic, October 28, 2020, https://

www.nationalgeographic.com/travel/article/the-strange-and-controversial-history-of-mount-rushmore.

13   Courtney Flatt, "Northwest Tribes Call for Removal of Lower Columbia River Dams," OPB, October 14, 2019, https://www.opb.org/news/article/pacific-northwest-tribes-remove-columbia-river-dams/.

14   Fred Shapiro, "Radwaste in the Indians' Backyards," *Nation*, May 7, 1983.

15   Bull, "Program 304—Elder Wisdom, Wisdom of the Elders."

16   "Russell Jim Talk at University of Washington" TalkingStickTV, accessed February 2, 2021, https://www.youtube.com/watch?v=wTLCSFN2fH4.

17   Michelle Tolson, "Yakama Nation Tells DOE to Clean Up Nuclear Waste," International Press Agency, April 14, 2014, http://www.ipsnews.net/2014/04/yakama-nation-tells-doe-clean-nuclear-waste/.

18   Robert Gottlieb, *Forcing the Spring: The Transformation of the American Environmental Movement* (Island Press, 2005), 237.

19   Spencer Heinz, "Nuclear Safety Questions Unresolved," *The Oregonian*, May 19, 1985.

20   Heinz, "Nuclear Safety Questions Unresolved."

21   Marjane Ambler, "Russell Jim is Pro-Safety; Not Anti-Nuclear," *High Country News*, July 7, 1986.

22   "Russell Jim Talk at University of Washington," TalkingStickTV, accessed February 2, 2021.

23   Ken Olsen, "At Hanford, The Real Estate Is Hot," *High Country News*, January 22, 1996.

24   Ward Churchill, *Struggle for the Land, Native American Resistance to Genocide, Ecocide, and Colonization,* (City Lights Books, 2002): 257-260.

25   Maggie Degnan, "Line 3 to Begin Operation This Weekend, Violating Treaties with Indigenous Peoples," *Badger Herald*, October 5, 2021.

26   Ray Levy Uyeda, "The Red Deal Is an Indigenous Climate Plan That Builds on the Green New Deal," *Teen Vogue*, November 1, 2019.

27   "Competing Visions for the Future of Hanford," Columbia Riverkeeper, June 2018.

28   Lauren Goldberg, "Behind the Hanford Cleanup: Yakama Nation," Columbia Riverkeeper, September 28, 2018.

29   Goldberg, "Behind the Hanford Cleanup: Yakama Nation."

30   Goldberg, "Behind the Hanford Cleanup: Yakama Nation."

31   Lora Shinn, "As the DOE Abandons a Toxic Mess Threatening the Columbia River, the Yakama Nation Fights Back," National Resource Defense Council, September 18, 2019, https://www.nrdc.

org/stories/doe-abandons-toxic-mess-threatening-columbia-river-yakama-nation-fights-back.

32 Atwai is a term used by the Yakama and other Indigenous peoples for a person who has passed on.

33 Goldberg, "Behind the Hanford Cleanup: Yakama Nation."

CHAPTER EIGHT

1 Working Group, "AR6 Climate Change 2021: The Physical Science Basis," Intergovernmental Panel on Climate Change, August 2021.

2 Katarina Zimmer, "Paleoclimate Data Raise Alarm on Historic Nature of Climate Emergency," *Scientific American*, August 12, 2021, https://www.scientificamerican.com/article/paleoclimate-data-raise-alarm-on-historic-nature-of-climate-emergency/.

3 Jeff Tollefson, "IPCC Climate Report: Earth Is Warmer Than It's Been in 125,000 Years," *Nature*, August 9, 2021, https://www.nature.com/articles/d41586-021-02179-1.

4 Eugene F. Mallove, "The Living Organism We Call Earth," *Washington Post*, February 1, 1987.

5 Arnold Gundersen, "An Open Letter to Bill Gates About his Wyoming Atomic Reactor," *CounterPunch*, August 23, 2021, https://www.counterpunch.org/2021/08/20/an-open-letter-to-bill-gates-about-his-wyoming-atomic-reactor/.

6 George Monbiot, "Why Fukushima Made Me Stop Worrying and Love Nuclear Power," *Guardian*, March 21, 2011, https://www.theguardian.com/commentisfree/2011/mar/21/pro-nuclear-japan-fukushima.

7 Monbiot, "Why Fukushima Made Me Stop Worrying and Love Nuclear Power."

8 World Health Organization, "Chernobyl: the True Scale of the Accident," September 5, 2005.

9 Alexey V. Yablokov et al, "Chernobyl: Consequences of the Catastrophe for People and the Environment," New York Academy of Sciences, November 2009.

10 Matt Reimann, "The First Fatal Nuclear Meltdown in the US Happened in 4 Milliseconds," *Timeline*, December 19, 2016.

11 J. C. Reindl, "Did We Really 'Almost Lose Detroit' in Fermi 1 Mishap 50 Years Ago?" *Detroit Free Press*, October 9, 2016.

12 US Nuclear Regulatory Commission, "Backgrounder on the Three Mile Island Accident," June 21, 2018.

13 M. Schneider, "An Account of Events in Nuclear Power Plants Since the Chernobyl Accident in 1986," Greens in the European Parliament, May 2007.

14 Joe Lemar, "Japan's Worst Nuclear Accident Leaves Two Fighting for Life," *BMJ*, October 9, 1999.

15 James Brooke, "Four Workers Killed in Nuclear Plant Accident in Japan," *New York Times*, August 10, 2004.

16 John LaForge, "Move Over Chernobyl, Fukushima is Now Officially the Worst Nuclear Power Disaster in History," *CounterPunch*, April 27, 2018, https://www.counterpunch. org/2018/04/27/move-over-chernobyl-fukushima-is-now-officially-the-worst-nuclear-power-disaster-in-history/.

17 Abubakar SadiqAliyu et al, "An Overview of Current Knowledge Concerning the Health and Environmental Consequences of the Fukushima Daiichi Nuclear Power Plant (FDNPP) Accident," *Environment International* 85 (December 2015): 213–28.

18 Bhaskar Sunkara, "If We Want to Fight the Climate Crisis, We Must Embrace Nuclear Power," *Guardian*, June 21, 2021, https:// www.theguardian.com/commentisfree/2021/jun/21/fight-climate-crisis-clean-energy-nuclear-power.

19 US Army Corps of Engineers, "Army Nuclear Power Program 1954-1976," accessed August 15, 2017.

20 Cassandra Jeffery, M. V. Ramana, "Big Money, Nuclear Subsidies, and Systemic Corruption," *Bulletin of the Atomic Scientists*, February 12, 2021, https://thebulletin.org/2021/02/big-money-nuclear-subsidies-and-systemic-corruption/.

21 Doug Koplow, "Nuclear Power: Still Not Viable without Subsidies," Union of Concerned Scientists, February 2011, 20, https://www.ucsusa.org/sites/default/files/2019-09/nuclear_subsidies_report.pdf.

22 Associated Press, "Russian Shelling Caused a Fire at a Ukrainian Nuclear Power Plant – How Close Did We Actually Come to Disaster?" March 4, 2022, https://theconversation.com/russian-shelling-caused-a-fire-at-a-ukrainian-nuclear-power-plant-how-close-did-we-actually-come-to-disaster-178549.

23 Robert Hunziker, "15 Nuclear Reactors in the Midst of Battle," *CounterPunch*, February 28, 2022, https://www.counterpunch. org/2022/02/28/15-nuclear-reactors-in-the-midst-of-battle/.

24 International Atomic Energy Agency, "Update 15: IAEA Director General Statement on Situation in Ukraine," March 8, 2022, https://www.iaea.org/newscenter/pressreleases/update-15-iaea-director-general-statement-on-situation-in-ukraine.

25 International Atomic Energy Agency, "Update 17: IAEA Director General Statement on Situation in Ukraine," March 10, 2022, https://www.iaea.org/newscenter/pressreleases/update-17-iaea-director-general-statement-on-situation-in-ukraine.

26 Francois Murphy, "All Chernobyl Staff Who Wanted to Leave Are Out, UN Nuclear Watchdog Says," Reuters, March 21, 2022.

27 Oliver Milman, "Forest Fires Erupt around Chernobyl Nuclear Plant in Ukraine," *Guardian*, March 22, 2022, https://www.

theguardian.com/world/2022/mar/22/chernobyl-forest-fires-ukraine-nuclear-plant.

28   David Roberts, "How to Save the Failing Nuclear Power Plants That Generate Half of America's Clean Electricity," *Vox*, May 11, 2018, https://www.vox.com/energy-and-environment/2018/5/10/17334474/nuclear-power-renewables-plants-retirements-us.

29   Keith Barnham, "False Solution: Nuclear Power Is Not 'Low Carbon,'" *Ecologist*, February 5, 2015, https://theecologist.org/2015/feb/05/false-solution-nuclear-power-not-low-carbon.

30   Andrea Wallner et al, "Energy Balance of Nuclear Power Generation," Austrian Institute of Ecology, 2011, https://www.energyagency.at/fileadmin/dam/pdf/publikationen/berichteBroschueren/Endbericht_LCA_Nuklearindustrie-engl.pdf.

31   Maya L. Kapoor, "A New Era of Uranium Mining Near the Grand Canyon?" *High Country News*, June 12, 2018, https://www.hcn.org/issues/50.11/energy-and-industry-a-new-era-of-uranium-mining-near-the-grand-canyon.

32   Eric Feigl-Ding, "Uranium Mining and the U.S. Nuclear Weapons Program," Federation of American Scientists, November 14, 2013.

33   Feigl-Ding, "Uranium Mining and the U.S. Nuclear Weapons Program."

34   C. Arnold, "Once Upon a Mine: The Legacy of Uranium on the Navajo Nation," Environ. Health Perspect. 122, A44 (2014).

35   C. Zanbak, "Heap Leaching Technique in Mining," Euromines, November 2012.

36   Peter H. Woods, "Uranium Mining (Open Cut and Underground) and Milling," Uranium for Nuclear Power, 2016, Pages 125-156.

37   Trip Jennings, "Remembering the largest radioactive spill in U.S. history," *New Mexico in Depth*, July 7, 2014, https://nmindepth.com/2014/07/07/remembering-the-largest-radioactive-spill-in-u-s-history/.

38   John Sadler, "Native American Tribe Claims Nuclear Waste Can't Be Stored on Its Land," *Las Vegas Sun*, August 15, 2019, https://lasvegassun.com/news/2019/aug/15/native-american-tribe-claims-nuclear-waste-cant-be/.

39   Jennifer Solis, "Western Shoshone Step Up Resistance to Yucca Project," *Nevada Current*, May 14, 2019, https://www.nevadacurrent.com/2019/05/14/western-shoshone-step-up-resistance-to-yucca-project/.

40   James Conca, "Do New Nuclear Reactor Designs Change The Nuclear Waste Issue?" *Forbes*, April 27, 2021, https://www.forbes.com/sites/jamesconca/2021/04/27/do-new-nuclear-reactor-designs-change-the-nuclear-waste-issue/.

41 David Biello, "Spent Nuclear Fuel: A Trash Heap Deadly for 250,000 Years or a Renewable Energy Source?" *Scientific American*, January 28, 2009, https://www.scientificamerican.com/article/nuclear-waste-lethal-trash-or-renewable-energy-source/.

42 Nicole Greenfield, "Alaska Natives Lead a Unified Resistance to the Pebble Mine," Natural Resource Defense Council, April 20, 2021, https://www.nrdc.org/stories/alaska-natives-lead-unified-resistance-pebble-mine.

43 Vijay Prashad, "After Evo, the Lithium Question Looms Large in Bolivia," *CounterPunch*, November 13, 2019, https://www.counterpunch.org/2019/11/13/after-evo-the-lithium-question-looms-large-in-bolivia/.

44 Mark Z, Jacobson, "No, We Don't Need 'Miracle Technologies' to Slash Emissions—We Already Have 95 Percent," The Hill, May 20, 2021, https://thehill.com/opinion/energy-environment/554605-no-we-dont-need-miracle-technologies-to-slash-emissions-we-already.

45 Kingsmill Bond et al. "The Sky's the Limit: Solar and Wind Energy Potential is 100 Times as Much as Global Energy Demand," Carbon Tracker, April 2021.

CHAPTER NINE

1 US Department of Energy, "Evaluation of Potential Opportunities to Classify Certain Defense Nuclear Waste from Reprocessing as Other than High-Level Radioactive Waste," December 2020.

2 US Department of Energy, "Evaluation of Potential Opportunities to Classify Certain Defense Nuclear Waste from Reprocessing as Other than High-Level Radioactive Waste."

3 Hanford Challenge, "Why Grout Failed at Hanford," June 2021, 2.

4 US General Accounting Office, "Hanford Tank Waste Program Needs Cost, Schedule, and Management Changes," March 1993, 30.

5 US General Accounting Office, "Hanford Tank Waste Program Needs Cost, Schedule, and Management Changes," 31.

6 US General Accounting Office, "Hanford Tank Waste Program Needs Cost, Schedule, and Management Changes," 31.

7 Anna King, "Hanford Waste Still On The Big To-Do List For Incoming Biden Administration," NWNews, January 19, 2021, https://www.nwnewsnetwork.org/environment-and-planning/2021-01-19/hanford-waste-still-on-the-big-to-do-list-for-incoming-biden-administration.

8 Hanford Challenge, "Why Grout Failed at Hanford," 2.

9 Annette Cary, "This Way to Treat Hanford Radioactive Waste Could Save $210 billion. But Is It Safe Enough?" *Tri-City Herald*, January 8, 2021.

10   Annete Cary, "Hanford Nuclear Cleanup 'on the Cheap' Won't Work, Cantwell Tells Biden's Energy Secretary," *Tri-City Herald*, June 16, 2021.

11   Lynn Simross, "Chernobyl and Hanford: Nuclear Author Draws Parallels," *Los Angeles Times*, May 7, 1986.

12   Nicolas K. Geranios, "Hanford Begins 1st Large-Scale Treatment of Nuke Tank Wastes," Associated Press, February 2, 2022, https://katu.com/news/nation-world/hanford-begins-1st-large-scale-treatment-of-nuke-tank-wastes.

13   Nicholas K. Geranios, "Workers at Some Hanford Radioactive Waste Tank Farms Stop Work in Dispute over Vapors," *Associated Press*, July 11, 2016, https://www.seattletimes.com/seattle-news/environment/workers-at-some-hanford-tanks-stop-in-dispute-over-vapors/.

INDEX

ABOUT HAYMARKET BOOKS

Haymarket Books is a radical, independent, nonprofit book publisher based in Chicago. Our mission is to publish books that contribute to struggles for social and economic justice. We strive to make our books a vibrant and organic part of social movements and the education and development of a critical, engaged, international left.

We take inspiration and courage from our namesakes, the Haymarket martyrs, who gave their lives fighting for a better world. Their 1886 struggle for the eight-hour day—which gave us May Day, the international workers' holiday—reminds workers around the world that ordinary people can organize and struggle for their own liberation. These struggles continue today across the globe—struggles against oppression, exploitation, poverty, and war.

Since our founding in 2001, Haymarket Books has published more than five hundred titles. Radically independent, we seek to drive a wedge into the risk-averse world of corporate book publishing. Our authors include Noam Chomsky, Arundhati Roy, Rebecca Solnit, Angela Y. Davis, Howard Zinn, Amy Goodman, Wallace Shawn, Mike Davis, Winona LaDuke, Ilan Pappé, Richard Wolff, Dave Zirin, Keeanga-Yamahtta Taylor, Nick Turse, Dahr Jamail, David Barsamian, Elizabeth Laird, Amira Hass, Mark Steel, Avi Lewis, Naomi Klein, and Neil Davidson. We are also the trade publishers of the acclaimed Historical Materialism Book Series and of Dispatch Books.

ALSO AVAILABLE FROM HAYMARKET BOOKS

Digging Our Own Graves
Coal Miners and the Struggle over Black Lung Disease
Barbara Ellen Smith, photography by Earl Dotter

An Enemy Such as This
Larry Casuse and the Fight for Native Liberation in One Family on
Two Continents over Three Centuries
David Correia, foreword by Melanie K. Yazzie

How We Go Home: Voices from Indigenous North America
Edited by Sara Sinclair

Kivalina: A Climate Change Story
Christine Shearer

No Planet B: A Teen Vogue Guide to the Climate Crisis
Edited by Lucy Diavolo, foreword by Lindsay Peoples Wagner

Rehearsals for Living
Robyn Maynard and Leanne Betasamosake Simpson
Foreword by Ruth Wilson Gilmore
Afterword by Robin D.G. Kelley

The Tragedy of American Science
From the Cold War to the Forever Wars
Clifford D. Conner

ABOUT THE AUTHOR

Joshua Frank is an award-winning California-based journalist and coeditor of the political magazine *CounterPunch*. He is a co-author of several books with Jeffrey St. Clair, most recently *The Big Heat: Earth on the Brink* (AK Press).